The Marxian Concept of Capital and the Soviet Experience

THE MARXIAN CONCEPT OF CAPITAL AND THE SOVIET EXPERIENCE

Essay in the Critique of Political Economy

Paresh Chattopadhyay

Praeger Series in Political Economy
Rodney Green, Series Editor

Westport, Connecticut
London

Library of Congress Cataloging-in-Publication Data

Chattopadhyay, Paresh.
    The Marxian concept of capital and the Soviet experience : essay
in the critique of political economy / Paresh Chattopadhyay.
        p.   cm.—(Praeger series in political economy, ISSN
1072–2882)
    Includes bibliographical references (p.   ) and index.
    ISBN 0–275–94530–8 (alk. paper)
    1. Soviet Union—Economic conditions. 2. Marxian economics—
Soviet Union.   I. Title. II. Series.
HC333.C45   1994
338.947—dc20   93–37881

British Library Cataloguing in Publication Data is available.

Library of Congress Catalog Card Number: 93–37881
ISBN: 0–275–94530–8
ISSN: 1072–2882

First published in 1994

Praeger Publishers, 88 Post Road West, Westport, CT 06881
An imprint of Greenwood Publishing Group, Inc.

Printed in the United States of America

The paper used in this book complies with the
Permanent Paper Standard issued by the National
Information Standards Organization (Z39.48–1984).

10 9 8 7 6 5 4 3 2 1

Copyright Acknowledgments

Grateful acknowledgments are due to the following publishers and journals for permission to use our previously published articles:

JAI Press Inc., Greenwich, Connecticut, for "On the Marxian Category of 'Competition of Capitals' and its relevance for the 'Post-Revolutionary' Economy," *Research in Political Economy* 10 (1987), and "Economics of Shortage or Specificity of Capital Accumulation," *Research in Political Economy* 13 (1992) (Chapters 2, 3, and 4).

Kluwer Academic Publishers, Boston, for "Bureaucracy and Class in Marxism," In *Bureaucracy*, edited by Neil Garston. 1993 (Chapter 6).

Union for Radical Political Economics, for "The Economic Content of Socialism: Marx vs. Lenin," *Review of Radical Political Economics* 24, 3/4 (1992) (Chapter 6).

Sameeksha Trust, Bombay, for "Rise of Social Capitalism in the USSR," *Economic and Political Weekly*, June 13, 20-27 (1981), and "Which Socialism is in Question?", *Economic and Political Weekly*, December 16 (1989) (Chapters 1, 3, 6, and 7).

People's Bank, Colombo, for "Did the Bolshevik Seizure of Power Inaugurate a Socialist Revolution -- A Marxian Inquiry," *Economic Review* 17, nos. 6 and 7 (September/October 1991) (Chapter 8).

Centre d'étude des pays de l'Est, Brussels, for "Post-Revolutionary Society: Bureaucracy or Social Capitalism?", *Revue des Pays de l'Est*, 1/2 (1983) (Chapters 3, 5 and 6).

CONTENTS

LIST OF TABLES

PREFACE

Though the USSR has now passed into history, its impact on the twentieth-century world -- judged negatively or positively -- is beyond dispute. The present work analyzes the Soviet *economic* experience in the light of the Marxian concept of capital. The subject of the book is Soviet economy, where economy is understood in its specific Marxian sense of a complex of social relations of production. Entirely subscribing to the materialist point of view, we hold that it is the economy, that is, basically the relations between the immediate producers and their conditions of production, that formed the foundation of the Soviet society and ultimately determined its politics and other elements of its edifice. Correspondingly, our work is an essay in the critique of political economy -- in the Marxian sense of the expression -- and not an exercise in economics or even in political economy. All the basic categories employed in the book are Marx's, as they appear in his original texts.

Soviet economy here refers, by and large, to the Soviet economic experience under the so-called administered economic system that took shape and consolidated itself beginning in the late 1920s. It is this economy which, with no major modification, continued to prevail almost to the end of the regime and was taken everywhere as the standard Soviet model. We study it here as a basically closed economy, abstracted from its international economic relations. The moving forces of the Soviet society, as well as the insoluble contradictions in which it increasingly got enmeshed, are analyzed, without recourse to the Soviet economy's relations with the rest of the world, in terms of its *own* social relations of production and the specific phenomenal forms in which those relations manifested themselves. Here a word of clarification is in order. In our employment of the term "Soviet" for the old regime, we have simply bowed to the term's common usage in order not to create any confusion in the readers' minds. As a matter of fact, the soviets, as the working peoples' independent organs of power, were systematically destroyed by the Party-State beginning as early as 1918. To maintain the distinction, the term Soviet, with the "S" capitalized, is used in the book with reference to the old post-1917 *regime*, including its economy.

The debate on the Soviet question -- wherever it appears in the book -- is basically with the tendencies within the broad spectrum of the left. For those on the right, neither Marx nor an analysis of the Soviet economy in the light of Marx's theoretical categories has been of any importance except perhaps as scholastic curiosities. Needless to add, there is nothing personal about this debate. The individuals concerned appear here uniquely as representatives of certain tendencies, and, in the debate, issue is taken with those tendencies. In the book considerable space is devoted to the debate with Paul Sweezy. Much more than the general indebtedness which I, like many others studying Marx's "Critique," owe to him, I am personally indebted to him and his distinguished colleague Harry Magdoff in so many different ways that it is not possible to sufficiently acknowledge my gratitude to them here. Let me stress that in my arguments with Sweezy I, following an ancient Indian tradition, have remained well within the bounds of debate between a master and his pupil.

The writings of Karel Kosik, Roman Rosdolsky and Maximilien Rubel have, in their different ways, considerably helped me in my Marx reading. I have also learnt a great deal from Charles Bettelheim's works on the USSR as well as from my personal association with him over a long period. He particularly helped by his unfailing observations on a large portion of the manuscript which I had the occasion to send him in parts over a period of time. I am also grateful to the following friends and colleagues who either commented on parts of the manuscript or helped in various other ways: Kevin Anderson, Asit Bhattacharyya, Rosalind Boyd, Adam Buick, Antonio Callari, Guglielmo Carchedi, Bernard Chavance, Iona Christopher, Walter Daum, Neil Garston, Peter Hudis, Louis Gil, Michael Goldfield, Rodney Green, John McDermott, Fred Moseley, Frank Thompson, John Weeks, Tom Weisskopf, John Willoughby, Behzad Yagmaian, and Paul Zarembka. I owe a special debt to Dr. James Ice, Praeger's acquisitions editor for economics, for his suggestions concerning the formal aspects of preparing and submitting the manuscript.

A word about the citations in the book from the non-English sources. I have preferred to translate them from their original versions, wherever available, even when their English versions existed. This preference is explained by my respect for the original texts, as well as a sense of dissatisfaction felt with regard to their existing English versions. This is particularly the case with Marx's texts. To remain close to Marx's texts, I have tried to translate them as literally as possible. I should point out, in this connection, that Marx's language was not completely free from what is considered today as sexism. In order not to tamper with his texts I have retained that language in the translation.

A final word. Throughout the manuscript I have used first person plural ("we"), instead of the first person singular ("I"), referring to its author. The basic reason is that I do not think any author can really claim that all the ideas in the particular work are wholly his/hers. Knowingly or unknowingly, we take, and make our own, the ideas of our predecessors and contemporaries. So I find the usage of "I" for an author immodest and not entirely honest.

INTRODUCTION

THE RELEVANCE OF MARX

In any endeavor to analyze the Soviet economy within a Marxian theoretical framework, one is immediately confronted with an apparently formidable problem. Are Marx's method and categories at all relevant for an inquiry into the Soviet economy? After the much proclaimed "defeat" of socialism, any effort in that direction would appear futile to most people. Leaving aside the non-Marxists, for whom such a stand is understandable, among Marxists, such reservations already aired earlier, can be summed up in four distinguished cases, which we discuss below.

THE CRITICS

One and a half decades ago, the French Marxist philosopher L. Althusser underlined the "quasi-impossibility of furnishing a satisfactory Marxian explanation" for the latter day Soviet developments, and Marxism's "difficulties, contradictions, shortcomings" leading to a veritable "crisis of Marxism" faced with the latter day Soviet phenomenon (1978: 244, 249). At about the same time P. Sweezy opined that while the part of Marxism dealing with "global capitalism and its crisis. . . works as well as ever," anomalies were appearing in the other part of Marxism, that which is concerned with the future society, inasmuch as there was a gap between "observed reality and the expectations generated by (Marxist) theory." More specifically, contrary to Marx's original ideas, the reality has shown that "a proletarian revolution can give rise to a non-socialist society, . . . a new form of society, neither capitalist nor socialist." Thus the "anomalies have been so massive and egregious that the result has been a deep crisis in

Marxian theory," Sweezy concluded (1980: 136, 137). In the same way, but from a different point of view, C. Bettelheim observed that "Marxian concepts" have become "insufficient" in view of the "new forms of capitalist relations" in the Soviet type societies (1985a: 31). Finally, we have the well-known "analytical Marxist" J. Roemer, whose conclusions concerning Marx were the most far-reaching. After adopting the "semantic convention" that the USSR was a "socialist society" and, at the same time, observing that exploitation persisted in that society, Roemer concluded that the Marxists were "incorrect in assuming that the absence of private ownership implies the abolition of exploitation." Indeed, as Marxism denied the existence of exploitation under "public ownership" of the means of production, "no materialist theory of the laws of motion of socialist societies is produced." After all, "Marxism is the application of historical materialism to the nineteenth-century society." Consequently, "Marxian theory is in a Ptolemaic crisis." It cannot "explain the developments of late twentieth-century society." Given this difficult situation in which Marxism finds itself, it is of course natural that Roemer's "work contributes . . . a foundation for Marxian economic theory," striving to "separate the historical-materialist kernel from its specific application as Marxism, the theory of nineteenth-century capitalism" (1981: 6,208-10).

In sum, the observations of these Marxists seem to lead to the conclusion, in the words of some Hungarian scholars, that "the very conceptual framework of Marxist theory" would "require significant revisions and modifications" before applying to the Soviet type societies (Feher, Heller, and Markus 1983: 8). Let us consider these arguments.

We start with Althusser. From the context of Althusser's discussion, it appears that he was speaking as a communist party member, basically as a Leninist and in terms of the "crisis of the international communist movement" (1978: 245,248). Althusser would prove correct if he could show that the Marxism, which the Communists, including Lenin, claimed as essentially realized in the Bolshevik seizure of power in 1917, and the construction of the society which issued therefrom, *was* the Marxism of Marx himself in the first place. If, on the contrary, it is seen -- as we shall argue in our concluding chapter -- that both the way in which the "socialist revolution" was represented and claimed to have been realized by the Bolsheviks, and the way in which the construction of socialism was undertaken in Russia, were exactly the *opposite* of what Marx had conceived them to be, then obviously Marx is not being judged within his own universe of discourse, and the judgment cannot be accepted as valid. Again, a word of precision. When Althusser underlines the "crisis of Marxism," the Marxism he, as a party person, is referring to, is the Leninist brand of Marxism. But why should the Leninist Marxism be identified with Marx's Marxism (to use R. Dunayevskaya's felicitous term)? It is well-known that all along there have been non-Leninist currents within Marxism which were, by and large, denounced, unilaterally, as anti-Marxism by Lenin and his followers. We do not see any reason to yield to this ideological fundamentalism and then attribute the crisis in question to Marx's Marxism.

In the same way, Sweezy is assuming that what is generally known as the October (1917) revolution *was* a "proletarian revolution." True, the October seizure of power was claimed by Lenin and his followers as a proletarian revolution. But we see no reason to accept this *subjective* claim a priori. If the the proletarian revolution is claimed made in the name of Marx -- which the Bolsheviks, as Marxists, did -- then, whether the event in question really amounted to a proletarian revolution has to be judged strictly by the criteria for such a revolution set out in Marx's own writings. Otherwise no justified critique can be addressed to Marx on this score. As we argue in the concluding chapter, the Bolshevik seizure of power was very different from what Marx conceived as the conquest of political power by the proletariat. Secondly, even the latter was not equated by Marx with the proletarian revolution itself. The installation of the proletariat as the ruling class, the "conquest of democracy," was specifically thought to be only the "first step in the workers' revolution," as the *Communist Manifesto* declares. Even the political configuration, immediately issued from the Bolshevik seizure of power, was far from "the proletariat organized as the ruling class," in the sense of Marx, demonstrating the "political form at last discovered under which to work out the economic emancipation of labor," as Marx thought of the state under the Communards of 1871 (1971: 75). Socialism, even as a concept, appearing in Lenin's *State and Revolution*, contains elements, such as "state" and "hired employees" earning "wages," that are alien to Marx's socialism conceived as a free Association.

We are also unable to accept Bettelheim's contention of "insufficiency" of Marx's concepts in view of the rise of new forms of capitalist relations. If these new forms are still forms of *capitalist relations* in the sense of Marx, then they would certainly be "adequate to the concept" of capital, to use one of Marx's often-used (Hegelian) expressions. Nowhere does Marx speak of a unique form of capitalist relations, though, only for illustrative purposes, he most often refers to English capitalism (of course, in its historically changing forms). In other words, whatever be the new forms of existence, if they are all shown to be based on the laborers' *separation* from the conditions of labor -- the very concept of capital in Marx -- then the Marxian (theoretical) categories are sufficient to deal with those forms.

We now come to Roemer's critique of Marxism in relation to the Soviet phenomenon. In what one could call his Copernican-Keplerian endeavor to save the Marxian theory from its "Ptolemaic crisis," this model builder, we submit, shows a surprising lack of rigor of presentation and, at the same time, demonstrates an astonishing innocence of Marx's texts. He accepts the Soviet system axiomatically as socialist simply because of a certain "convention," without any rigorously established criteria. (Maybe this is the most convenient way for him to debunk socialism). In the same way, he uses "capitalism" and "private ownership" without any precision. Again, we do not know what exactly he means by Marxism. We have only an idea, from a more recent publication, in which he seems to include within this term the ideas of Marx as well as those of Marx's self-proclaimed followers -- again, uncritically, as if the ideas of the master and those of his followers are basically the same (Roemer 1992). He makes a distinction between Marxism and "historical-materialist method," neither defining the terms nor making the distinction clear, and his following proposition remains undemonstrated: "Marxism is the application of historical materialism to nineteenth-century society" (1981: 208). As a matter of fact, there is no historical materialism in Marx. What Marx has is the "materialist method" that studies "the immediate process of production of material life" as the "origin of social relations and the ideas or intellectual conceptions which follow therefrom" (1962a: 393; 1965: 915). This is the method that Marx employed for studying human history and sometimes called it, not historical materialism but more appropriately, the materialist "conception of history" (1973b: 37). We do not understand what is specifically nineteenth-century about Marx's simple materialist proposition that "the economic categories are only the theoretical expressions, the abstractions of social relations of production" (1965: 78). Or, take the celebrated proposition of 1859: "the mode of production of material life conditions the social, political and spiritual life process in general" (1958: 13). We have no evidence, and Roemer does not offer any, to show that this proposition was valid only for nineteenth-century society, but became invalid in the late twentieth century. Interestingly, Marx had already encountered a Roemeresque critic who maintained that Marx's materialistic principle, that "the economy forms the material basis of society," was valid for (at that time) nineteenth-century capitalism but invalid for both the antiquity and the middle ages, the former being governed by politics, the latter by Catholicism. Marx replied that "the middle ages did not live on Catholicism, neither did the ancient world on politics," and that the specific roles of politics and Catholicism in the respective cases "are explained, on the contrary, by the economic conditions" (1962a: 96; 1965: 616).[1] It is well known that nineteenth-century Marxists like E. Bernstein had already questioned the validity of Marx's "Critique" in regard to the nineteenth-century society itself.

Finally, Roemer's unrigorous statement that "public ownership of the means of production" or, equivalently, "state's control of the firm's policies and entitlement to its profits" is the "sine qua non" of Marxian socialism(1992: 261,262) is absolutely unwarranted by Marx's texts. He seems to be unaware that socialism according to Marx is a free Association of producers without state, without commodity production, and without wage labor. When Marx speaks of abolition of private property, it is not in the sense of individual private property, contrary to the Marxist Vulgate, but in the sense of "class property," as is seen in texts as temporally distant as the *Communist Manifesto* (1848) and the *Civil*

War in France (1871). The reason is simple. It is precisely capitalism's "historical mission" to destroy individual private ownership in the means of production, and in the remarkable chapter on the function of credit in capitalist production in the third volume of *Capital* (of which Roemer seems to be blissfully innocent) Marx refers to the "abolition of capital as private property within the limits of the capitalist mode of production itself" and of the genesis of "directly social capital." (We develop the theme at length in Chapter 1 of this book). There is no text by Marx which would warrant the elimination of exploitation under "public ownership of the means of production," simply because exploitation continues while capital continues, and capital can continue both under private and public ownership. In fact, Marx explicitly mentions State as capitalist in *Capital* as well as in *Notes on Wagner* (which will be mentioned later). According to Marx, it is only the collective (direct) *social appropriation* of the conditions of production -- and not "public ownership of the means of production" -- that alone would replace capitalist "class (private) property." This would of course imply elimination of capital itself along with the state.

RELEVANCE OF MARX'S METHOD

The irrelevance or insufficiency of Marx, faced with a particular economic -- social formation, would imply the inadequacy of Marx's materialist method, and of the categories arising uniquely from this method, for investigating and characterizing the formation in question. This is the method which Marx had in mind when he claimed that "the method of analysis which I have employed had not yet been applied to economic subjects" (1965: 543). At the same time, Marx qualified this method as "dialectical," "taking every finished form in the flow of its movement," after having "discovered the rational kernel" from inside the "mystical shell" of Hegelian dialectics (1962a: 27,28). According to this method, the fundamental criterion for characterizing an economy -- corresponding to a social formation -- is the specificity of the social relations of production -- the "definite relations into which human beings enter" in course of the "social production of their lives" (1958: 13). These relations show the "specific way in which laborers and the means of production" -- the invariant "factors of the social form of production" -- are "combined for production" (1973a: 42), that is (in the case of a class society), "the specific form in which the unpaid surplus labor is pumped out from the immediate producer," where one must "find the innermost secret, the hidden foundation of the whole social edifice" (1964: 799).

The application of the materialist method to the Soviet case implies that, as the Soviet society, like any other society, could not have lived on politics or ideology -- to paraphrase Marx -- one has to see how the Soviet people gained their livelihood, that is, inquire into the specificity of the social relations of production on which the society was based and the way of appropriating and utilizing society's surplus labor (including its "specific economic form"), arising from those relations, in view of their enlarged reproduction. This also includes, at the same time, the inquiry into how, as in any other economy, it is the needs of enlarged reproduction of the relations of production that determined the specific existential forms of ownership, exchange, and distribution in the Soviet economy. Contrary to the scholars who have been discussed, we find this materialist method and the categories corresponding to this method adequate for analyzing the Soviet economy. Following this method, we argue the capitalist character of the Soviet economy in the light of the Marxian concept of capital. The Marxian concept of capital is analyzed at some length in the chapter that immediately follows.[2]

We would stress here one vital point. Marx's (theoretical) categories, as developed in his principal theoretical works -- abstracted from the historical illustrations -- are not directly applicable to any economy -- Soviet or Western -- in its existential form at any time (including the nineteenth century). After all, "the bourgeois economy in its (inner) depth is totally different from what it appears to be on the surface [*auf der Oberfläche scheint*]" (Marx 1958: 59). In each case, one has to go behind the phenomenal forms which, though necessarily manifesting the essence, do conceal as well as reveal the latter. In other words, one has to grasp what Marx calls the "inner interconnections" of the reality -- precisely determined by the relations of production -- and see if and to what extent the reality in question is "adequate to the (Marxian) concepts."[3]

From the general materialist proposition, that an economy is adequately characterized by its own social relations of production, it follows that characterizing the Soviet economy does not require comparing its phenomenal features with those of any other existing economy, whatever other values such a comparison might provide. Each existential form of a particular mode of production is specific, and capital should offer no exception in this regard. Thus there is no reason to think, for example, that Western capitalism, as it appears on the surface at a particular epoch, is the unique form of the capitalist mode of production, and that any economy (or society) that does not manifest similar phenomenal characteristics cannot be considered capitalist. On the contrary, whatever be the different forms of manifestation of an economy, if the latter is based on the laborers' separation from the conditions of labor, necessarily rendering labor wage labor, then the economy in question is capitalist. What is essential is to grasp that "the *same economic basis* -- the same as to the principal conditions -- through innumerable different circumstances can phenomenally show *unending variations and gradations* which only through the analysis of these empirically given circumstances can be understood " -- where economic basis precisely stands for the "totality of production relations" (Marx 1964: 800; 1958: 13; italics added).

GENERAL OUTLINE

The first two chapters analyze Marx's concept of capital. Capital has a double existence -- an economic existence and a juridical existence. Capital's economic existence is that it is not a "thing" but a social relation of production given by the *separation* between labor and the conditions of labor, rendering the former wage labor and the latter capital. Capital's economic existence, again, has a double dimension: an essential reality where capital is a social totality -- existing as "social total capital" (hereafter STC) -- and a phenomenal reality, existing as reciprocally autonomous singular capitals, the "fragments" of STC. An immediate consequence of capital's totality -- singularity configuration is that laborers are "free" (separate) only with respect to individual capitals, but are attached to STC as "accessories."

Capital's juridical existence is the ownership relation of capital. Capital as juridical property is defined negatively as the non-property of the laborers -- arising from separation -- rendering capital the private property of a *class*. This is the basic sense of capitalist private property in Marx, though this private property is unrecognized by jurisprudence. Individual private property -- a specific form of capitalist (class) private property -- is the secondary sense of capitalist private property, recognized juridically, and commonly considered as private property *tout court*. Capitalist private property in the first (basic) sense is invariant with respect to its changes in the second (secondary) sense and goes out of existence only with the economic existence of capital. Starting with the unity of ownership and function of capital in the same hands at the initial stage of capital accumulation, capitalist private property arrives at a stage of accumulation where that unity is split, making non-(property) owning pure functionaries of capital -- the employers of wage labor -- the "active" (real) capitalists. This is the stage where capital increasingly negates itself as individual private property and becomes common capital of the associated capitalists. Ultimately the centralization of capital could reach a point where there is one single national capital, its individual units remaining reciprocally autonomous -- functionally speaking -- ensuring the continuation of the competition of capitals. Finally, the accumulation of capital has to be understood as essentially the enlarged reproduction of the laborers' separation from the conditions of production taking the form of self-expanding values. Capital accumulation can take place under (largely) unchanging methods of production as well as under "continuous metamorphosis" of the methods of production. The accumulation of capital is the independent variable, the employment of labor the dependent variable.

The next three chapters examine the Soviet economy -- statically and dynamically -- in the light of Marx's concept of capital. The social relation of production in the Soviet economy was marked by the laborers' separation from the conditions of production, ensured by juridical abolition of (individual) private property in the means of production and the control of the economy (and society) by the completely autonomized Party-State on the one hand, and the laborers' freedom with respect to individual units of production (for most of the period) on the other. An immediate consequence of this separation was the wage labor character of the Soviet labor. The reciprocal autonomy of the individual units of production working with wage labor ensured the competition of capitals (including the exchange of products of labor in value form). Naturally, the enlarged reproduction of the productive apparatus and labor power assumed the form of accumulation of *capital*. Spurred by the attempt of "catching up with and surpassing" the advanced capitalist countries in the shortest period, this accumulation followed the path of quantitative expansion of production with more capital under the same conditions of production and not the path of continuous revolutionalization of the methods of production. This particular mode of capital accumulation finally reached the limit point of absolute over-accumulation of capital which served as the basis of the regime's final collapse.

The two chapters that follow confront the widely-held idea that the Soviet economy was non-capitalist. The Soviet economy was held to be non-capitalist by those who accept it as socialist, as well by those for whom it was neither socialist nor capitalist (hereafter NSNC). Non-capitalism is conceptualized as the negation of the dominant existential features of contemporary Western capitalism. Thus a specific juridical form of ownership in the means of production, a specific form of exchange of the products of labor (including the means of production), and a specific form of remunerating labor, associated with modern Western capitalism, are taken as uniquely representing the capitalist forms of ownership, exchange, and distribution, the absence of which is equated with non-capitalism. Thus, by ignoring the question of (social) relations of production and by confining itself to the phenomenal world of forms of existence, the non-capitalist theoretical approach appears as a-historic and empiricist-positivist. As to socialism within this non-capitalist approach, it is not conceived as a society of free and associated producers without state, commodity production, and wage labor. It is conceived, on the contrary, as a society ruled by a workers' state which owns the means of production, after having juridically eliminated their private ownership character and thereby (supposedly) capitalism itself. In other words, socialism, within this non-capitalist approach, loses its emancipatory character.

In their representation of the Soviet *economic reality*, the non-capitalist tendency stresses the following features, supposed to distinguish it from capitalism: state ownership of the means of production, the non-spontaneous character of exchange of products, alleged absence of competition of capitals, and guaranteed full employment. Now, state ownership turns out to be -- when its real basis is examined -- only a specific form of juridical ownership in which means of production appear as *capital*. Similarly, if the exchange of products takes commodity form -- which it admittedly did in the USSR -- then, for the purposes of commodity production, spontaneity or non-spontaneity of exchange is of little importance. Thirdly, as respects the competition of capitals, wage labor producing commodities, which were exchanged between reciprocally autonomous enterprises (each considered as a juridical person) ensured competition of capitals in the Soviet economy. Finally, the strategy of "catching up with and surpassing" within the shortest period, based on extensive accumulation, signified that the needs of capital exceeded the supply of labor and thereby guaranteed the full employment of *wage labor.*

The book concludes by arguing the invalidity of the generally accepted idea of "restoration of capitalism" in the ex-USSR The Soviet regime, almost from the beginning, was not a regime ruled by the workers themselves. The autonomized Party-State exercised dictatorship over the proletariat (in the latter's name) from Lenin's days. The Bolsheviks had effectively destroyed the earlier pre-capitalist production relations and increasingly transformed the producers into wage laborers (whose freedom from individual production units was curtailed for a limited period). Given this essentially capitalist reality, there is no question of restoration of capitalism in the ex-USSR.

NOTES

1. The expressions "society" in the first quotation, and "the economic conditions" in the second, appear in the French version replacing, respectively, "world" and "the mode by which they gained their living" in the German edition.

2. It is not clear whether Althusser accepts Marx's materialist method at all. For he seems to virtually reject (1969: 21) what he calls Marx's "profoundly Hegelian-evolutionist" "Preface" [to the *Contribution to the Critique of Political Economy* of 1859] which *is* the text where Marx magisterially lays down his specific method, and to which he explicitly refers in *Capital,* considering it as the text where "I discuss the materialist foundation of my method" (1962a: 25,96).

3. For a clear exposition of Marxian abstraction, see Ollman (1993).

Chapter 1

CAPITAL'S DOUBLE EXISTENCE

Despite the fact that Marx's lifelong preoccupation was the investigation and analysis of the "economic law of motion" of the capitalist society and of the working of the forces destined, according to him, to undermine and eventually destroy it, there has surprisingly been little satisfactory discussion of the Marxian category of capital as such. Marx emphasizes the necessity of developing an "exact concept of capital," because it abstractly mirrors the "bourgeois society" with all its contradictions, and, at the same time, shows the limit where the "bourgeois relation is driven to supersede itself" (1953: 237). In order to develop an exact concept of capital (in Marx), it is necessary to analyze what Marx calls capital's "double existence," or the "economic property" and the "juridical property" of capital (1962b: 456, 460), where the first refers to the production relation and the second to the ownership relation of capital.[1] In this chapter, this relatively unexplored aspect of Marx's critique of political economy is analyzed. The chapter is divided into two sections corresponding to capital's two existences. Section one analyzes the economic existence of capital, first as a pure social relation and then as a social totality. Section two deals with the juridical existence of capital in the two very different senses of private property in capital: as private property of the capitalist class and as private property of the individual capitalist.

CAPITAL'S ECONOMIC EXISTENCE

The economic property of capital, compared to political economy, undergoes a double rupture in Marx. First, capital is not a *thing*, but a social *relation* of production, a historical and not a natural category. Secondly, capital, as a social relation, is, in *essential* reality, a social totality representing the capitalist class in opposition to the wage-laboring class but, in *phenomenal* reality, the social total capital (hereafter STC) appears only through its fragments, as reciprocally independent, singular capitals.

CAPITAL AS A SOCIAL RELATION AS SUCH

Political economy considers capital as a "thing." This is not only true of vulgar political economy, but it is also true of classical political economy (both in the sense of Marx). Of course, the former with the "evil design of the apologetic roves only within the apparent connections" and "feels at home" in (their) phenomenal forms, while the latter, as "science," studies the economic conditions impartially and disinterestedly -- "inquires into the inner connections of the bourgeois production relations" (Marx 1962a: 21,95; 1964: 838). However, the approach to capital as a category even in classical political economy -- not to speak of vulgar political economy -- is basically different from that in Marx. Thus, in classical political economy, capital -- "stock" -- is, in its "real" (non-financial) aspect, considered as "the effect of past labor" (Petty 1963-1966: 110), or as simply "a certain quantity of labor stocked or stored up" (Smith 1937: 314), "accumulated labor" (Ricardo 1951: 410), in the same way as it is regarded as only "machines and instruments" (Smith 1937: 325) or "implements" (Ricardo 1951: 26). Consistent with this approach, the classical political economy considers the capitalist mode of production as a natural and everlasting mode of production. Classical political economy, opines Marx, conceived as capital "the general elements of labor process appearing in capitalist production independently of their social form, making thereby capitalist mode of production an eternal, natural form of production" (1956: 10). In Marx, on the other hand, capital is considered not as a mere (produced) means of production, a thing, but as a specific social relation of production represented in a thing and appearing at a particular phase of human history (1964: 822).

By treating capital as a thing and capitalist production as natural and eternal, political economy succeeded, Marx points out, only in showing how production is carried on within capitalist relations but was unable to explain how these relations are themselves produced, that is, "the historical movement which has begotten them" (1965: 74). Political economy saw "how production is carried on *within* the capitalist relation but not how this *relation* itself is produced and simultaneously how it produces the material condition of its dissolution and thereby the removal of its *historical justification* as a *necessary form* of economic development" (1982: 2160; 1969: 89; italics in original).[2]

As with every other mode of production appearing in history, capitalist production is characterized, according to Marx, by the specific way in which the

"Man of Labor" is related to the "Instruments of Labor" (1970: 208), in other words, how the laborers are combined with the means of production. In capitalist production this combination is effected in a specific way. Here the starting point is the separation of the free laborers from their means of production. As the "productive mode of existence of capital, these two are united in the hands of the capitalist" (Marx 1973a: 42). This *separation* determines capital as a historically specific social relation of production. Here the objective conditions of labor, taking the form of alienation in opposition to living labor, directly appear as "arms against the living labor" (Marx 1982: 2057). As Marx emphasizes:

What imprints the *character of capital* on money or the commodity is not their nature of money or commodity, nor the material use value of the commodity as subsistence and means of production, but the circumstance that this money and this commodity, these means of production and subsistence, confront the *labor power*, denuded of all material wealth, as *autonomous powers*, personified in their possessors (1969: 30; italics in original).

It cannot be sufficiently stressed that capitalist production relation is basically a relation of separation between laborers and the conditions of labor, in other words, a relation of "absolute *divorce* [*Scheidung*], *separation* [*Trennung*] of objective wealth from the living labor power." This divorce appears as the product of labor itself, as objectification of its own moments. Labor appears in the capitalist production process in such a manner that "its realization [*Verwirklichung*] is equally its *negation* [*Entwirklichung*]. It posits itself objectively, but it posits its objectivity as its own non-being or the being of its own non-being -- of capital" (Marx 1966a: 76; 1982: 2238-39; italics in original). In this separation (opposition) labor appears in a contradictory form: negatively -- positively, simultaneously as "absolute poverty" and as "universal possibility": absolute poverty, insofar as labor is considered as "non-raw material, non-instrument of labor, non-means of subsistence, non-money, separated from al=nl means and objects of labor, . . . a complete denudation [*Entblössung*] of all objectivity;" universal possibility, in so far as labor is considered "not as object but as activity, not as value but as the living source of value," opposed to capital, the "universal wealth where it exists objectively as its universal possibility" (Marx 1953: 203; 1976a: 148).[3]

Before proceeding further one important point in Marx's "Critique" needs to be emphasized. Once capital is understood as a historically (specific) social production relation (and not as a thing), "capital", "capitalist production," "capitalist relation of production," "capitalist mode of production," and "capitalism" could be basically used equivalently. Similarly, from the relational point of view, there is strict reciprocal implication between "capital" and "capitalist." "[If there is] no capitalist production [there is] no capital and thus no capitalist" (Marx 1969: 32), and "capital [which] can only be a production relation is essentially capitalist. . . . *Capitalist is contained in the concept of capital*" (Marx 1953: 412-13; italics added). Indeed, this follows as a matter of course once the capitalist is conceived, as is done by Marx, simply as "personified capital," as "bearer of objectified labor," of "definite class relations," as the "necessary functionary of capitalist production" (1962a:16; 1962c: 359; 1964: 827; 1976a: 33).[4]

It should be stressed that separation (opposition) in its Marxian sense, that we have been discussing, signifies an *inversion* of the producer-product relation. Contrary to the earlier forms of domination, capitalist domination is not that of person over person. It is a domination of objectified labor over living labor, of the laborer's produce over the laborer. The relation of inversion is the general relation common to the different stages of capitalist production. It shows that the material conditions of production, including the means of subsistence, which are the product of labor, subsume the laborer, and, thereby, they are *capital*. "Capital *employs* labor" (Marx 1956: 354; 1969: 16; 1982: 2161; italics in original).[5] This universal domination of *thing* over *person* Marx qualifies as "fetishism" (1958: 45, 167; 1966a: 257; 1982: 2160).

Marx shows in an original way the specific character of labor under capitalism. The laborer, separated from all means and objects of labor -- which is specific to capitalism -- is a free laborer; "free in a double sense: a free person -- free from relations of clientship or bondage -- to dispose of his labor power as his commodity [and], on the other hand, having absolutely no other commodity to sell, free from all things necessary for the realization of his labor power" (1962a: 183; 1953: 406). An immediate and *necessary* consequence of this double freedom of the laborer -- itself conditioned necessarily by separation (inverse domination) -- is shown in the specific character of labor itself in capitalism (unlike in any other mode of production): *wage labor*.

Marx notes that the classical political economy (not to speak of the vulgar political economy) had taken over from everyday life "naively," and "uncritically," what appears on the surface of the bourgeois society to be the laborer's wage as the value or price of labor, and thereby "got into unsolvable confusions and contradictions" (1962a: 561). The wage-form, "this phenomenal form," effaces all traces of the division of the working day into necessary labor and surplus labor, into paid labor and unpaid labor, and "makes the real relation [between capital and labor] invisible and, indeed, shows its opposite" (1962a: 562).[6] It is only by going behind this "irrational expression," this "category for the phenomenal form arising from the production relation itself," that one discovers the true nature of wage labor. Marx claims that he is the first to go behind the mystery of the wage of labor (1962a: 559,562).[7]

Wage is that part of the laborer's own product that appears as alien income, but, not being spent as income, "confronts the laborer as *capital* in exchange of not merely an equivalent but against more labor than that objectified in the product" (Marx 1962b: 421; italics in original). A mere sale and purchase of labor power does not yet, as Marx emphasizes, constitute wage labor. The "proletarian, economically speaking," is the "wage laborer who produces and valorizes capital" (1962a: 642). In other words, "in the strict economic sense of the term" wage labor is only "the labor which *posits and produces capital [Kapital setzende, Kapital produzierende]*" (1953: 367). What Marx calls "productive labor" (under capitalism), that is, "labor that directly posits surplus value" (1956: 357), is wage labor in this "strict economic sense". Alternatively speaking, the laborers, freed from the conditions of labor and selling their labor power in order to produce commodities, that is, "labor as activity positing value" (1953: 185) for the purchaser of labor power -- the possessor of these conditions -- are wage-laborers "in the strict economic sense."[8]

The simple sale and purchase of labor power does not yet reveal the nature of capital. Marx distinguishes "two essentially distinct -- though conditioning each other -- moments of capital-labor exchange." The first moment is that of pure exchange between the possessor of money and the possessor of labor power as a commodity, taking place in the sphere of circulation, "on the surface, full of noise and visible to all eyes." Here the capitalist and the laborer confront each other as buyer and seller of commodities *exchanging equivalents*. This is the "veritable Eden of inherent rights of man." In this "*formal process* capital appears as money and labor power as commodity (where). . . materialized labor in its general social form, that is, money, is exchanged against *labor which exists only as power [Vermögen]*." The second moment ("act") in the capital-labor relation is "a process that is qualitatively different from exchange." Here "there is no exchange, strictly speaking" (1956: 360,361; 1962a: 189; 1976a: 146; italics in original).

The second moment of capital labor relation is really the specific process of appropriation of labor by capital. It is only after the possessor of money and the laborer have ceased to be the buyer and the seller of the commodity (labor power), it is only with the "actual absorption [*Einsaugung*] of labor, that labor is transformed into capital and the advanced sum of values is transformed from capital *as a possibility [aus möglichem Kapital]* . . . *into acting and actual capital*". (1969: 84; italics added). Incapable of showing how the exchange of more living labor against less materialized labor corresponds to the law of commodity-exchange, the classical political economy, Marx argues, "confounded the exchange process between variable capital and labor power with the process of absorption of living labor by constant capital" (1969: 36).

The second moment constitutes, in fact, a process of *double consumption*: on the one hand, the objectivity in which capital consists must be put to work, that is, "consumed by labor," and, on the other hand, the possessor of money (must) consume the commodity that has been bought, that is, "the subjectivity of labor must be abolished and objectified in the material of capital" (Marx 1953: 206; 1956: 362). The process of double consumption is comprehensible only when one quits the sphere of exchange and follows "the possessor of money and the possessor of labor power into the secret abode of production, on the threshold of which stands: no admittance except on business". (Marx 1962a: 189).[9]

Unable to distinguish between the two determinations (moments) of capital-labor relation -- namely, the alienation [*Veräusserung*] of labor (power) and its actual manifestation [*Äusserung*] as use value -- the "economists", as Marx emphasizes, cannot understand the veritable nature of the (combined) result of the "three moments of the production process, that is, materials, instruments and labor," the result being conceived as "simple consumption," as the *simple end* of the process. However, "in the product are simultaneously reproduced the moments of the production process which have been consumed [*aufgezehrt*] in it. The whole process appears as consumption which does not end in nothing nor in simple subjectification of what is objective, but which itself is, again, posited as an object" (1962a: 188; 1953: 208).

A correct perspective on the two moments of capital-labor relation, and on the productive consumption as the process of arriving at a new positing is not possible as long as one understands only "how capital produces" but not "how it is itself produced," that is, capital as producing only material things, but not as what it essentially is, namely, a *relation of production reproducing itself*, where "the condition of production is (also) its constant result," where the "preconditions of production appear in the *reproduction* itself as its past results, and the result of production appear as its precondition" (Marx 1962a: 189; 1962b: 488; 1982: 2243; italics in original).

From his concept of capital, as the separation of the living from the materialized labor, Marx arrives at his two alternative formulations for characterizing capitalism which might appear at first sight as not quite mutually consistent. "Capitalist production," says Marx in one formulation, "is in fact commodity production as the general form of production, . . . because labor itself appears as a commodity here, because the laborer sells his labor, that is, the function of his labor power, at a value determined by the cost of its reproduction" (1973a: 119-20).[10]

A second formulation is in following terms:

Two characteristic features [*Charakterzüge*] distinguish the capitalist mode of production from the start. First, it produces its products as commodities . . . . Commodity constitutes the dominant and determining character of its product. This first of all implies that the laborer himself appears only as the seller of commodity and thus as free wage laborer, and therefore labor appears as wage labor in general . . . . Secondly, what specially distinguishes the capitalist mode of production is the production of surplus value as the direct objective and determining motive of production. Capital produces capital and this it does only in so far as it produces surplus value (1964: 886-88).

Now, a reading of the two formulations would show that the first formulation contains only what appears as the first characteristic feature in the second formulation, omitting the latter's second characteristic feature, namely, the production of surplus value, without which, of course, there is no capitalist production. In other words, the first formulation seems, at best, incomplete and, to that extent, inconsistent with the second. However, a careful reading of Marx's text, where the second formulation appears, shows that the second characteristic feature is not a separate feature -- on a par with the first, as it were -- but a *necessary consequence* of the first which in fact contains all the essential conditions of capitalism. In that particular text, immediately after speaking of the dominance of commodity production with labor appearing as wage labor as capitalism's first characteristic feature, and *before* going on to mention the second, Marx emphasizes that "the relation between capital and wage labor determines *the whole character* [*den ganzen Charakter*] of the capitalist mode of production"; and a few paragraphs later he adds that "*only because* labor in the form of wage labor and means of production in the form of capital pre-exist [*vorausgesetzt sind*], . . . does a portion of value appear as surplus value and this surplus value as profit . . . . [And only because of this] do the additional means of production . . . appear as new additional capital" (1964: 886-87; italics added). Thus the second formulation, in so far as it lays down the essential conditions of capitalism, is equivalent to the first formulation.

We can go even further. From Marx's discussion of capital's economic property we could conclude that the relation between generalized commodity production (hereafter GCP), wage labor, and capitalist production is one of reciprocal implication. First we note that when labor becomes wage labor in the strict economic sense, commodity production is generalized. On the one hand wage labor implies GCP. Only when labor becomes wage labor does the value form of the product of labor become generalized, inasmuch as wage labor signifies that, along with the material products, labor power itself, reproduced by labor, becomes a commodity. Thus the "positing of social labor in the form of capital-wage labor opposition . . . is the final development of value relation and production founded on value" (Marx 1962a: 184,185; 1953: 592). This is clear from what we presented above as Marx's first formulation on the specificity of capitalism. On the other hand, GCP implies wage labor. This appears textually in the very first characteristic feature of capitalism in what we called Marx's second formulation above. Again, Marx shows, as we saw earlier, that capitalist production is commodity production as the general form of production while, at the same time, emphasizing that it is only on the basis of the capitalist mode of production that all or even the majority of products of labor assume commodity form (1962a: 183-84; 1976a: 33-34). Finally, the relation of wage labor and capital is also one of reciprocal implication for Marx. Capital is a production relation between the immediate producers and their conditions of production which, separated from them and passing under the control of non (immediate) producers, dominate them as capital. The necessary consequence of this "forcible separation [*Diremtion*]," posited by the difference between objective labor and living labor, in other words, "forcible separation, pertaining to their very concept [begriffsmässige], between objective and subjective conditions of labor, arising out of the nature of the (capitalist) labor process" (1953: 207; 1969: 9), is, of course, wage labor. Thus capital necessarily implies wage labor. On the other hand, the fact that wage labor is characterized by Marx as labor that "produces and posits capital," signifies that wage labor necessarily implies capital. Hence the relation of reciprocal implication between the two. As Marx emphasizes, "Labor produces its conditions of production as capital and capital produces labor as wage labor as the means of its realization as capital," each one "reproduces itself while reproducing the other, its negation." Indeed, "labor as wage labor and conditions of production as capital . . . are the expression of the same relation, only viewed from different poles" (1969: 85; 1953: 362; 1962b: 488). This identity of opposites Marx expresses by equating wage labor with capital.[11]

Once we understand the relation of reciprocal implication between GCP, wage labor, and capitalist production -- a kind of tri-symmetric relation, if we could call it -- the rest of the features of capitalism could be seen as the necessary resultants following from any one of these essentially equivalent central categories.

CAPITAL AS TOTALITY

The second specificity of Marx regarding capital's economic property is his conception of capital as a *social totality*. Generally political economy has considered capital from the point of view of the individual capitalists. Among his predecessors, Marx credits the Physiocrats not only for the first systematic conception of capitalist production but also for establishing the first rational concepts concerning "capital in general," as well as for showing the whole productive process of capital as a "total movement" (1956: 306-7; 1973a: 360; 1976a: 42). Indeed, beginning with A. Smith, there is a systematic impoverishment of the point of view of totality. This is one of the reasons why Marx considers the Physiocrats to be superior to Smith as respects the analysis of the process of reproduction.

For Marx, on the other hand, the point of departure is the category of *totality*, the domination of the whole over the parts. "The relations of production of every society constitute a whole," he stresses (1965: 79). Following from this basic position, Marx's starting point in the treatment of capital is conceiving capital as a social totality, capital representing a *class* opposed not so much to the individual laborers as to the wage laborers as a *class*. For "capital is not a personal but a social power" (1966b: 71). An individual capital is not what it seems to be in phenomenal reality. It does not lead an (absolutely) independent existence. Each particular capital "constitutes only an autonomous fraction, with an individual life as it were, of the total social capital just as each particular capitalist is only an element of the capitalist class," and hence the movement of individual capitals is "simultaneously their individual movement and an integral part of the movement of (social) total capital" (1973a: 351-52,391).

This insistence on the priority and primacy of the whole over the parts is indissolubly associated with Marx's basic (materialist) position that it is only from the class point of view and not from the point of view of the individual, taken in isolation, that the social reality is fully comprehensible.[12] To understand the (antagonistic) reality of capital as a specific social relation, one must start with what Marx alternatively calls, total capital, social capital, social total capital or capital in general, signifying "the totality of buyers of labor power" (1969: 30), the "collective capitalist" (1962a: 243), the "whole capitalist class" (1964: 389), that is, *"capital as class"* (1953: 337; italics added) - in other words, with what constitutes the essential reality of capital, before dealing with individual capitals. This specificity of Marx's method, *totally different from the method of political economy*, has been little understood by most of his commentators, including the Marxists.[13]

Marx shows, contrary to political economy, that "social total capital" (hereafter STC) has an existence different from that of individual capitals. As he says: "Capital in general has a real existence different from the particular, real capitals" (1953: 353). Marx first studies STC, or capital in general, and then arrives at the concrete forms engendered by it -- that is, the individual capitals as they appear in competition "on the surface of the bourgeois society."
As he emphasizes:

The finished form of economic relations such as they show themselves on the surface in their real existence, and consequently also in the representations by which the bearers and agents of these relations seek to make a clear idea, is very different from, and in fact *contrary* to, their internal and *essential*, but *hidden* kernel [*Kerngestalt*] and the concept corresponding to it . . . . All science would be superfluous if the appearance and the essence of things coincided immediately (1964: 219,825; italics added).

From a Marxian perspective it is only the point of view of capital as essentially a social totality that reveals the exploiting character of capital while the point of view of individual capital, underlying "free competition" in political economy, obscures it. First, in the relations between individual capitals we are -- as Marx points out repeatedly -- only at the level of *exchange* relations which do not allow us to see the relation between capital and labor at the level of *production*. Secondly, as we shall argue in the next chapter, at the level of individual capital, the origin of profit and, thereby, labor's exploitation, is mystified, inasmuch as the profit of the individual capitalist is not the surplus value extracted by the latter but is derived as an individual share from the total surplus value that the social total capital, that is, capital as class, has extracted from labor as class. At the same time, the consideration of capital as a social totality shows that the servility of the laborer under the capitalist system is not basically different from that under other historical systems. Thus in capitalism, compared to the earlier economic social formations, the immediate producer seems to be free in relation to the masters of the conditions of production, and the exploiting character of his/her labor remains invisible on the (competitive) surface of the capitalist society. But things change as soon as we "penetrate the phenomenon (of competition) and go behind the appearances" and "discover the inner essence and the intimate structure of the (capitalist) process," that is, as soon as we seize capital as a social totality, capital representing a class. From that vantage point we discover that "the working class is . . . like the dead instrument of labor, an accessory of capital . . . . The Roman slave was bound to his proprietor by a chain. The wage laborer is bound to his proprietor by invisible threads. Only his *owner is not the individual capitalist*, but the capitalist class" (1964: 178; 1962a: 598,599; italics added).[14]

In the same way, the point of view of social totality also clarifies the real nature of a laborer's remuneration under capitalism. That the laborer's wage is nothing but a part of the product "constantly reproduced by the laborer himself" is obscured and disguised by the commodity form of the product and the money form of the commodity. However, this is an "illusion" which "immediately vanishes as soon as, instead of individual capitalists and individual laborers, the capitalist *class* and the laboring *class* are considered." (1962a: 593; italics added).

This totality -- singularity configuration of capital vis-à-vis the laborers -- clarifies a very important point. We saw earlier that according to Marx, the separation of the immediate producers from their conditions of production constitutes the very concept of capital. Now this separation -- equivalently "double freedom" -- of the laborers in relation to capital is really true in so far as the laborers relate to *individual capitals*, not to the STC, as we saw just now. In other words, though capital, considered as a social totality, remains non-property of the laborers, the latter are not separated from it, they are only its accessories, being part of it, exactly like the slaves in relation to their individual masters -- who also had no property but who themselves formed part of the means of production. (That is why Marx calls wage laborers "wage-slaves"). It is in relation to individual capitals only that the laborers are really "free", *separated*. In this case, capital is of course their non-property but, at the same time, they are not an accessory of capital. What the free laborer sells is always "a definite, particular magnitude of manifestation of (labor) power . . . to a particular capitalist in opposition to whom he stands as an independent individual. This is not his relation to the existence of capital as capital, that is, the class of the capitalists" (Marx 1953: 368). Hence wage labor implies individual capitals in their reciprocally autonomous relations, which implies, again, GCP and *conversely*; the same conclusion we reached earlier through an alternative argument.

CAPITAL'S JURIDICAL EXISTENCE

Our starting point here is how Marx relates property to production. In the broadest sense, production is only an appropriation of nature by individuals as social beings. It is "appropriation through labor, (which is) real economic process of appropriating," which, again, is the same thing as "property over objectified labor." Thus "what appeared as a real process is *recognized* as a juridical relation." In this sense "it is a tautology to say that property is a condition of production" (Marx 1953: 413,9, italics added). Here relations of production, considered as real economic relations, are equivalent to the relations of property, the second being only the juridical expression of the first. "Juridical relations arise from production relations," and "the juridical forms as simple forms cannot determine the content itself, they can only *express it* [*drücken ihn nur aus*]" (1966b: 177; 1964: 352; italics added). Inasmuch as property relations only reflect economic relations which are their content, to consider property relations as a "category apart" is a "metaphysical or juridical illusion" (1962a: 99; 1965: 118). The capitalist appropriation process is simply the "capital-wage labor relations expressed as property relations" (1953: 373).

PRIVATE PROPERTY AS CLASS PROPERTY

In all class societies, the objective conditions of production are basically the property of the dominant class or classes. Naturally, capitalism is not different from other class societies in this regard. In all modes of production, and particularly also in capitalism, the objective conditions of labor belong to one or more classes and the simple labor power belongs to the laboring class, that is, outside of the case where laborers are simultaneously producers and sellers of their commodities, and where, consequently, "the value of labor is equal to the value of products of labor" (Marx 1956: 37,38). In this sense, the objective conditions of labor are the "*private property* of a part of society" (Marx 1956: 21; italics added), that is, *class property*. Marx's general expression "capitalist private property" would, then, simply signify that the character of capital is assumed by the "means of production monopolized by a distinct part of society" (1964: 823). This is what Marx calls "monopoly of capital" that enables the capitalist to extort surplus labor from the laborer (1973a: 85). Thus when the *Communist Manifesto* declares that the communists can sum up their theory in a single expression: "abolition of private property," the latter is expressly used in the sense of "disappearance of class property " [*Aufhören des Klasseneigentums*] (1966b: 71,73). Private property, again, is clearly used for class property in Marx's well known statement, "The knell of the capitalist private property sounds" (1962a: 791), Marx even substituting "capitalist property" for "capitalist private property" in the French version of *Capital* (1965: 1239).[15]

This class monopoly over the conditions of production which are *capital*, or this class property of the bourgeoisie, is of course equivalent to, nay, identical with, its very opposite, the "non-property" [*Nichteigentum*] or "alien property" [*fremdes Eigentum*] of the (wage) laborers in respect to the (objective) conditions of production, which Marx stresses in many places of his "Critique." Simply, "the *opposite existence [Dasein] of these conditions against labor makes their proprietor capitalist*" (1962b: 458; italics in original). The sense of class property/non-property stands out clearly in the following lines:

Let us consider the total capital, that is, the totality of buyers of labor power on one side and the totality of sellers of labor power, that is, the total labor on the other. The laborer is constrained to sell, instead of a commodity, his own labor power as a commodity. . . because all the *objective wealth* as the property of the possessor of commodities *stands against him* [*gegenübersteht*] . . . . The laborer labors as *non-proprietor* [*Nichteigentümer*] and the *conditions of his labor* stand against him as *alien property* [*fremdes Eigentum*] (1969: 30; italics in original).

Naturally, with all the changes *within* capitalism -- and the latter "cannot exist without constantly revolutionizing the instruments of production, the relations of production and [therein] the whole social relations" (1966b: 62) -- private property in capital, in this first and fundamental sense of Marx, remains invariant, though completely *unrecognized as such juridically*.[16]

PRIVATE PROPERTY AS INDIVIDUAL PROPERTY

Although capitalist property as the simple juridical expression of the capitalist production relations are by definition private, that is, class property of the capitalists, the latter does not and need not, according to Marx, always assume a *particular juridically recognized form of property*. Thus, as Marx observes in connection with his discussion of ground rent, capital, at the initial stage of its development, finds itself in the presence of a form of landed property which does not correspond to it, and "by subordinating agriculture to itself capital creates the form corresponding to it . . . *however diverse are its juridical forms*" (1964: 630; italics added).[17] In effect, it is in the context of the specificity of the *form of property* within class property that capitalist private property takes on a second meaning in Marx. Here the starting point is private property considered simply as the "opposite [*Gegensatz*] of social, collective property," and private property in this sense refers to the property of "private individuals" [*Privatleute*] in the conditions of production which, again, can have two different "characters," according as these "private individuals" are "laborers or non-laborers" (1962a: 789). Corresponding to these two characters, Marx speaks of "two laws" of (private) property. "The first [law] is the identity of labor and property," that is, "private property based on one's own labor" (1953: 373; 1962a: 802). The second law is the law of "bourgeois" (private) property into which the first law is "transformed" [*umschlägt*] "by its own inner, unfailing dialectic" (1953: 373; 1962a: 609). According to this second law, the "product of one's own labor appears as alien property [and] contrariwise, alien labor appears as the property of the capitalist", that is, labor appears as "negated property." Capitalist private property "necessitates [*bedingt*] the annihilation of private property based on one's own labor". Thus the "separation of property from labor becomes the necessary consequence of a law that apparently started out from their identity" (1953: 373; 1962a: 802,610).

Before proceeding further, let us stress that capital(ism) has not invented the juridically recognized private property in this sense. Capital(ism) just took over the institution of private property, considered juridically, from pre-capitalism, that is, from the Roman law (Marx 1973b: 63; 1953: 916). Thus private property in the means of production, either in its class sense (considered above) or in its individual sense, is not specific to capital. Private property becomes *capitalist* private property only when the means of production are capital, that is, only when the workers are separated from the conditions of production (at the level of individual units of production). Truly, capital's juridical existence arises from its economic existence.[18]

Now, this second law of private property negating the first law, looks, in fact, like the negation of private property as such (in the second sense of Marx). This seems to be the meaning of some striking observations that Marx makes in (almost) identical terms in at least two texts. There Marx mentions that one of the "principal facts of capitalist production" is that the means of production through [their] concentration in a few hands cease to appear as the property of the immediate laborers (individually) and are transformed, contrariwise, into "social powers of production"; thereby "the capitalist mode of production *abolishes/sublimates private property* -- [*hebt das Privateigentum auf*] even though *at first* these means appear as the private property of the non-laboring capitalists" (1962b: 422; 1964: 276; italics added).[19] Thus it seems that it is really the first law of private property that corresponds strictly to private property as such -- in the sense of property of private individuals -- taking its "adequate classical form" not in capitalism but in petty mode of production (Marx 1962a: 789).[20]

Capitalist private property in Marx's first sense -- that is, as class property -- is of course invariant with respect to changes within the capitalist mode of production. However, private property in capital in the sense of individual property (Marx's second sense) changes its form corresponding to the needs of capital accumulation. At the initial stage of capital's existence, the needs of accumulation seem to be best served by uniting capital as property with capital as function in the same (individual) hands.

The first split in this property-function unity, dictated by the needs of accumulation, manifests itself with the appearance of money capital as loan capital -- the "interest bearing capital" -- with the advance of money capital by its owner to the non-money capital owning "industrial capitalist."[21] Here, for the first time, the "double existence of the capitalist" is laid bare: as the pure "proprietor of capital," and as the "industrial capitalist who really transforms money into capital" (Marx 1962 b: 456). Correspondingly, the total (gross) profit is divided between "interest" and "entrepreneurial gain," or "industrial profit". Compared with the *non-owning* active [*fungierende*] capitalist who receives entrepreneurial gain the receiver of interest is simply the passive, *non-functioning* owner of capital as "idle property" [*nur als träges Eigentum*] (Marx 1964: 393). The same capital undergoing this "double and totally different movement" thus results in the "purely quantitative division" of its remuneration -- the gross profit -- being "transformed into a *qualitative* one" (*in eine qualitative umschlägt*) (Marx 1964: 385; italics added).[22] Here Marx notes a contradiction: whereas the conditions of labor are capital only to the extent that, as (separated) *non-property* of the laborers, they stand and function in opposition to the latter, with the remuneration of "capital-property" taking the interest form, "this opposition is *effaced* [*aufgelöscht*]", inasmuch as the capitalist representing "simple ownership, anterior to and outside of the production process", faces the capitalist "simply active and nonowner of capital", and, consequently, "interest bearing capital stands in opposition not to wage labor but to the functioning capital" (1962b: 458; 1964: 387,388,392; italics in original). The process of "inversion" -- inherent in the capitalist mode of production -- here manifests itself in that "interest appears as surplus value that is due to capital as capital, . . . *independently of the process of production*, . . . [whereas] industrial profit as part of the surplus value is earned by the capitalist, not because he is the proprietor of capital but because . . . his *capital functions*." To the capitalists, it seems natural that interest is due to (sheer) proprietorship of capital, whereas industrial profit is the "product of their *labor*"; in other words, "the functionaries of capital, the real agents of production, are there as *laborers* confronting themselves or others as *proprietors*" (1962b: 474-75; italics added). Thus, in the transaction of money capital between the lender and the borrower, "the veritable movement of capital, . . . the mediation [*Vermittlung*] is effaced, [becomes] invisible," and the "simple form of capital without its mediation [is] only the *irrational form* [*begriffslose Form*] of the veritable movement of capital" (1964: 361; 1962b: 519-20; italics added).

In this first form of split in capital's (erstwhile) apparently unitary existence, though money capital belongs to the passive, non-functioning capitalist, the material instruments of production -- obtained through borrowed money (capital), nevertheless, belongs to the functioning or industrial capitalist, and thus capital's ownership is not yet fully separated from capital's function. On the other hand, the owner of money capital and the owner of material instruments of production (as capital) are still private owners of capital in Marx's second sense. In other words, capital has not yet transcended the bounds of private property in Marx's second sense.

The dissolution of private property under capitalism assumes a new character with the further accumulation of capital. Through the "play of the immanent laws of capitalist production," the process of capital accumulation entails concentration of capital, given that conditions of production require massive use of capital, as well as centralization of capital, necessitating "decapitalization [*Entkapitalisierung]*) of smaller capitalists by bigger ones" (1962a: 790; 1964: 256). This ultimate form of expropriation within capitalism, "expropriation of capitalist by capitalist" (1962a: 654) -- "separation between laborers and conditions of labor raised to its second power" (1964: 256) -- finally reaches a point where capital is negated as property of private individuals/households and transformed into common capital of what Marx calls "associated capitalists" (1962a: 655). Thereby capital which is social in essential reality becomes, along with production itself, social in phenomenal reality. Share capital of the joint stock companies is the first concrete form of common capital to which Marx pays a good deal of attention.

Marx's analysis of the significance of this first form of appearance of the "capitalist collective" is of considerable importance, the full implications of which have been little appreciated even by the avowedly Marxist scholars. In this connection Marx observes:

Capital which in itself is based on the social mode of production and presupposes social concentration of the means of production and labor, *directly* assumes here the form of social capital in opposition to private capital. This is the *abolition/sublimation [Aufhebung] of capital as private property within the limits of the capitalist mode of production itself* (1964: 452; italics added).

Together with this abolition/sublimation of private property -- that is, property of private individuals/households -- in the means of production *within capitalism* itself there is the "transformation of the capitalist really exercising his functions into a simple manager and of the owners of capital into simple owners, into simple financiers" (1964: 452).

Share capital is the first form of "directly social capital" (hereafter DSC); in this first form of DSC, the property-function split in capital, that is already inaugurated with the appearance of loan capital, is widened further in that, as opposed to the simple proprietor of capital entitled to dividends including interest and entrepreneurial gain, that is, *total profit*, the functionary of capital - the active capitalist -- is no longer even the industrial capitalist -- still the individual proprietor of material instruments of production and obtaining entrepreneurial gains -- but the simple director of the capitalist collective who, as an "administrator of *alien* capital," as a *non-proprietor*, receives only a "wage of administration [*Verwaltungslohn*] *fully separated* from entrepreneurial gain." Thus, for the first time, "the ownership of capital is totally separated [*ganz getrennt*] from the function of capital in the actual process of production" (Marx 1964: 401,452; italics added).

What the first split between capital's ownership and capital's function already inaugurated -- appearing in loan capital -- now becomes palpable, that is, the exploitation process itself appears as a simple labor process in which the functioning capitalist only performs a labor different from the labor of the worker. As labor, "exploiting labor and exploited labor are identical," where, of course, the capitalist is a "laborer as a capitalist, that is, the exploiter of the labor of others," and where the wage worker is obliged to produce his/her own wage as well as the "wage of direction and superintendence" of the functioning capitalist (1964: 396,399,401). Marx, indeed, contrasts this new "real [*realiter*] separation" between function and property of capital with their initial separation and calls the latter, following the English socialists, "*sham separation* between industrial capitalist and moneyed capitalist" (Marx 1962b: 494, italics added).[23] Private property -- in Marx's second sense -- is, for the first time, shown to be irrelevant for the means of production to be *capital*. It is no longer "adequate" (in the Hegel-Marx sense of "corresponding to") for the new stage of capital accumulation; it is in fact revealed as the "*old form* in which the social means of production appears" (Marx 1964: 456; italics added). The total separation of ownership from the process of production signifies that the ownership of the means of production is not only separate from the labor of immediate producers -- a characteristic of capitalism from the very beginning -- but it is also separate from *all labor* connected with the process of production, including the labor of the active capitalist, the non-owner of capital, such that "only the functionary remains, the capitalist [that is, the owner of capital] disappears from the process of production" (Marx 1964: 401).[24] In other words, this is the separation of "juridical property of capital from its economic property," showing "a contradiction between capital as function and capital as property," an "inversion [*Verkehrung*] and reification of the production relation at its maximum . . . . In this form the *fetishist configuration* [*Fetischgestalt*] of capital is completed just as the representation of capital-fetish" (Marx 1962b: 460; 1964: 394; italics in original).

DSC in its first form, as discussed, though it veritably "annihilates [*vernichtet*] private industry "(Marx 1964: 454) -- in Marx's second sense -- within capitalism, it does not, however, yet *completely* transcend the juridically recognized private property form inasmuch as each separate "capitalist collective" under this configuration is still recognized juridically as the *private owner* of capital under its jurisdiction. Marx also envisages the case of the "state itself as capitalist producer [with] its product as a commodity" (Marx 1962c: 370), "to the extent that [it] employs wage labor" (Marx 1973a: 101). Here the "functionaries of capital" are at the same time the (salaried) functionaries or agents of the state, extracting surplus value from the immediate producers who remain separated from and opposed to their own product, that is, the conditions of labor which, by this fact, continue to be capital. Thus "state capital" represents the second form of DSC -- logically, not necessarily chronologically, in relation to the first -- where all the contradictions appearing with the first form are exacerbated to the maximum.[25] Here production and property appear to lose whatever private character they had earlier. Juridically recognized as public property, this second form of DSC completely casts off capital's old form of existence as juridically recognized private property and reveals its essence in the starkest form as a pure (social) exploitation relation of production -- the pure economic property of capital, though, in the absence of traditional form of existence, the mystification and obfuscation of this relation, as Marx would say, reach, at the same time, their maximum.

Let us add that state capital could be, as it usually is, an individual capital in the sense of a fraction of STC (Marx 1973a: 101), though juridically it would be recognized as belonging to public ownership, while the other fractions of STC, including those in which DSC has appeared, and those where the old form still prevails, would continue to be juridically recognized as belonging to private ownership. Alternatively, the state could very well take over the totality of society's capital in which case the "centralization of capital would reach its last limit . . . where the total national capital would constitute only a single capital in the hands of a single capitalist" (Marx 1965: 1139), that is, STC would be under the single juridical public ownership of the state.

With DSC (in the form of share capital or state capital), capital is supposed by Marx to have reached the ultimate phase of its existence from the point of view of capital's juridical property, where state capital, in particular, is indeed logically the last configuration of the juridical capitalist (1962b: 456), where property is defined -- let us emphasize -- not as private but as public. Capital, originally starting out with the expropriation of the immediate producers "at last realizes," under DSC, "its objective: the expropriation of all individuals [*Expropriation aller einzelnen*] from their means of production which . . . cease to be means as well as products of *private production*" (1964: 455-56; italics in original).

Concurrently with the abolition (sublimation) of private property in capital, and integrally connected with it, "the enormous extension of the scale of production and of enterprise" signifies that "*the labor of the individual* is transcended in its immediate existence and particularity and is posited as *social labor*" (1964: 452; 1953: 597; italics in original). With property, production and labor all ceasing to be private, their non-private character, let it be stressed, is "still imprisoned within the capitalist confines" (Marx 1964: 456), that is, still within capitalist private property in Marx's *first sense* -- DSC, it seems, brings capital to its final point and, "while appearing to accomplish the domination of capital, announces, at the same time, its dissolution." Thereby this last form of capital's juridical existence is, as Marx emphasizes, an objective preparation for the "transition from the capitalist mode of production to the associated mode of production" (1953: 544-45; 1964: 456).[26]

It is clear from this that capital as property is basically different in Marxian "Critique" compared to political economy. With Marx, capitalist property is not necessarily the property of private individuals (households) over capital, which is only the property form of capital at a *particular (old) stage* of the latter's development. At a later stage, capitalist property assumes a directly social character eliminating private property in this sense. In a fundamental sense, of course, capitalist property for Marx always remains private property as *class property* of the capitalists over the conditions of labor. In political economy, on the other hand, the only form of capitalist property is private property, and the only form of private property is the property of private individuals/households. (This accords with political economy's recognition only of separate, singular capitals, and not of capital as a social totality, not of capital as class). Even when jurisprudence recognizes corporate property as private (for the corporation), it remains by and large true that "the large corporation [with ownership-control split] has never been assimilated into the main body of economics" (Galbraith 1978: 370). Even those few who, in contrast with the dominant trend in economics, have recognized the empirical reality of ownership -- control separation in modern capitalism, conclude that this fact constitutes a revolution in capitalism, virtually amounting to the abolition of capitalism itself, inasmuch as they identify capitalist property with the property of private individuals/households over the (produced) means of production.[27] It is remarkable that the Marxist tradition, beginning with the Second International, has, on the whole, uniquely held capitalist private property as individual, and not *class* (private) property of the capitalists, and a capitalist as the *individual* owner of capital (Kautsky 1965: 115; Hilferding 1973: 154; Lenin 1982b: 300,302; Trotsky 1972: 233), F. Engels's important distinction between "capitalist production" and "capitalist private production" -- made in his critique of the Erfurt Program (1891) -- notwithstanding.

NOTES

1. The common term "property" in both the expressions in this case is not to be interpreted in the usual *juridical* sense of ownership or possession. It has another meaning here. It refers to quality or power belonging specially to something (e.g., the soap has the property of removing dirt). The term *"Eigentum"* that Marx uses in both the expressions is exactly property in this sense: "what belongs to one" [*"was einem gehört"*]. See *Der Sprach-Brockhaus* (Wiesbaden 1956: 154).

2. The French philosopher L. Althusser cites the passage from *Misère de la philosophie* as given here but, preoccupied with (anti) "historicism," dismisses it as unimportant (1965: 31-32). Thereby, it seems, he misses this basic Marxian specificity in relation to political

economy. Marx's "discovery of the difference as well as the connection" between capital as a social relation and capital as a (material) thing has been termed by the Russian economist V.P. Shkredov as "constituting . . . a *revolutionary upheaval* [*revolyutsionnogo perevorota*] in political economy" (1973: 165; italics added).

3. This Marxian meaning of "absolute impoverishment" of labor under capitalism has, by and large, escaped the Marx scholars. "The process of impoverishment of the laborer" is simply "his creation of *value*, [remaining] *alien to himself*" (Marx 1969: 16; italics in original)

4. The well-known Hungarian scholar Istvan Meszaros, trying to distinguish between "capital" and "capitalism," has pointed out that in *Capital* Marx focuses on the "domination of *capital* and not of capitalism," and has faulted Engels for allegedly translating "production of capital," as it appears in Marx's *Capital*, as "capitalist production." This Engelsian lead, according to Meszaros, was followed by the later Marxist tradition which "mixed up and confused" these two "very different things" (1978: 135; italics in original). Space does not permit us to go into this argument at length. We simply submit that there is confusion, rather, in the eminent scholar himself. As a matter of fact, in the "Foreword" to the very first edition of *Capital* (vol. 1), Marx himself writes about "capitalist production" and "capitalist mode of production," and not of production of capital or the mode of production of capital (1962a: 12). Similarly, in the posthumously published so-called sixth chapter of *Capital*, Marx speaks of the "development of capitalist production, that is, of capital" (1969: 92). In fact, the identity of "capitalist production" and "capital" appears many times in Marx's early 1860s manuscripts. This is, of course, as it should be if capital is understood as what it is -- a (social) relation of production and not a thing. On the testimony of the well-known Marx scholar M. Rubel (1968: 1661), Marx seems not to have used capitalism as a term before 1870. Once we take capitalism and capitalist as a specific production relation, Meszaros's assertion that "post revolutionary societies" were not capitalist even though "capital maintained its domination [there]" (1978: 136, 137), appears self-contradictory.

5. The sentence appears in English in the original.

6. The expression within parenthesis was inserted in the French version (1965: 1036).

7. Marx faults "political economy" as being the only science which takes things as they appear in their everyday existence without bothering to go behind these phenomenal forms in order to seek their "contradictory essence" (1962a: 559; 1982: 2117).

8. Thus even though the mercenaries in the Roman army freely sold their labor power to the state against wages, this institution of mercenaries was essentially different from wage labor inasmuch as "the exchange of money as income, as simple means of circulation against living labor, can never posit money as capital, therefore labor as wage labor in economic sense" (Marx 1953: 371,428).

9. The final phrase is in English in the original.

10. For a somewhat shorter version of the same formulation see Marx (1962a: 184).

11. Thus "capitalist production" is explicitly used by Marx as an alternative expression for "wage labor" (1962b: 257), in the same way as "society of wage laborers" is made to stand for capitalist society (1962a: 231), and "wage system" [*système du salariat*] for the capitalist system (1965: 1113-14).

12. Cf. G. Lukács: "The category of totality, . . . the domination of the whole over the parts, is the essence of the method that Marx took over from Hegel. . . . Marx considers, particularly in *Capital*, every problem from this point of view" (1970: 94,96).

13. R. Luxemburg, justly appreciating Marx's uniqueness in this respect, observed that "Marx, for the first time, has brought out with classic clarity the fundamental distinction between the individual capital and the social total capital in their movements" (1966: 436). In modern times, R. Rosdolsky was one of the few who had properly appreciated Marx's specificity in this regard (1968: 61-71). For an interesting analysis of capital's totality-singularity configuration in Marx, following Rosdolsky's lead, see H. Reichelt (1970: 73-95).

14. The last sentence was inserted by Marx in the French version (1965: 1076), not reproduced in the later German editions. Let us recall that Marx reproached Proudhon's "imitation of bourgeois economics" in holding that "when a society of the capitalist mode of production is considered en bloc as a *totality*, . . . it would lose its specific historically determined character." Proudhon did not understand that "we are dealing with the collective capital" (1973a: 431; italics added).

15. Capitalist private property, again, appears as class property a few years later in Marx's defense of the Paris commune: "The Commune, they exclaim, intends to abolish property, the basis of all civilization! Yes, gentlemen, the Commune intends to abolish that class property, which makes the labor of the many the wealth of the few" (1971: 75).

16. Even in his earlier writings Marx considers "opposition between capital and labour" as *equivalent* to the "opposition between property and propertylessness" -- where he uses "property" and "private property" synonymously (1966a: 96-97) -- in the same way as he considers private property as the "antithesis of the proletariat" and as "producing the proletariat as proletariat" (1972a: 37).

17. Here the "form" of property corresponding to capital -- resulting from laborers' separation from land -- is obviously used by Marx in a general sense, in the sense of capitalist *property relation*, corresponding to the capitalist production relation, as distinguished from specific *forms of property within this property relation*, as it appears in the last sentence.

18. This is the sense of the remarkable insight shown by the young Marx: "[Capitalist] *private property* is the product, the result, the necessary consequence of *alienated labor* . . . . *Private property* is derived from an analysis of the concept of *alienated labor*" (1966a: 84; italics in original).

19. Another "principal fact" of capitalism that Marx mentions is the "organization of labor itself as social labour" resulting in the "abolition/sublimation of private labor."

20. The term "adequate" was changed into the stronger term "integral" in the French version (1965: 1238).

21. Here "industrial capital" refers to productive capital as such, independently of the specific sphere of capitalist production (Marx 1973a: 114,120).

22. Elsewhere Marx approvingly refers to the "correctness of the law, discovered by Hegel in his *Logic*," that "simple quantitative changes are transformed at a certain point into qualitative differences" (1962a: 327).

23. The whole phrase, excepting the word "between," appears in English in the original.

24. Paraphrasing Aristotle, Marx writes: "The capitalist bestirs as such not in the ownership of capital. . . but in the employment of labor" (1964: 398).

25. Though Marx specifically speaks of "state capital" [*Staatskapital*] (1973c: 101), where capitalist production continues with the state as the *juridical owner* of capital, he does not, unlike in the case of the first form of DSC, go into any length on the question. However, once given the concept itself, the essential elements for constructing the basis of the relevant analysis could easily be gathered from his discussion of the first form, just as he himself bases the latter on his analysis of the initial property -- function separation of capital.

26. Cf. Hegel: "The highest maturity and stage, which something can attain, is that in which it begins to disappear" (1963b: 252).

27. See, among others, Berle and Means (1968: xxxvii, 115, 305); J.R. Hicks (1971: Ch. IX); J.K. Galbraith (1978: xiv, 45).

Chapter 2

ACCUMULATION OF CAPITAL, COMPETITION OF CAPITALS

Consideration of capital as a category remains incomplete without a consideration of accumulation of capital and competition of capitals. As regards the accumulation of capital, which we take up in the first section, we focus on a specific type of accumulation in Marx which has been largely neglected in the relevant literature. We shall see in Chapter 4 that the Soviet accumulation process largely accords with this type. In the second section, we explore the Marxian category of competition of capitals which, we argue, is qualitatively different from competition as envisaged in political economy (classical or otherwise). This is another aspect of the Marxian concept of capital that has been virtually ignored by most of the writers on Marx. Later we shall see, again, how very relevant this category is for the Soviet case.

ACCUMULATION OF CAPITAL

There are two types of capital accumulation in Marx's theoretical scheme: one based on continuous revolutionization of the method(s) of production, the other based on unchanging method(s) of production. To each of these types corresponds a specific type of over-accumulation. Economists -- including those of Marxist persuasion -- have, by and large, concentrated their attention on the first type of accumulation and over-accumulation, virtually neglecting the second type.[1] The present chapter explores the distinction between the two types and more specifically focuses on the second type of capital accumulation in Marx.

Capital, as previously stated, is essentially the laborers' separation from their conditions of labor. Consequently, the accumulation of capital is basically the enlarged reproduction of this separation. Inasmuch as the original accumulation of capital is simply the original separation of laborers from the objective conditions of labor, and their subsumption under these conditions in the latter's autonomized existence, the accumulation of capital represents only as a continuous process what appears in the original accumulation (of capital) as a particular historical process. As Marx emphasizes: "What is produced and reproduced anew is not merely the *existence* of these objective conditions of living labor, but their *existence alien* to the laborer, their existence as independent values belonging to an alien subject against this living labor power" (1982: 2284; italics in original).

On the other hand, the process of enlarged reproduction does not appear as the accumulation of capital "so long as the means of production of the laborer and therefore his product and his means of subsistence do not stand opposed to him in the form of capital" (1962a: 624). Alternatively speaking, accumulation of capital is the reconversion of a part of the (unpaid) surplus labor of the (immediate) producers -- taking the *value form* -- into additional means of production and subsistence toward additional labor power on the basis of this relation of *separation -- opposition*.

Given the specificity of the capitalist mode of production, Marx derives the accumulation of capital from capital's "drive for measureless absorption of labor power," its tendency to "draw out infinitely the volume of surplus labor," its "ravenous appetite [*Heisshunger*] for surplus labor" (1962a: 249,253; 1976a: 158). If the technique or (equivalently) method of production remains unaltered, the mass of surplus value can be increased either by prolonging the working day or, if the latter is given, by employing more laborers (in case a labor reserve exists), "by simultaneous employment of more laborers; by simultaneously multiplying the working day" (1953: 290). In other words, in such a case the mass of surplus value will depend on the mass of available labor power in the market, therefore, on the magnitude of the laboring population and the proportion in which it increases, such that "the natural growth of the population forms the basis of the growth of the absolute quantity of surplus value" where, therefore, "the increase of population constitutes the mathematical limit of the production of surplus value by total social capital" (1962a: 325; 1976a: 165). Marx, however, did not consider that the absolute prolongation of the working day could be a constant means of (capital) accumulation (1959: 474). Hence *given* what could be considered a "normal working day," determined physically or socially (1962a: 325; 1976a: 164), the only alternative -- with a *given* technique of production -- is to increase the number of laboring population (with a view to increasing the mass of surplus value). The latter could increase without the increase in population as such when some parts of the population who were independent producers like small peasants and artisans are transformed into wage laborers or, in more general terms, when the laborers who were earlier "unproductive are transformed into productive laborers" and/or when parts of the population who did not work earlier, like women and children, are drawn into the process of production (1959: 474; 1976a: 167). Thus, given the *unchanging method of production*, demand for labor will increase with the accumulation of capital. "Each year will furnish employment to a number of wage laborers which is higher than that of the preceding year" (1962a: 641).

In the development of capitalism, though "the absolute movements of the accumulation of capital . . . *appear* to be due to the exploitable labor power's own movement," it is really "the magnitude of the accumulation which is the *independent variable* [while] the magnitude of wages is the *dependent variable*" (Marx 1962a: 648; italics added). As Marx elucidates in the French version of his work, "the movement of expansion and contraction of capital with a view to accumulation therefore produces, alternatively, relative insufficiency or superabundance of labor offered" (1965a: 1130). Now, the stationary state of the method of production holds, by definition, during the phase of "formal subsumption" of labor under capital, when, that is, capital simply takes over from the pre-capitalist epoch the existing technique of production. Here the development of capitalism, exclusively based on the expansion of absolute surplus value, naturally signifies that "the demand for wage labor increases rapidly with every new accumulation of capital while the supply of labor follows only slowly" (1962a: 766).[2] It is only with the "real subsumption" of labor under capital, that is, when the existing technique of production is changed -- which leads "the social man to produce more with less labor," thus enabling capitalism to advance on the basis of the increase in relative surplus value -- that the demand for labor relatively diminishes, with the "corollary of absolute increase in the demand for labor following a diminishing proportion" resulting in the "industrial reserve army of labor" (1962a: 673; 1965: 1162). Thus the creation of the "reserve army of labor" or, alternatively speaking, the "relative surplus population" in capitalism, is postulated on the "progress of the productivity of social labor" resulting from "technical changes that revolutionize the composition of capital" (1962a: 674; 1965: 1145).

However, the real subsumption of labor under capital -- corresponding to accumulation based on the increase in relative surplus value -- though generally associated with the transformation of the (old) method of production, can also be envisaged in the context of an *once-for-all and not continuing* transformation of the method of production. In other words, once capital makes the transition from the stage of formal to that of real subsumption of labor on the basis of a change in the earlier method of production, the latter can remain *stationary* over a period. This happens during the intervals of the development of capitalism "where technical revolutions are less perceptible" and where "*accumulation presents itself more as a movement of quantitative extension on the new technical basis once acquired*" (Marx 1965: 1145; italics added). Here, given the increase in capital with a stationary technical composition of capital, the number of employed workers rises as the "demand for labor increases in the same proportion as capital" (Marx 1962a: 650,473; 1965: 1145). As Marx observes: "In this case the mass of commodities produced increases, because more capital is used, not because it is more productively used . . . . [This is] reproduction on an extended basis, . . . appearing only as a *quantitative expansion of production with more capital under the same conditions of production*" (1959: 518; italics added).

Here the productivity of labor remains the same, (and) the increase of capital costs the same labor as the production of capital of the same amount last year (1959: 473-74), that is, accumulation of capital necessitates an increase in the magnitude of labor demanded. On the other hand, given the stationary state of the technique of production, a certain length of the working day, and the number of laborers, the mass of surplus value could be increased by raising its rate through a greater intensity of labor used. To the extent that a higher intensity of labor used *necessarily* implies that "more products are obtained from additional expenditure of labor," that "each parcel of time is filled with more labor" and that "magnitude of labor increases within a given parcel of time" (1962a: 547; 1976a: 307), we would maintain that, in this case of a rise in the rate of surplus value, its absolute element dominates its relative element and that, in this sense, it is a variant of the case of accumulation of capital by increasing the absolute surplus value. This was the case, as Marx mentions, of the weaving sector of English textiles in the 19th century where a higher labor intensity rendered a higher value along with a larger quantity of products *without* "any change in the objective conditions of production" (1962a: 434), that is, without any change in the technique of production. As a matter of fact, the two methods of increasing the mass of surplus value -- that is, prolongation of the working day and the increase in the intensity of labor -- were in *simultaneous* operation in English factories for half a century (1962a: 432).

Now, when the accumulation of capital is based on "extensive growth," when, with the increase of capital, "the number of its subjects increases," and when, eventually, there is an "increase of capital greater than the increase in the supply of labor, the wage rate rises." However, a rise in wages at best can mean "a quantitative diminution in unpaid labor" which may "not in any way interfere with the capitalist domination" and in any case is never allowed "to go far enough to threaten the capitalist system itself." On the other hand, if through suitable measures the bourgeoisie could "*durably lower the minimum wage*, surplus value would increase in its relative magnitude exactly as if the productivity of labor has increased" (Marx 1962a: 645,646,647-48; 1965: 1129; 1976a: 171; italics added).

It should be emphasized that in the context of a change in the method of production it is the *technical composition of capital* -- understood as the ratio of the mass of the material means of production to the quantity of living labor --

and not its value composition that is relevant, inasmuch as the former is the "real [*eigentlich*] basis of the composition of capital," and a change in the value composition "only *approximately [nur annäherend]* indicates the change in the composition of (capital's) material components" (Marx 1964: 154; 1962a: 651; italics added). Now, a change in the technique of production is not necessarily equivalent to a change in the technical composition of capital. According to Marx accumulation of capital could take place either with changing or with unchanging technique of production as we saw above. Technical composition of capital could, however, behave differently under each of these two types. This requires some elucidation.

As regards accumulation of capital with changing technique of production, Marx envisages two cases of change in the technique of production -- both associated with an increase in relative surplus value through higher productivity of labor: change in "technical labor process" and change in "social combination of labor" (1962a: 532-33; 1965: 1003, 1136). In other words, one is the *technological change*, the other is the *organizational change*. Though, in general, the two types of change march hand in hand, there are certain phases of capital accumulation when they are not (necessarily) associated. This is the case particularly at the *initial stage* of real subsumption of labor under capital where there are changes in the technique of production due only to changes in "social combination of labor" giving rise to higher productivity of social labor *without there being any change in the technical composition of capital*, when "concentration" of working population through "association" -- imposed by capital -- as well as "concentration of capital" in place of its "dispersion" take place. This association/concentration is the *"first transformation* of formal subsumption of labor under capital in a real change in the method of production itself, . . . the first level when subsumption of labor under capital no longer appears as a purely formal subsumption" (1976a: 235,237; italics added). This is basically an organizational and not a technological change in the (capitalist) method of production. Initially, for a higher productivity of social labor, it is sufficient that there is this concentration of capital and *not* its growth, that is, "not its accumulation." Any progress of accumulation at this stage -- where "concentration is [still] indistinguishable from accumulation" involves only "a *quantitative and simultaneous* growth of the divers elements of capital," that is, *no change in the technical composition of capital*, even though the earlier technique of production has changed through change in the "social combination of labor," giving rise to a higher productivity of social labor (1953: 479; 1956: 133; 1965: 1134; 1982: 2223; italics added).

In the second case of a change in the method of production, that is, where there is a change in the "technical labor process," the "enlarged reproduction, accumulation . . . has a *qualitative* aspect" (1959: 518; italics added). Here the technical composition of capital is no longer stationary. That is, in the case of production "the mass of tools and materials increases more and more in comparison with the sum of labor force necessary to operate them" (1965: 1135), this quantitative change in the technical composition of capital being (simultaneously) associated with the *qualitative* changes in this composition; "the accumulation of capital takes place [here] under a progressive *qualitative change in its composition.*" This is manifested in the "development of productivity of social labor which becomes the most powerful lever of [capital] accumulation" (1962a: 650,657; 1965: 1135; italics added).[3]

As regards the accumulation of capital with unchanging technique of production -- discussed above -- Marx envisages, again, two situations: in the one, technical composition of capital remains stationary while in the other it changes. In either of these cases the productivity of social labor is non-increasing, generally speaking. Change in the productivity of (social) labor is generally associated positively with change in the technique of production (1959: 470, 473) (an exception to be noted presently), not with change in the technical composition of capital *as such.* Productivity of (social) labor increases generally with a transformation in the technique of production, which could entail a change in the technical composition of capital as well, when the transformation in the former involves the technical labor process. But a rise in the technical composition of capital as such, on the basis of an *unchanging* technique of production, does not result in a higher productivity of (social) labor.

Now, technical composition of capital remains stationary with unchanging technique of production during the formal subsumption of labor under capital as well as during certain periods of real subsumption of labor -- noted earlier -- when magnitudes of materialized and living labor move together along with the expansion of production, when demand for labor increases proportionately with capital, when, in other words, "with the growth of total capital *the composition of capital and the production conditions remain constant [seine Zusammensetzung konstant bleibt, weil die Produktionsbedingungen]*" (1962a: 473,641; italics added). An increase in the productivity of labor -- unaccompanied by changes in the technique of production as well as technical composition of capital -- due *only* to a greater *intensity* of use of existing labor and equipment (employed), faced with a resource barrier, would constitute a special (nondurable) case of this situation of capital accumulation.[4] However, *given* a situation of non-increasing productivity of labor and the limitation of the working day, technical composition of capital tends to grow with an unchanging technique of production when, under the impulsion of the capitalists' "ravenous appetite for surplus labor," the "needs of capital accumulation outgrow the usual supply of labor," when "the increase of capital makes exploitable labor power insufficient" (1962a: 641, 648). This is a case of purely *quantitative* change in the technical composition of capital -- under non-revolutionization of the technique of production -- when there is a simple increase in the *same type* of the means of production in relation to the mass of living labor.[5]

Corresponding to each broad type of capital accumulation -- that is, one based on continuous revolutionization of the method of production and the other based on (largely) stationary method of production -- there is a specific type of over-accumulation of capital as a logical outcome of the process. In general, Marx holds that over-accumulation of capital and overproduction of commodities go hand in hand, because capital, as it accumulates, leads to the growth of productive powers of social labor which bring about, periodically, overproduction of commodities. Hence, in general, "over-accumulation of capital implies overproduction of commodities" (1964: 261). Capital is over-accumulated here because the production engendered by it is overproduced in the sense that the quantity produced is more than can be disposed of at an acceptable rate of profit, given the absence of proportionality of the diverse branches of production as well as limitations of consumption capacity based on "antagonistic distribution relations" (1964: 254).[6] Here overproduction of commodities is the outcome of capital's tendency to promote an "unlimited increase in production," which itself is the immediate result of the "tendency [of capital]" to an "absolute" or "unconditional development of productive powers of social labor" (1964: 259, 260). This latter tendency is, in its turn, uniquely associated with the "continuous revolutions in the methods of production," a *qualitative* transformation of the technical composition of capital, "reflected" in the rise of the organic composition of the average social capital, "only another expression for the progress of the social productive power of labor" (1964: 254,222), engendering in the process a relative surplus population, the latter being *"inseparable* from the development of the productivity of labor" (1964: 246; italics added). Thus capital is overaccumulated, that is, it is excessive only in relation to the so-called "effective demand,"[7] that is, in relation to the possibility of realization of surplus value (1964: 255). This is the over-accumulation of capital of the first type corresponding to the tendency of continuous process of "technical metamorphosis" of the (capitalist) methods of production (1965: 1144). Given that "modern [capitalist] industry never considers and never treats as definitive the existing mode of production" and that "its basis is revolutionary" (1962a: 510-11), Marx naturally pays a great deal of attention to this type of over-accumulation/ overproduction of capital, and it plays a considerable role in Marx's theoretical scheme of capitalist crisis.

There is, however, another type of over-accumulation of capital in Marx's analysis of capitalism. This type corresponds to the *quantitative* -- as distinct from the qualitative (noted earlier) -- accumulation of capital, that is, accumulation of capital *without* a revolutionary change in the method of production. This over-accumulation of capital is *not* associated with overproduction of commodities and hence it is not (at least not directly) related to the problem of realization of surplus value. Here capital is over-accumulated in *relation to the employed labor force,* because the method of production remains (largely) stationary. Accumulation of capital here being based on sheer quantitative increase in the material means of production (taking the form of capital), given its continuous process, a moment arrives when "the needs of accumulation start to surpass the supply of labor," when "the growth of capital renders exploitable labor power insufficient" (1962a: 641,648). Capital is over-accumulated here "from the moment when capital increases in relation to the laboring population in such proportions that neither the absolute labor time furnished by this population could be prolonged [that is, neither the number of workers nor their working time could be increased] nor relative surplus labor time extended" (precisely because of the stationary method of production), and this is called by Marx "absolute over-accumulation" or "absolute overproduction of capital" (1964: 261-62). This over-accumulation of capital, unlike the over-accumulation in the first case, is not associated with overproduction of commodities as such inasmuch as *"this time . . . the change in the composition of capital would not be due to the development of the productive power,"* unlike the first case, where *"the productive power and the composition of capital develop simultaneously"* (1964: 262,259,260; italics added). Here over-accumulation of capital is in relation to the non-increasing labor power and non-revolutionization of the method of production.

Thus the over-accumulation of capital is *absolute* in this case because there is no way that the mass of surplus value could be raised in *the production process* (leaving aside the question of its *realization*), inasmuch as "neither the mass of labor power used could be increased nor the rate of surplus value raised" (1964: 262). In other words, "when the increased capital would produce a mass of surplus value at best equal to or even less than what capital produced before its increase, there would be absolute overproduction of capital" (1964: 261).[8]

Necessarily associated with and in fact indicating this absolute over-accumulation of capital, is the *non-utilization* of a part of society's existing capital. (In *this* respect the situation is similar to the one produced by the over-accumulation of the first type). Capital, becoming "incapable of exploiting labor at a degree required by 'healthy and normal' development of the capitalist production process," would cease to function as capital, that is, there would be an "effective destruction of the means of production," they would "no longer act as capital," or (equivalently), they as capital "would cease to act as means of production" and would "lie fallow [*brachgelegt*]" (1959: 492; 1964: 266,264). Let us emphasize that this "absolute over-accumulation of capital," being the outcome of the process of accumulation based on (largely) *stationary* method(s) of production, would logically be associated with the *underproduction* (as opposed to the overproduction) of commodities -- contrary to the case of the first type of accumulation of capital -- or, in other words, with the "economy of shortage."

COMPETITION OF CAPITALS

Competition of capitals has been one of the least explored categories of Marx's "critique of political economy," numerous contributions on the so-called transformation problem notwithstanding. Though most economists on the left correctly distinguish between the classical and the neoclassical positions on competition, they, on the whole, seem to hold that the classical and the Marxian positions on the question are similar if not identical.

Competition of capitals, as a specific category, appears only in Marx's "Critique." The classical political economy speaks, in general, of "free competition," of course meaning thereby (unimpeded) competition among the capitalists. "However, so firmly were they [classical economists] convinced that the competitive case was the obvious thing that they did not bother to analyze its logical content [that is, of free competition] . . . . Competition just meant the absence of monopoly and of public pricing" (Schumpeter 1954: 545). Though the later neoclassical concept of "perfect competition" is different in many respects from the classical concept of "free competition,"[9] the basic starting point of both the versions of competition in political economy is the absence of monopoly (Schumpeter 1954: 545; Stigler 1967: 262; McNulty 1968: 639). Indeed, as Marx observes, competition of capitals arose historically as a negation of various kinds of monopolies, corporations, and regulations that sprang from the mode(s) of production that preceded capitalism and restricted the mobility of capital from one sphere of the economy to another. Corresponding to this historical tendency, bourgeois (classical) political economy conceived of competition of capitals *purely negatively,* as epitomized in the celebrated Physiocratic slogans of *laissez-faire, laissez-aller* (1953: 542). Marx rejects the classics' purely negative way of looking at competition of capitals, and emphasizes that competition is also positive; it belongs to capital itself, showing capital in its *phenomenal reality.* Competition is the "relation of capital to *itself* as another capital" (1953: 543), the relation which shows how capital "necessarily repels itself" [*stösst es sich notwendig sich selbst ab*] (1953: 324). Competition -- the reciprocal interaction of many capitals -- is the *necessary mode of manifestation* of the "limitless urge of capital to increase surplus value"; to create the "biggest possible surplus of labor time over the time necessary for the reproduction of wage" (1976a: 158).

This "inner nature of capital," and "essential determination of capital" can *appear* only in the reciprocal interaction of different capitals, that is, in competition, and thus *shows* itself as an *external necessity* (1953: 317). It is a misinterpretation of Marx to make him say that competition is the inner nature of capital.[10] The "inner nature of capital", or, equivalently, the "inner tendency of capital" is not competition, it is to "surpass all existing proportions by creating surplus value and increasing productive forces" (Marx 1953: 317). This inner tendency of capital only *appears* and is *realized* in phenomenal reality as reciprocal actions of many capitals, as a constraint imposed (on individual capital) by another capital, inasmuch as "capital can exist only as a plurality of capitals". "Competition [only] executes the inner laws of capital, realizes them," but "does not establish them." What appears to be on the surface of the capitalist society, the reciprocal actions of many capitals, is nothing but "capital's *own determination.*" (1953: 317,450,638; italics added). In *essential reality* capital is only *one*, representing the capitalist *class* as a whole or what Marx calls, "capital as such," "capital in general," "total social capital," or "social capital." However, since capital does not exist without valorization, and since "value which constitutes the basis of capital can only exist necessarily through the exchange against another value" showing the state of "permanent repulsion," it is "absurd to imagine a universal capital which would not find itself confronting other capitals to realize exchanges" (1953: 324). Hence capital shows itself in phenomenal reality through its fragments, through many capitals. From this point of view, it should be stressed that there is no monopoly capitalism as distinct from competitive capitalism. All capitalism is *competitive* since capital can appear only as many capitals (in their reciprocal interactions). That which is popularly called the monopoly phase of capitalism is only a particular phase of socialization of capital (in the sense of Marx), reached through the increasing concentration and centralization of capital, independently of *the forms of competition* of capitals. Monopolies are excluded by competition *only* to the extent that they arise and are a hangover from the precapitalist modes of production. Free competition being nothing but "free movement of capitals within capital's own conditions," monopolies, "arising out of the capitalist mode of production itself," are considered by Marx as "natural," falling within the competition of capitals. "Unlimited competition" only signifies "the full reality and realization of the bourgeois relations of production in their *differentia specifica*" (1953: 544,450; 1964: 206).

Marx's way of looking at competition of capitals as something positive, as well as negative, belonging to capital itself, where *one capital* (in essential reality) *simply appears as many capitals* (in phenomenal reality), is absent in political economy (vulgar as well as classical). This is basically because the point of view of *totality*, crucial to Marx's method and the starting point of his analysis of capital, is, by and large, alien to political economy as we saw in the last chapter. Indeed, A. Smith's non-recognition of social total capital as a reality, independently of singular capitals -- in effect, taking the point of view of individual capitalist -- leads him to suppose that competition imposes laws on capital that are *external* and does not belong to itself (Marx 1953: 637). This is of course an aspect of the classics' negative view of competition. In Ricardo, capital as a social totality is dispensed with. In the last chapter, we cited R. Luxemburg's correct assessment of Marx's singularity in this regard. Indeed, a consideration of capital's simultaneous existence as a social totality and as plurality of capitals -- this two-level analysis of capitalist reality, Marx's singular contribution -- is indispensable for a proper understanding of competition of capitals.

With the point of view of totality as his crucial methodological point of departure Marx shows -- contrary to the political economists -- that each capital is *not* an independent entity in an *absolute* sense. A particular capital is an organic part of, and hence *dependent* on, the social total capital.

A contemporary economist has correctly observed that "[Smith's] invisible hand creates society as a whole out of a world of individuals. The key to this creation is the absence of any determination by the social totality outside of the activities of its parts, the individual units and their products" (Levine 1977: 141-42). Political economy's position on individual capitals as being undetermined by, and hence being independent of, social total capital is not fortuitous. It arose from what Marx calls the "eighteenth century illusion of robinsonade" which was fully shared by Smith and Ricardo as illustrated by their point of departure, namely, "the singular and singularized [*einzelne und vereinzelte*] hunter and fisher" (1953: 5). On the other hand, Marx emphasizes individual capitals' dependence on social total capital simultaneously with their "indifference to *one another* and independence *from one another*" [*Gleichgültigkeit gegeneinander und Selbständigkeit voneinander*] (1953: 323; italics added). In other words, individual capitals are only *relatively independent*, only in relation to other capitals. Marx points out two aspects of this reciprocal indifference and autonomy of capitals -- completely ignored by political economy, with its standpoint of individual capital as the ultimate reality of capital -- both of which obscure the essence of capitalist exploitation. First, the individual capitalist behaves with another capitalist *not as capitalist* but as a simple commodity producer, inasmuch as the sale-and-purchase relation between capitalists that appears in competition, and through which surplus value is realized, "is not a capitalist relation, it is the relation of simple exchange." Individual capitalists "confront one another as mutually independent and competing commodity producers" (1953: 323; 1962a: 654). Moreover, in the process of circulation, as shown in competition of capitals, "capital coming out of its internal organic life . . . *disguises [verkleidet]* the (initial) form in which capital is opposed to labor" (1964: 54; italics added). Secondly, the individual capitalist confronts -- and considers -- all workers except one's own *not* as wage-laborers but as simple consumers of his/her products, as "simple centers of circulation" in which the latter's "specific determination as workers is completely effaced" (1953: 323).[11] This illusion obscuring the essence of capitalist exploitation -- created by competition of capitals -- disappears only when we consider not the individual capital, but the total social capital, represented by the capitalist *class* as a whole, confronting the working *class* as a whole, as we argued in the last chapter.

The *apparent* character of the individual capitalist's "independence" is brought out by Marx at each of the two levels of competition of capitals that he analyzes -- competition within the same sphere of production, and competition across different spheres of production. At the first level of competition, the market value of the product -- the same for all the capitalists of the sphere -- is not determined by the particular labor time necessary for an *individual* capitalist but the "labor time necessary for producing the *total mass*, the *total sum* of the commodities corresponding to this sphere of production." It is only through such imposition of socially necessary labor time that the "singular capital is really placed in the conditions of capital in general," [*des Kapitals überhaupt*], and "it is precisely the apparently independent action of singularities, . . . the reciprocal action of capitals, that posits them as more general and supersedes their apparent independence and autonomous existence" (1953: 549-50; 1959: 195; italics in original).

Similarly, analyzing the second level of competition of capitals, Marx shows that the bourgeois economists failed to see that the profit of the individual capital is precisely mediated by "the total exploitation of labor by the total (social) capital," that it comes out of the "global surplus value extracted from the workers by the social total capital." Indeed, "the [individual] capitalists strive to share the [total] quantity of unpaid labor that they extract from the working class. The capitalists share as brothers, as brother-enemies, the loot of the labor of others appropriated in the way that on an average one appropriates as much of unpaid labor as another." Marx calls this "striving" of the singular capitalists at *sharing the total unpaid labor* "competition" (1964: 180, 219; 1959: 21). However, viewed from the point of view of the *individual capital* -- which shows, on the surface of the capitalist society, its "apparent independence in the face of the other," the origin of profit is mystified. "Surplus value transformed in profit has in fact itself disowned [*verleugnet*] its origin and lost its character; it has become *unrecognizable*" (1964: 177; italics added).

The whole process of the establishment of the general rate of profit for the economy as a whole takes place behind the back of the individual capitalist, thereby completely hiding from the capitalist (as well as from the worker) the real nature and origin of profit. To what extent the average profit of the individual capitalist is engendered by the *global* exploitation of labor by *total* (social) capital, that is, "by all his capitalist colleagues, all this interconnection is a complete mystery to him," and "this inability to penetrate the phenomena and recognize beyond the appearances *the inner essence and the inner configuration of the process "* is not only true of the individual capitalist, it is also true of the "political economists themselves" who have not "till now revealed this inner connection." Marx claims that it is he who has revealed this inner connection for the first time. No wonder that the "basic law of capitalist competition" remained "uncomprehended by political economy hitherto" (1964: 178,180,47; italics added). Even the best representatives of political economy, such as Smith and Ricardo, basically partake of the point of view of the *individual capitalist*. For the individual capitalist "the rate of profit [along with the wage rate] . . . is given and appears as given; how and why, does not interest him." Adam Smith, "sharing the crude empiricism" of the latter, "places himself entirely in the midst of competition and continues to argue sense and nonsense [*räsoniert und deräsoniert*] with the *individual capitalist's own logic*" (Marx 1959: 210-11; 1973: 190; italics added). Ricardo, in his turn, assumes the general rate of profit (as between different spheres) as *given* whereas he should have first analyzed *how* this general rate of profit itself is found. Thus Ricardo fails to see that "this latter operation already presupposes . . . the *partition of the whole social capital between its different spheres of employment* determined by competition" (1959: 200; italics in original).[12] This is connected with Ricardo's confusion between two meanings that he offered for "natural price": natural price as the labor-value of the commodity and natural price as the cost of production of the commodity, different from its labor-value. As a matter of fact, instead of discussing how competition of capitals "transforms values into cost prices" (in the sense of Marx's prices of production), Ricardo, following Smith, analyzes how competition reduces actual market prices to cost prices. In other words, Ricardo, accepting the Smithian tradition uncritically, follows a "false route" and is preoccupied with only *one* aspect of competition of capitals, "the most superficial," namely, "the rotation of actual market prices around cost prices or natural prices, . . . the equalization of the market prices in different trades to general cost prices." Ricardo's "blunder" comes from the fact that "knowing the nature of neither profit nor surplus value," he does not separate surplus value from profit, nor does he clearly differentiate value from "natural price." Basically, Ricardo does not understand the process of genesis and reproduction (of capital), believing as he does that capital is the result of saving. That "it is explained by the *differentia specifica* of capital," Ricardo does not understand. Indeed, "the creation of surplus value can never be clearly understood by the bourgeois economists" because "it coincides with the appropriation of the labor of others without exchange" (1953: 450; 1959: 201,204,208).

Contrary to political economy, Marx does not necessarily associate competition of capitals with the juridical private property in capital. What, in Marx, is essential for the competition of capitals is not the existence of capital as juridical private property as such, but, its existence as *individual capital* confronting other individual capitals as *reciprocally autonomous* entities independently of the question of juridical ownership. This is of course a consequence of the Marxian distinction -- analyzed in the last chapter -- between the economic property and the juridical property of capital, "capital in process [of production] as opposed to capital outside the process, capital as process as opposed to capital as ownership" (1962b: 487), and, following therefrom, the basic Marxian *dissociation* of capital as a specific social *relation* of *production* (the capitalist being conceived as a simple bearer of this relation) from the particular *forms* of juridical ownership in which it *appears*.

Consequently, competition of capitals is perfectly conceivable without the existence of juridically recognized private ownership in the means of production. For competition of capitals to exist it is sufficient that there exist different, reciprocally independent, units of (commodity) production, based on wage labor exchanging their products, independently of the question of legal title to ownership over the particular unit. Each unit is then a center of *effective appropriation* of surplus value, a (reciprocally) autonomous profit center, where profit is conceived as "excess of sales price over cost price," the *form* in which surplus value appears (Marx 1964: 54). In this regard, Marx's discussion of competition in Chapter 9 of *Capital* volume 3 is of an extreme importance. In the numerical example, with which the chapter opens, Marx considers five (competing) capitals as being fractions of "one single capital," alternatively, the different capitalists are considered as "simple share holders of one [single] joint stock company." Finally, all five capitals (investments) are considered to be "belonging to one man" -- obviously in the sense of juridical property -- who fixes the cost of production for each capital differently, that is, following the different organic composition each one entails. "As regards the different masses of surplus value or profit, produced [by five capitals], the capitalist [their legal owner] could very well count them as profit, engendered by *his total* advanced *capital in such a way as to attribute an aliquot part of it to each fraction of 100 of capital."* The cost prices of the commodities in the particular investments I - V would therefore be different but the fraction of the sales price coming from the profit added to each fraction of 100 of capital would be the same for all the commodities. The total prices of commodities I - V would be equal to their total values "in the same way as when, in the society, the totality of all branches of production is considered, the sum of prices of production of the commodities produced is equal to the sum of their values" (1964: 164,168,169; italics added). In other words, in this extremely significant example Marx envisages five singular capitals, each exchanging its product against the products of other capitals in its capacity as a *reciprocally* autonomous appropriation/profit center, but all of them juridically belonging to *one* owner. This is a clear case of *competition of capitals without there being a separate [private] owner for each separate capital.*[13]

This discussion also helps us to understand an apparent puzzle in Marx's position on the form of existence of capital. We cited above Marx's statement about the absurdity of there being a universal capital without any other capital confronting it. On the other hand, in the last chapter, Marx's other statement about the tendency of the "total national capital" to become one "single capital" was referred to. At first blush, these two statements may seem to be mutually inconsistent. However, this apparent inconsistency is easily resolved if we remember Marx's important distinction between the juridical property and the economic property of capital, referred to earlier. Here the oneness of capital is obviously with respect to its juridical property. Total social capital even under a single juridical ownership (under one person or one company) is clearly envisaged by Marx as fragmented into many *reciprocally autonomous* capitals in the sense of appropriation/profit centers confronting one another through exchange of the products of human (wage) labor taking commodity form -- in other words as *competing capitals*.[14] This follows logically from the concept of capital. The existence of capital necessarily implies the existence of wage labor. To ensure laborers' "double freedom" -- without which there is no wage labor -- laborers must be shown to be free with respect to individual capitals, as we argued in the last chapter. This freedom with respect to individual capitals would necessarily imply the functional division of the single national capital and reciprocal independence of its units as individual capitals transacting their products as commodities -- in other words, competition of capitals.

NOTES

1. A notable exception in this regard seems to be the (ex)Czechoslovak economist M. Toms who has, at some length, discussed what we have called the second type of accumulation of capital in Marx (Toms 1976: 19-70).

2. Marx faulted Ricardo for obscuring the origin of surplus value by ignoring absolute surplus value through his assumption of a fixed working day, which meant, in effect, ignoring the "historical justification of capital" (1959: 403,405). In an important paper, N. Georgescu-Roegen has reproached "every standard economist" for neglecting the lengthening of the factory working day as a significant factor of economic growth, and has credited Marx for being an exception in this respect (1974).

3. The original word "*Produktivität*" (productivity) was changed by Marx into "*pouvoirs productifs*" (productive powers) in the French version (1965: 1132). The changed expression, we believe, catches better the spirit of *qualitative* change in the composition of capital.

4. To be more exact, let us note that in the case of an increase in the intensity of labor only, and not in the employment of labor, the quantity of (capital) equipment does not increase, only its intensity of use increases, whereas the quantity of raw materials used increases in the same proportion as the intensity of labor in the absence of any change in the technique of production (Marx 1962a: 630; 1965: 1110).

5. The accumulation of total social capital, discussed above, could be conveniently summed up by the following 2x2 "accumulation matrix":

$$A = \begin{bmatrix} a_{00} & a_{01} \\ a_{10} & a_{11} \end{bmatrix}$$

where the first subscript refers to the technique of production and the second to the technical composition of capital, each taking the value (0) or (1) depending on whether it is stationary or changing. As can be seen, each row of the matrix symbolizes a particular type of accumulation of capital.

6. Marx is careful to point out that under capitalism too much of wealth is not produced, only "too much of wealth under capitalist, contradictory forms," and that "overproduction of commodities" does not mean "overabundance of products," considering the real needs of the immense majority. "On the contrary, on the basis of capitalist production, there is always *underproduction* in this sense" (1959: 524; 1964: 268; italics in original). In other words, capitalism, by its very nature, is really an "economy of shortage."

7. In his notebooks on Ricardo, Marx used the term "active demand" (1953: 832).

8. Using (partially) Marx's notations, the situation of absolute over-accumulation of social capital could be depicted in the following way:

$$C' > C, \quad M' \leq M, r' < r$$

where C is the initial capital, M the mass of profit (the same as the mass of surplus value) produced by C, and $C' = C + \Delta C$; $M' = M + \Delta M$; $r = M \div C$ $r' = M' \div C'$; all the variables having positive values.

9. For a clear exposition, see P. McNulty (1967).

10. See Ben Fine (1983: 90). Fine's misreading of Marx is also exemplified by his misunderstanding, in the same text, of Roman Rosdolsky's important discussion of the Marxian categories of "capital in general" and "many capitals".

11. Marx shows that what distinguishes capitalist domination from other modes of domination is that the immediate producer under the former constitutes "an autonomous centre of circulation," an "exchangist positing exchange value and obtaining (subsistence) through exchange" (1953: 322), thereby mystifying the exploitation relation.

12. The italicized portion is in English in the original.

13. Again, while discussing capital's rotation, Marx significantly shows the similarity between the case of two capitals, each "belonging to a different capitalist totally independent of the other," but being equally "parts of social capital," and the case of two capitals being parts of the "same private capital" (1973a: 271,273).

14. After citing the *Grundrisse* passage on the absurdity of a universal capital Roman Rosdolsky significantly remarks: "Therefore a state capitalism would be possible only in so far as several state organized capitals confront one another" (1968: 62).

Chapter 3

THE SOVIET ECONOMY VIEWED STATICALLY

After exploring the concept of capital in Marx we now propose, in this and the next two chapters, to investigate the Soviet economic experience in the light of that concept and the associated categories. This chapter briefly analyses the *essentials* of production and ownership relations, as well as the relations of exchange and distribution of the Soviet economy from a *static* point of view in the light of the Marxian categories discussed earlier. In fact, the Soviet economy that finally collapsed did not differ in its basic functioning from the one that had emerged during the Stalinist period (Davies 1980a: xiv; Kuromiya 1988: 312; Shmelev and Popov 1989: 44). Some of the points touched upon here will be further elaborated later in the book.

PRODUCTION AND OWNERSHIP

The locus of power in the USSR was codified by Article 6 of the Soviet Constitution (1977) which stated that the Soviet Communist Party was the leading and guiding force of the Soviet society and, more specifically, of all State and public organizations, as well as the authority determining the general perspectives of society's development. The party itself was, of course, subject to no outside control. To paraphrase the oft-quoted expression of M. Fainsod, the true parliament of the USSR was the Party Central Committee, the true government was the Political Bureau, and the true Prime Minister was the General Secretary. Completely contradicting the principle of election and recall of *all* officials by the citizens -- so loudly proclaimed by the Bolsheviks on the eve of October

(1917) -- all the important officials in the Soviet economy and polity were the party nominees through a system, taken over from the Tsarist table of ranks, the so-called *nomenklatura* -- a system of list of appointments under the direct control of the party authorities (Levitski 1961; Mathews 1975; Voslensky 1980). Thus at the most general level of society, the Soviet (immediate) producers were completely alienated from all real power which controlled and dominated them.

Coming to the *economy* as such which is our basic concern, we first observe that by the late 1930s when the "victory of socialism" was proclaimed in the USSR, the Soviet state, through juridical measures, had deprived practically the totality of the immediate producers from their individual (private) ownership of the means of production, bringing the latter under "public" (mainly state) ownership -- the proportion of the independent commodity producers having been reduced to less than three percent of the total (working) population (*Narkhoz* 1987: 11). In other words, as the state was completely autonomized in relation to the immediate producers, the so-called public property of the means of production simply signified the *non-property* of those producers over the means of production -- that is, private property in the primary sense of Marx.

Naturally, the working people were excluded from all power starting at the highest economic level -- the level where all effective decisions on the functioning of the economy were made. About three years before the First Five Year Plan had started, a Soviet planning document had already asserted: "The state is becoming the real master of its industry. It is only the state economic agencies which can construct the industrial plan . . . the industrial plan must be constructed *not from below but from above*" (Carr and Davies 1974: 875; italics added). Indeed, the immediate producers were totally alienated from all decision-making concerning what one could consider, following O. Lange, as the three fundamental elements that characterize the "planning and effective direction of the economy's development" -- namely, the division of national income between accumulation and consumption, the distribution of investments among different branches of the national economy, and the co-ordination of the activities of these different branches (Lange 1969). In a word, the producers had little to do with what, how, and for whom to produce. The highest planning body, the *Gosplan* (State Planning Committee), received instructions only from the Party-State authorities, particularly from the party's Political Bureau and the Soviet Council of Ministers, with whom lay the power of all basic decision making well beyond the reach of the producers (Davies 1966).

For most of the Soviet period, the workers' non-property (in the means of production) and their exclusion from all decision making went hand in hand with their *separation* from the conditions of production at the level of the *individual* units of production. In other words, for most of this period, the selling of their labor power was subject basically to *economic constraints* (in the sense of Marx).

However, it should be pointed out that during the period roughly between the late thirties and mid-fifties, the industrial workers were subject to non-economic constraints, such as labor books, legal prohibition from leaving jobs, severe penalties for absenteeism, compulsory transfers for the skilled workers -- leaving aside the question of 10 to 15 million prisoners working from inside the labor camps (Brown 1966: 16; Nove 1982: 234-35,261-62,279; Shmelev and Popov 1989: 64-65).

Much worse, undoubtedly, was the situation of the agricultural laborers. First of all, the laborer in the so-called "collective farm" (*kolkhoz*) was "a citizen with lesser rights (and) lived in the lower and outer half of the Soviet society," with a standard of living well below the average Soviet standard of living (Wädekin 1969: 41). The collective farm laborers, for a considerable period, were subjected to compulsory state corvées like road building and timber cutting, which did not apply to the city dwellers, and they were "subjected to a labor system which reminded them of conditions from which the revolution seemed to have redeemed them for ever," and, indeed, for a long time, they were legally bound to their workplace (Lewin 1985: 176). Similarly, the apparently cooperative and democratic principles enunciated in the *kolkhoz* charter were a fiction.[1] The *kolkhoz* administration was thoroughly subject to the Party-State control through the system of *nomenklatura*, the kolkhoz president being simultaneously powerless in relation to the superiors and all-powerful in relation to the inferiors in the system (Wädekin 1969: 178-81). As regards the remuneration of the *kolkhoz* members, it did not take the regular wage form (like the case of the rest of the Soviet workers) until 1966. Before that date, the peasant had the status of a residuary legatee, receiving the payment -- based on the so-called *trudoden'* (labor day unit) -- after all other requirements of the *kolkhoz* were met (Wronski 1957; Davies 1980b; Pouliquen 1982; Zaleski 1984). In short, one could say that the Soviet agricultural laborers remained under pre-dominantly *non-economic* constraints for a much longer period compared to the industrial laborers.

However -- anticipating somewhat our argument -- these predominantly extra-economic constraints on the immediate producers, limited to a particular period of Soviet history, do *not* contradict the existence of capital in the Soviet Union. On the contrary, it is precisely under the exigencies of *capital accumulation* that the "division of the power of disposition over social property between the state and the cooperatives" was reduced to a "fiction", just like the "free labor contract in which the conscription of the labor force clothed itself" (Hofmann 1956: 223). Indeed such "extra-economic direct violence" toward "forcing the laborers to sell their labor power voluntarily" perfectly corresponds to the stages (of capitalism) *preceding* the organization of the "*developed* process of capitalist production" (leaving aside its common use in wartime capitalism), as Marx clearly shows (Marx 1962a: 765; italics added). For the greater part of the Soviet period, however, it remains true that the immediate producers -- at least in their great majority -- were neither the owners of the means of production nor a part of them, that is, they were "doubly free."

Though the means of production in the USSR had virtually a single juridical owner -- the state -- in relation to which the Soviet workers were necessarily just "an accessory of capital" (Marx 1962a: 598), these workers were, however "free," that is, *separate* in relation to the *individual* units of production. It was not the state which employed the workers. The latter were hired by the individual enterprises in their (reciprocally) autonomous capacity, given that these enterprises were considered to be "juridical persons" through the "possession of separate property" (*Legislative Acts* 1983: 106). Moreover, according to the Soviet labor legislation, "the labor contract is an agreement between the worker and the [particular] *enterprise* whereby the person employed undertakes to do work. . . while the enterprise undertakes to *pay the worker a wage or salary*" (*Legislative Acts* 1982: 66; italics added). The enterprise of course was represented by its management, functioning under the principle of "one-person management" [*edinonachalie*], nominated and subject to dismissal by higher administrative organs (Polyakov and Rakhmilovich 1977). The workers had the duty to "carry out the orders of the management promptly and accurately" and were subject to the management-imposed "disciplinary penalties" including "dismissal" (*Legislative Acts* 1982: 80-81).

That the Soviet workers (in their vast majority) were free from the means of production at the level of the individual units of production and that they did not have a unique employer is clearly seen in their "right to choose their trade or profession and the type of job" (*Constitution*: Art. 40; *Legislative Acts* 1982: 63) as well as their "right to cancel a labor contract," and leave a particular job (and enterprise) subject to one month's prior notice to the enterprise management (*Legislative Acts* 1982: 68). As a matter of fact, there was a fairly high rate of labor turnover in the Soviet economy (Rusanov 1971; Sukhov 1974; Kotliar 1984). "Outside of the migration of collective farm laborers," about a fifth of the Soviet labor force, in general, changed their workplaces annually (Manevich 1985a: 46; *Narkhoz* 1987: 412), the majority changing jobs, in many cases, due to unsatisfactory working conditions and wages (Kurman 1971). It has been shown that the Soviet separation rates in industry were of the same order of magnitude as those of the United Kingdom and (West) Germany (Granick 1987: 14-16).

However, a mere sale and purchase of labor power against a remuneration does not, as we saw earlier, constitute *wage labor* in what Marx calls the "strict economic sense of the term." In order to qualify as wage labor, the sale and purchase of labor power must be shown to have as its objective the production of *commodities*, that is, "labor as activity positing value" for the purchaser of labor power (Marx 1953: 185). To this aspect of the Soviet economy we now turn.

EXCHANGE

The products of labor in the Soviet economy *were*, in general, commodities "to the extent that these products are [were] not produced as immediate means of subsistence for the producers themselves, but as values, as products which only by being transformed into exchange value [money] through alienation become [became] use values" (Marx 1964: 650). The products of labor taking commodity or *value form* and thence appearing as *exchange values* is independent of the question of *how* their prices are actually determined -- "administratively," or by the (spontaneous) "market forces." It is the specific form (which is the value form) itself in which these use values become -- and have to become -- exchange values that is fundamental in this connection. On the other hand, the exchange of the products of human labor in commodity form is not invariably related to the existence of juridically *separate properties* in the means of production. For the existence of the commodity form of these products it is enough that they are exchanged as products of "private [that is, non-directly social] labors executed independently of one another" (Marx 1962a: 87), in other words, it is sufficient that the total social labor be fragmented in reciprocally autonomous units of production, independently of the specific (juridical) form of the latter's ownership.

Law in a society can never be higher than the economic formation of the society in question (Marx 1966b: 179), and the juridical act of the Soviet state resulting in a (quasi) single ownership in the means of production and the institution of central planning could not overstep the reality of *reciprocal (organizational) separation* of the units of production relating to one another through exchange in *money-commodity form*. "Soviet planning," observes a well known authority, referring to the Stalinist planning, "did not do away with the market . . . it has [had] introduced new rules of the game" (Zaleski 1962: 297).

According to two contemporary Russian economists, even in the 1930s, "under widespread directive planning, commodity-money relations did not disappear from real life. There emerged a gap between theory, which rejected the functioning of the law of value and the existence of commodity-production under socialism, and reality, where money could not be driven out despite concerted efforts" (Shmelev and Popov 1989: 286). In fact, the commodity sphere of production in the Soviet economy had widened rather than narrowed over the years. A contemporary Yugoslav economist, referring to what he called "several socialist countries" (including the USSR), wrote that "in spite of the organized economic, political and sometimes even physical pressure, commodity production maintained itself, it spread, renewed itself and extended to many fields," and that those countries were "now more of a commodity producing nature than they had been before the revolution" (Vacic 1977: 233). Similarly R. Bahro, in his widely discussed work, pointed out that "eventually the entire 'socialist' economy had necessarily to be recognized as one of commodity production and the law of value had again to give sway" (Bahro 1978: 135). An important quantitative index of the enlargement of commodity-production in the USSR was what the Soviet statisticians called "commodity traffic for the totality of the means of public transport." It increased from a mere 28 billion ton-kilometers in 1922 to a vast 8192 billion ton-kilometers toward the end of the eighties (*Narkhoz* 1987: 341). At least beginning with the 1950s, the Soviet spokespersons, yielding before the reality and the exigencies of the extended reproduction of the system, recognized that the Soviet economy was basically a commodity economy in all its sectors (Kronrod 1959; Lavigne 1960; Lewin 1974).[2]

Commodity production in the Soviet economy was, of course, not "simple commodity production" not to speak of the absurd "socialist commodity production"; given the "double freedom" of the Soviet workers in the (reciprocally) separate units of production, the commodity production in the USSR was *capitalist* commodity production, independently of the question of formal-juridical ownership. In other words, it was a case of "exchange of capitals in their multiplicity" (Marx 1953: 618), that is, *competition of capitals* (in the sense of Marx).

It was argued earlier that competition of capitals in the sense of Marx exists whenever the process of total social production is split among *reciprocally* autonomous units of production each of which, based on the double freedom of the producers, exchanges with other units the products of labor in (money) commodity form, whatever be the specific juridical *form* of property in the means of production or the specific *form* of exchange of commodities (including labor power as a commodity). The fact that in the Soviet economy, the products of labor were not just directly appropriated and physically distributed among the production units but were mutually exchanged in money-commodity form, and the fact that these units were the independent employers of labor, show that these units were reciprocally separate (autonomous) units of the total social capital. On the other hand, law itself recognized that these enterprises (associations), though under the ownership of and, hence, dependent on the center, were *reciprocally* autonomous. Thus the state enterprises deeming to "possess separate property" and "operating at their own account, having fixed and circulating assets assigned to them, and a separate balance sheet," were considered juridical persons (*Legislative Acts* 1983: 106).[3] According to a Soviet *uchebnik*, "Enterprises enjoy the right of a juridical person, i.e., establish economic relations and conclude agreements with other enterprises. . . . For the purposes of economic activities they hire workers, organize the production process, purchase the necessary means of production and sell the produced output" (Khudokormov 1985: 103).

We know from Marx that it is reciprocal, that is, *relative*, and not absolute independence of different capitals (such absolute independence cannot exist in any case) that is relevant for competition among them. It is this "reciprocal autonomy and indifference" -- as Marx would call it -- of the production units in relation to one another combined with the exigencies of plan fulfilment (in fact the plan serving as the mediating instrument for the accumulation of capital) that was the basis of the exchange of commodities, including the means of production, among these units.[4]

More than three decades ago a leading Soviet economist noted that the state enterprise used a part of the monetary income, received as a result of the sale of products, to acquire the indispensable means of production and for the payment of wages of the enterprise workers. "This form of state property" served as the basis of the "*money-commodity relations between State enterprises*" *[tovarno-deneznykh otnoshenii mezhdu gosudarstvennymi predpriyatiyami]* (Zaostrovtsev 1959: 101; italics added). In the same vein, we are told of the "market for means of production" as being the "most important link in the process of circulation" where "*commodity exchange of the means of production takes place between public enterprises*" (Kozlov 1977: 314, 315; italics in original), and of "commodity turnover" (in general) showing "sales value of the means of production [*stoimost' prodazh sredstv proizvodstva*] as well as the articles of consumption," the former representing the "commodity link" between enterprises (Markina and Orlov 1977: 40).[5] An important quantitative indicator of the growth of inter-enterprise commodity exchange in the Soviet economy is the increase in bank credit -- short term and long term taken together -- from 64 billion rubles in 1940 to 521 billion rubles in 1985 (*Narkhoz* 1989: 627).

It has been a received idea that in the USSR money was "neutral" or "passive", and that there were two systems of monetary circulation -- cash and non-cash -- remaining in two "water-tight compartments" allegedly unlike what is found in capitalism (Garvy 1966; Grossman 1966). However this purely empiricist way of analyzing the Soviet monetary phenomenon neglects the important point that the Soviet bank credit involving non-cash or scriptural transactions, far from having a non-capitalist character, rather shows itself as another form of *money* -- the "general equivalent for all commodities" (Marx 1973a: 36) -- which had in fact greatly facilitated the mobility of capital from one sphere to the other. "The system of clearing accounts," wrote a well-known official text book, "facilitates rapid and regular movements of commodities from producer [enterprises] to consumer [enterprises]" (Kozlov 1977: 347). Indeed a Soviet economist while noting the "cross streams" [*vstrechnye potoki*] of cash and non-cash transactions had emphasized that "through credit organs the observance of the principle of equivalent exchange is guaranteed" and that "in this way the action of the law of value [*zakona stoimosti*] finds expression in banking operations" (Zakharov 1982: 8, 10). Thus "in actual economic practice non-cash turnover and cash circulation are not separated by the Great Wall of China" (Shmelev and Popov 1989: 195), which means that in the Soviet economy "*book entries and ready cash together constitute a single money turnover. Unity of the two forms is realized* through the mechanism of the conversion of the one into the other" (Kozlov 1977: 348; italics in original). Marx had remarked that though different forms of money could correspond more suitably to the different stages of social production, as long as money remained an essential relation of production, "no form can eliminate the contradictions inherent in money, at best one form can represent them differently than the other [just as] no form of wage labor can eliminate the defects of wage labor itself" (1953: 42-43).

We can now say that the selling of labor power by the Soviet worker to the reciprocally autonomous production units toward production of commodities against monetary remuneration rendered the worker a *wage laborer* "in the strict economic sense." On the other hand, the exchange of the means of production, taking commodity form, between Soviet enterprises based on wage labor, signified *competition of capitals* in the Soviet economy. Let us emphasize again that for competition of capitals to exist it is necessary and sufficient that each individual capital -- while naturally dependent on social total capital -- is independent relative to other individual capitals such that these "other capitals confront it" and "it exchanges values with them," where the "mutual repulsion of capitals . . . is already contained [*liegt schon*] in capital as realized exchange value" (Marx 1953: 324).

DISTRIBUTION

We come now to distribution. Wage labor being the basis of Soviet material production, *wage form*, that is, "workers' own product appearing as alien income" -- as Marx would put it -- was naturally the basis of the distribution of the means of consumption in the Soviet economy. "The individual who participates in production in the form of wage labor, participates in the results of production in the form of wage" (Marx 1953: 16), where wage simply signified, as a Soviet economist observed, the "value of the necessary product, . . . what basically ensures the reproduction of the labor power expended by the working people" (Manevich 1985a: 187).

In response to the exigencies of capital accumulation, spearheaded by forced industrialization, it was the differential wage structure as the incentive mechanism that became the basis of the allocation of "free" labor in the Soviet economy (Bergson 1944, 1964, 1984; McAuley 1979). Wage differentiation, particularly between the unskilled and the skilled laborers, which was declining toward the end of the 1920s, greatly increased following Stalin's denunciation of "wage equalization" in 1931. In the 1930s wage differentials in the USSR were about as great as those in the USA at a comparable stage of economic development (Bergson 1964: 110-18). "In the years when the USSR was rapidly building industry, large differences in wage rates were decisive in ensuring the training of a skilled labor force . . . . In many enterprises skilled workers earned 300 to 700 percent more than unskilled workers" (Manevich 1985a: 192). There was some reduction of differences beginning with the late 1950s. However, until the end of the Soviet period (when there was a renewed campaign against "wage equalization") wage differentials continued, based on the system of three six-grade rate scales in industry (McAuley 1979; Manevich 1985a). It is interesting to note that on the basis of studies of percentile ratios of frequency distribution of wage-and-salary earners classified by their pay -- spread over several years -- A. Bergson found that there was a "striking similarity between the USSR and western countries" (1984: 1065).

Wage took the forms of both piece wage and time wage. However, on Lenin's insistence, reinforced later by Stalin's so-called six-point speech in 1931, and perfectly corresponding to the need for increasing intensification of labor, the piece wage system became the preferred mode of wage payment (Dobb 1966: 463-64). By the late 1930s three-quarters of all industrial workers worked under this system, and, for the Soviet period as a whole, workers paid by piece rate remained a majority among the industrial workers (Dobb 1966: 464; Malle 1991: 184).[6]

As regards the non-immediately consumed part of the social product (taking value form), that is, surplus value, the individual unit of production in the Soviet economy, in order to produce and realize it, had to go through capital's general cyclical process represented in Marx's well-known formula:

$$M - C \begin{smallmatrix} \nearrow MP \\ \searrow LP \end{smallmatrix} \ldots P \ldots C' - M';$$

where M is money, C is commodity, MP and LP are, respectively, material means of production and labor power, P is product, and

$$C' = C + \Delta C, \quad M' = M + \Delta M$$

that is, with surplus value added, the dots indicating interruption in the circulation process (Marx 1973a). In other words, the enterprise transformed the sum of money (money capital) into productive capital by buying with it the material means of production and labor power, combined the dead and the living labor in the process of production giving rise to a new product which, as a (new) commodity containing the extra value created in production, was passed on to circulation which culminated in the realization of the product (as a commodity) having a money capital greater than the initial one.[7]

In the Soviet economy, the existence of (free) wage labor producing commodities in reciprocally autonomous units of production naturally ensured the *production* of surplus value. The *realization* of surplus value in the Soviet economy had its own specificities conditioned by the (quasi) single juridical ownership over the social total capital as well as by the economy's specific mode of capital accumulation. A Polish economist noted that unpaid surplus labor was the source of surplus value in both private enterprise economies and planned economies. The difference between them lay in the fact that in the planned economies, the surplus value was in the hands of the state rather than in private hands, and that the "state, as the collective owner of the means of production, has the ultimate say in determining how surplus value is to be obtained, in what form it should appear, and how it is to be used" (Zwass 1978-79: 7, 31). Following from the "cost-accounting" [*khozraschët*] principle -- an integral part of the Soviet economic system almost from the beginning -- each unit of production was supposed to cover its costs of production and obtain a profit out of its own sales (Basin 1968; Bornstein 1970, 1987; Polyakov and Rakhmilovich 1977; Popov 1984). However, the realization of surplus value did not always coincide with the production of surplus value at every individual unit of production.[8] As true "Marxists," the Soviet authorities considered surplus value as a social totality created in the economy as a whole so that, for maximizing this social (total) surplus value, the *particular* unit or units of production, where a part of this surplus value was created, was not of much importance.[9]

Indeed, the accumulation of capital in the USSR, under the battle cry of "catching up with and surpassing" the advanced capitalist countries in the shortest period, was greatly facilitated by the deliberate practice of two-level pricing of the industrial products: prices of producer goods -- particularly those of heavy industry -- were formed differently from those of consumer goods (Kurowski 1962: 15-16; Zwass 1978-79: 31-33). In the interest of industrialization, prices of the former were kept relatively low, just enough to cover the costs of production with a small profit margin. That is, the prices here did not contain a profit equal to the surplus value created. It could be that the sales of certain products -- depending on the planners' preference -- would have to be effected at prices that would not even cover the production costs, not to speak of obtaining a profit. Subsidized by the state, production would continue in such cases along with the creation of surplus value. Surplus value created in heavy industry but not included in their prices were built in the prices of consumer goods which were set at a relatively higher level excepting for some basic necessities where they would be low. "The view came to prevail that surplus value need not necessarily be tapped at the point at which it was created, but rather should be extracted at the point deemed most expedient from the point of view of the state budget" (Zwass 1978-79: 32). Surplus value was realized from the consumer goods not as profits but as "turnover taxes," called by the Soviet economists "a changed form of the part of the surplus product's value [*chasti stoimosti pribavochnogo pro-*

dukta]" (Ezhov 1982: 97). "Unlike Western sales taxes where consumers are generally aware of the tax rate they are paying," writes a well-known textbook, "the Soviet turnover tax is included in the retail price without the purchaser knowing how large it is" (Gregory and Stuart 1990: 222).

Turnover tax and profit together constituted around 90 percent of the total surplus value, called "monetary accumulation" [*denezhnye nakopleniia*], virtually all through the plan period. Over the same period, their joint contribution to the state budget was of the order of about 60 percent of the state revenue. Of the two, turnover tax played the dominant role in the accumulation process for the greater part of the period. However, their relative shares changed over time with the development of the country's industrial base. Thus their respective shares (in percentage) in monetary accumulation were 74:23 (1940), 46:44 (1965), 40:50 (1980), and 33:57 (1985), and in the state budget 59:12 (1940), 38:30 (1960), 31:30 (1980), and 25:30 (1985), where the first number stands for turnover tax, the second for profit, and the years appear within parentheses.[10] Along with the development of industries, there was an increase in the role of enterprise profit in relation to turnover tax in the accumulation process. It should be emphasized that through the differential price system, where the gap between the sales price and the cost of production was to a considerable extent covered by turnover tax, the "rates of profit from different products realized by different enterprises in the different branches of the Soviet economy were effectively equalized" (Kurowski 1962: 21).

In conclusion, in the Soviet economy the juridical abolition of private property in the means of production on the one hand, and control of the economy (and society) at all levels -- including one person management in the production unit nominated from and accountable to "above" -- by the (single) party on the other, the party itself remaining outside of any control by the (immediate) producers, ensured the producers' *non-property* of the objective conditions of production. At the same time, the producers were not a part of the means of production in their relations with the *individual units* of production (at least for the greater part of the Soviet period). This "double freedom" of the laborers in relation to the conditions of labor of course signified a relation of *separation* (opposition) between the two, and we know that *capital* is simply *this* separation (Marx 1953: 409,451; 1962b: 419; 1976a: 33-35). *Wage labor* was the natural result. On the other hand, the (quasi) single juridical ownership of the means of production, "forming [thereby] a single national capital" (Marx 1965: 1139), far from eliminating the *functional separation* between its units ("fragments"), had in fact facilitated this separation in a planned manner, thereby producing in a sense more favorable conditions compared to so-called private enterprise capitalism, for the mobility of the means of production, taking *money commodity* form, between the units of production, and had thus created the essential conditions for the *com-*

petition of capitals (in the sense of Marx). In a word, to paraphrase Marx, in the Soviet economy the laborers did not employ the means of labor, the means of labor employed the laborers (1962a: 674).

NOTES

1. The reality of Soviet collectivization is seen most vividly in the "Smolensk Archives" which show -- particularly through the letters of the poor peasants -- how widespread the discontent was among the peasantry *in general* on this question, accompanied often by active mass resistance (Fainsod 1958). See, in this regard, Davies (1980a: 255-59;410-11).

2. The unduly neglected Soviet economist V.P. Shkredov had the lucidity of correctly connecting the Soviet commodity production with the "not yet immediately social character" of labor at the level of society (1967: 56).

3. For an elaboration on this reciprocal separation of production units in the Soviet economy see, among others, Basin (1968); Polyakov and Rakhmilovich (1977); and Kuczynski (1978). Reciprocal autonomy of the units of production based on organizational separateness -- all producing and exchanging products as *commodities* -- existed even in the extremely centralized Stalinist period of the Soviet economy. See Baykov (1970: 170-73); Zaleski (1984: 46-48).

4. "In order to carry out the production assignments of the *tekhpromfinplan*," wrote J. Berliner, "the enterprise must enter into purchase and sale relationships with other firms" (1957: 20).

5. For examples of exchange of means of production between Soviet units of production, see Glushkov (1982).

6. Let us recall that "piece wage" as the "most fruitful source of wage deductions and capitalist swindling" is the "form of wage that corresponds most to the capitalist mode of production" (Marx 1962a: 576, 580).

7. An official Soviet text book applied Marx's formula for the capitalist cyclical process to the Soviet economy while wishing away the fact of the commodity character of labor power by the simple *assertion* that the laborers in the USSR were "themselves the owners of the means of production" (Kozlov 1977: 244).

8. Marx stresses that there is no necessary one to one correspondence between exploitation of labor and realization of the extorted surplus value. *"The conditions of immediate exploitation and its realization are not identical.* They not only do not coincide temporarily or spatially, conceptually also they are different" (1964: 254; italics added).

9. Thus the progenitor of the Soviet model underlined the great importance of the "higher form of profitability" that one obtains if one considers "profitability not from the point of view of individual enterprises and branches, nor from the point of view of only one year but from the perspective of the *whole national economy* and of [a period of] ten to fifteen years" which alone "guarantees an *incessant increase in production*" (Stalin 1980: 588, 613; italics added).

10. Calculated from *Narkhoz* (1922-1982): 549, 563; and *Narkhoz* 1987: 620, 628.

Chapter 4

THE DYNAMICS: THE PROCESS OF CAPITAL ACCUMULATION

There is a widely held view among the Marxists that the enlarged reproduction of labor power and the productive apparatus in the USSR had been the accumulation of *wealth* or *use values* and not of *capital* (Varga 1938; Hilferding 1972; Mandel 1986a). However, in the light of our discussion in Chapter 3, it could be said that the enlarged reproduction in question did take the form of accumulation of *capital* and not simply of wealth or use values. In this chapter we shall be concerned with the specificity of the Soviet accumulation process and the specific type of the over-accumulation of capital associated with this process.

THE INITIAL STAGE

The accumulation of capital in the USSR through time has been an amalgam of the elements of original accumulation of capital, formal subsumption of labor under capital, and *certain phases* of the real subsumption of labor as envisaged by Marx -- that is, *predominantly* based on the *extension* of productive resources employed and *not on the continuous revolutionization* of the methods of production.[1] The economy that the Bolsheviks inherited, had, it is well-known, all the basic features of pre-capitalism and backward capitalism, as generally understood. This, together with the initial hostile environment of the country, dictated the urgency of a rapid development of the economy. The stage was definitively set by the new authorities when they decided, at the 15th Party Conference (1926), that it was essential to "strive in a relatively minimum historical period to overtake and outstrip the levels of industrial development of the advanced [capitalist] countries" (*Resheniya* I 1967: 539). Given the deadweight of pre-capitalism, the development of the economy had to traverse the paths of original accumulation of capital and formal subsumption of labor. With around 80 percent of the country's total labor force working in agriculture (Eason 1963: 76), and "commodity producing peasant households constituting a small portion of the rural population," of which (again) "only 10 to 15 percent accumulated the means of production" (Prokopovitch 1952: 92,93) even at the end of the 1920s, the brunt of the original accumulation of capital naturally fell on the peasantry, illustrating in a striking manner Marx's statement that "the expropriation of the agricultural producer from land forms the basis of the whole process [of original accumulation]" (1962a: 744).[2]

Indeed, given the strategy of superindustrialization, agriculture was seen not only as the supplier of food and raw materials, but also -- being the biggest employer of labor -- as the main source of labor supply. However, the principal obstacle to what Stalin had called, in 1928, "reconstructing agriculture on a new technical basis" was the existence of individual peasant production in an overwhelmingly dominant form -- around 98 percent of the sown area being cultivated by individual peasant households in 1928 (Nove 1982: 150). According to one authority, the party leadership decided on forced collectivization of agriculture as a necessary part of the new industrialization strategy to facilitate central control over rural production and at the same time "sweep aside the individual peasant units" which stood in the way of increased production (Davies 1974: 261).

The rapidity of "original expropriation" (Marx's alternative expression for original accumulation) is seen in the fact that whereas the percentage of peasant households collectivized stood at 1.7 in 1928, it rose to 64.5 in 1932 and to 93 in 1937 (Prokopovitch 1952: 163). At the same time "individual farmers and non-cooperated handicraftsmen" (including non-working dependents) who constituted 75 percent of the country's total population in 1928 were reduced to 30.6 percent in 1932 and 5.5 percent in 1937 (Vinogradov et al, 1978: 467). Naturally, at the end of the First Five Year Plan it was claimed that the "capitalist elements in the town and countryside have been defeated," and, referring to the end of the Second Five Year Plan it was declared that "the first phase of communism has been attained" (*KPSS v resoliutsiyakh* 1971: 64, 335-36). "Peter the great," writes Lewin, "had to build his industrial plants on the basis of serf labor. Stalin carried on his industrialization, especially his industrialization of agriculture, on the basis of *forceful extraction of unpaid labor*" (Lewin 1985: 314; italics added). It seems that under the slogan of "liquidation of the kulaks as a class" it was "the peasant class that was liquidated" (Shmelev 1987: 146).

The twin goals of collectivization -- "to feed *gratis* the non-agricultural segments of the economy and at the same time provide a flow of labor for the public works of the government" (Gerschenkron 1966a: 148; italics added) were largely achieved.[3] State grain procurements more than doubled within three years -- rising from 10.8 million tons in 1928 to 22.8 million tons in 1931 (Nove 1982: 180). Similarly, as regards the supply of labor, "collectivization of agriculture was seen as the principal contributing factor toward the transformation of the whole system of country's manpower utilization to ensure a high tempo of industrialization " (Skorov and Danilov 1976: 173). Even observers as enthusiastic as the Webbs spoke of "the ruthless . . . removal of the occupiers and cultivators who were *stigmatized* as kulaks," and of the peasants being "*removed or deported* to lumber camps or employed in public works, or taken as laborers at gigantic industrial enterprises" (Webbs and Webbs 1944: 467,471; italics added). For example, in course of only a few months, between the spring and winter of 1931, five and a half million persons had been recruited; including 2.6 million for building and construction and 1.4 million for lumbering (Skorov and Danilov 1976: 174).

"Before everything capital smashes all legal or traditional barriers which prevent it from purchasing, at pleasure [*nach Gutdünken*] such and such kind of labor power or appropriating at will, this or that type of labor" (Marx 1969: 39). Though capitalism is based on the double freedom of the immediate producers, this double freedom is heavily enmeshed with restrictions at the initial stage of capitalism. "Capital made effective its ownership right over the free laborer through legal constraints" (Marx 1962a: 599). The expropriated masses do not, on their own, become wage laborers. They have, at first, to be "forcibly placed on the narrow road leading to the labor market" (Marx 1953: 406). In the same way the Soviet authorities understood the futility of relying on the "spontaneous influx of labor power" and underlined the necessity of "organized recruitment of workers for industry" (Stalin 1970: 204).

This organized recruitment meant, in fact, that "on the kolkhozy fell the *obligation* of supplying a definite volume of labor [to industry] and on the kolkhozian fell the *duty* of being employed in industry" (Schwarz 1956: 82; italics added).

The exigencies of capital accumulation spearheaded by the strategy of superindustrialization made huge demands on productive resources, *quantitatively speaking*. Thus, whereas for the whole of the pre-planning period 1918-1928 -- excluding the fourth quarter of the terminal year -- total investment in fixed capital amounted to 4.4. billion rubles, for a much shorter period of the First Plan, 1928-1932 (excluding the first three quarters of the initial year), it amounted to 8.8 billion rubles, and for the Second Plan period, 1932-1937, the figure more than doubled to 19.7 billion rubles (all in "comparable prices" of 1969) in spite of cutbacks in 1933 and 1937 (*Narkhoz* 1922-1982: 365). The same exigency is reflected in the growth of production/extraction of natural resources in which the USSR was initially in an unusually favorable situation. This is seen in Table 4.1.

TABLE 4.1

**GROWTH OF NATURAL RESOURCES
PRODUCTION, 1928-1940**

	1928	1932	1937	1940
Electricity (milliard KWh)	5.0	13.5	36.2	48.3
Coal (million tons)	3.3	6.2	14.5	14.9
Oil (million tons)	11.6	21.4	28.5	31.1
Natural gas (milliard cubic meters)	0.3	1.0	2.2	3.2
Iron ore (million tons)	6.1	12.1	27.8	29.9

Source: *Narkhoz* 1922-1972: 136-137.

As to (living) labor, the tempo of accumulation itself, combined with a series of measures undertaken by the Soviet authorities (not very different from those undertaken by the first bourgeoisie in Western Europe) "forcing the laborers to sell themselves voluntarily" (Marx 1962a: 765), resulted in raising the employment level, by more than two times between 1928 and 1932 -- from 11.4 million to 24.2 million (*Narkhoz* 1922-1972: 345), thus not only wiping out previous mass unemployment but also creating serious labor shortage. "From the beginning of the thirties the main problem became the labor shortage" (Skorov and Danilov 1976: 149). This immediately showed itself in the slowdown in the growth of employment, the increase over the Second Five Year Plan being only a quarter of that over the First -- about 4 million compared to about 13 million (*Narkhoz* 1922-1972: 345). In this situation, with no *continuous technological revolutionization* in the method(s) of production, the tempo of (capital) accumulation could be maintained by means of the prolongation of the total (social) working time, intensity of labor used including enforcement of discipline, and bringing into the fold of productive labor those who were still outside of it: mainly women, in other words, increasing the totality of absolute surplus value. The leading idea behind the Soviet labor economy, it has been observed, was the "maximization of the social share of labor time" in which "the process of accelerated economic accumulation was reflected" (Hofmann 1956: 197). Thus, governed by the principle of continuous production, the introduction of seven-hour day was coupled with three-shift work and uninterrupted work-week [*nepreryvka*] in the factories where, according to the Soviet official affirmation, "work was going on for 24 hours almost without interruption" (Schwarz 1956: 328).[4] At the same time methods of intensification of labor such as socialist competition, shock-brigade campaigns (including the much publicized "Stakhanovite" movement) and raising the work norms in the different branches of production were adopted (Lorenz 1976: 221,350-51; Nove 1982: 232-35; Kuromiya 1988: 119-34). One is immediately reminded of Marx's remark (cited earlier) that in the English factories "the prolongation of the [working] day and the increase in the intensity of labor went hand in hand."

Perfectly in keeping with the increasing intensification of labor was the use of piece wage as the preferred method of wage payment. Particularly following Stalin's so-called six point speech in its favor in 1931, the method was greatly extended to cover, by the late 1930s, three-quarters of all industrial workers (Dobb 1966: 464; Stalin 1970: 203-18). Here again Marx's remarks are particularly relevant: "Given piece wage it is naturally the personal interest of the worker to stretch his labor power in the most intensive way possible, which makes easier for the capitalist to raise the normal degree of labor intensity" (1962a: 577).

Referring to the proletariat at the initial stage of capitalism in Western Europe, Marx remarked that "[these people] suddenly uprooted from their habitual life could not so suddenly be amenable to the discipline of their new situation" (1962a: 762), and he mentioned a series of measures enforced by the state for disciplining the laborers. For example, a law asserted that "every man in good health between 16 and 60 years of age without means of living and without practising a profession is to be sent to the galleys" (Marx 1962a: 765). "Socialist full employment" policy was carried to the hilt by demanding in 1930 that "no reasons to refuse the work offered are to be taken into consideration excepting ill-health, confirmed by a hospital certificate" (Baykov 1970: 213). In fact, as in the first stage of capitalism in Western Europe, a whole series of measures were adopted by the Soviet authorities during the 1930s to discipline the newly recruited proletariat -- such as, measures concerning punishment against absenteeism, introduction of "labor books", prohibition of voluntary mobility as between work places (*Resheniya* II 1967: 662,665,757).

If the exploitation of the already employed laborers cannot be increased by raising the rate either of absolute or of relative surplus value, the capitalist class requires the enrollment of supplementary labor power to make the (material) elements work as capital (Marx 1962a: 607). Thus beginning with the early 1930s, women in the USSR were increasingly "subjected to the service of capital" as Marx would put it, thereby "increasing the number of wage laborers, independently of any increase in the absolute number of the population itself" (1976a: 166). As a matter of fact, the percentage of women in total employment steadily rose from 27 in 1932 to 39 in 1940 (Schwarz 1956: 100; *Narkhoz* 1984: 412). This was reflected in the rise in the growth of total employment again: by more than 5 million in three years (1937-1940), compared to a little more than 4 million in the previous five years (*Narkhoz* 1922-1972: 345). On the whole, even during the pre-war years of USSR's high population growth, its laboring population was growing at a faster rate than the population: the former increased threefold while the latter increased by 1.3 times between 1928 and 1940.[5] This was a clear case of the "increase of laboring population in relation to the population [itself] when along with the concentration of capital the old elements of the productive classes fall among the proletariat" (Marx 1956: 191).

The more or less symmetric increase in fixed capital and natural resources along with the employment of living labor in the USSR well illustrates what Marx had discerned as an important characteristic of the accumulation of capital with more or less a *stationary technique of production* where, moreover, the technical composition of capital remains largely unchanged (1976a: 165-66, 269). The symmetric growth as between constant capital and living labor, Marx emphasizes, implies "*the growth of capital without the growth and development of labor's productive power*", where capital "has assumed only formal domination" (1953: 633-34; italics added).

It has been pointed out that "productivity in the economy as a whole rose substantially in these years" (Nove 1982: 232). However, whatever rise there was in productivity seems not to have much to do with a *technological revolutionization* in the method(s) of production and a corresponding (qualitative) change in the technical composition of capital. In fact, with regard to the shortage of labor in the earlier years of planning, the Soviet spokespersons themselves note that "the shortage had arisen because the planned tempos for *increasing labor productivity had proved unrealizable* at the then scale of building and *low levels* of skill and poor *technical equipment* of the builders" (Skorov and Danilov 1976: 172; italics added). To the extent that there was a rise in productivity, it seems to have been due to the concentration of capital with corresponding changes in the "social combination of labor," to the "upward revision of the existing technological and labor norms" including "improved labor discipline" (Nove 1982: 233-35) and, more importantly, a change in the composition of output through shift of labor from agriculture to industry (Gomulka 1986: 171; Winiecki 1988: 209; Khanin 1991: 30: Hanson 1992: 43) -- the hall marks of the *initial* stage of the real subsumption of labor under capital where the absolute form of surplus value still dominates its relative form as we argued earlier.[6] It should be noted that the movement of a laborer from rural to industrial employment resulted in an absolute increase in labor time (Cohn 1987: 12). Even though the Soviet Union tried to utilize "the advantages of industrialization in conditions of backwardness" by "adopting the fruits of Western technical progress" (Gerschenkron 1966a: 149), and though "during the period from 1930 to 1945 Soviet technology was almost a complete transfer from Western countries," (Sutton 1971: 319),[7] the impact of even this borrowed technology was, taking the *economy as a whole*, rather moderate. According to a careful calculation, a little less than three-quarters of the economy remained outside of it in the period immediately preceding the Second World War (Moorsteen and Powell 1966: 294), due to, it seems, the "inability of the Soviet engineers and workers to master fully the intricacies of modern techniques (and) almost complete absence of indigenous self-generated innovation" (in sharp contrast with Japan) with the exception of military production (Sutton 1971: 324,329).

Though ordinarily one expects a "rising movement of the wage rate" when the "needs of accumulation begin to surpass the supply of labor" (Marx 1962a: 641), thus creating difficulties for further accumulation, the problem was solved without difficulty in the USSR. Facilitated by the single juridical ownership of social total capital, with no independent workers' organization to reckon with, the Soviet rulers did in fact *depress* the real wage level for a considerable length of time. "Real wages fell during the early 1930s and again during the war and only regained 1928 level in the early 1950s," observes a distinguished authority, correctly adding that "the very low level of real wages was undoubtedly an important factor in the large increase in participation in the labor force, particularly among wives" (Chapman 1977: 251).[8]

Summing up the initial accumulation-proletarianization process in the USSR an eminent historian noted that "the shift of labor force out of agriculture of the magnitude that occured in the USSR between 1928 and 1940 took from thirty to fifty years in other countries," and stressed that it was not so much the high level of "capital formation proportion" as its "concentration" and the "rapidity with which this level was attained," that set the Soviet economy apart (Kuznets 1963: 341,345,353,367-68).

THE OVER-ACCUMULATION OF CAPITAL

After dismissing for years all talks of crisis in "socialism" as only bourgeois "inventions" [*vymysly*], the Soviet spokespersons, toward the end of the regime, had to bow before the evidence and openly acknowledge the existence of "negative trends" [*neblagopriyatnye tendentsii*] in the (economic) development of their society (Gorbachev: 1986a: 4).

However, contrary to their assertion, the negative trends did not start in the middle 1970s; they started much earlier. In fact, the growth rate of perhaps the single most important economic indicator -- national income -- started to decline even before the Second World War: its annual average growth-rate, according to the Soviet official estimates, after attaining 16.2 percent in 1928-1932, as well as in 1932-1937, went down to 10 percent in 1937-1940 (Cohn 1972: 123). Though it again increased to 14.6 percent in 1946-1950 (Sorokin 1986: Table 2), it started its *secular slowdown* beginning with 11 percent during 1951-1955

(*Narkhoz* 1967: 671). However, though declining, the rate of growth of the economy was still high until the end of the 1960s on official estimates and could still be sustained by massive quantitative mobilization of productive resources.[9] For example, even as late as the seventh plan period (1961-1965), the average annual rates of growth of productive resources, though lower compared to those during the first two Plans, were, on the whole, certainly high as Table 4.2 shows.

TABLE 4.2

AVERAGE ANNUAL RATES OF GROWTH OF
THE PRODUCTIVE RESOURCES
IN PERCENTAGE (1961-1965)

Electricity	14.7
Oil	12.8
Natural gas	36.5
Iron ore	8.8
Coal	2.6
Cement	11.8
Fixed productive investment	6.2
Labor in material production	2.2

Sources: Rates of growth of non-labor resources computed from *Narkhoz* 1980: 154,156,157,158,176; labor growth rate computed from Anchishkin 1973: 179; investment growth rate as in UN -- *Economic Survey of Europe in 1984-85*: 139.

In fact even in the absence of the "revolutionization in the method of production," the mere existence of abundant natural resources, besides a large reserve of labor, within the territory of the USSR greatly facilitated the enlarged reproduction of the system at such a high tempo over such a long period. The natural resources in the USSR have been abundant enough not only to cover the costs of initial capital accumulation but also to yield an exportable surplus. As the Soviet authors have noted, "in 1930-1931, with a shortage of grain within the country, more than ten million tons of cereals were exported in order to pay for imports" which globally "grew by 55 percent," while "imports of machinery, metals and metal goods, electrical engineering items and precision machines rose by 243 percent" between 1926-1927 and 1931 (Skorov and Danilov 1976: 178-79). However, the extraction of tremendous amounts of mineral resources and fuel over a long period with a view to fulfilling high growth targets resulted in the decline in their rates of increase by the 1960s (Aganbegyan 1988: 112-14). At the same time there was a drastic slow-down in the rate of growth of fixed productive investment due, among other things, to the increasing difficulties of natural resource mobilization and to the increase, dictated by political necessity, of consumption fund share of national income, the growth rate of which itself was declining. (Consumption fund share of "utilized national income" had earlier come down from 74.8 percent during 1951-1955 to 72.1 percent during 1966-1970. From then on it increased gradually back to 74.8 percent for the Eleventh Plan and to 75.4 percent during 1986-1989. Data was obtained from Becker 1972: 98; *Narkhoz* 1987: 430; *Narkhoz* 1989: 15). On the other hand, the virtual exhaustion of labor reserve caused by the extremely high labor participation rate in the economy,[10] accentuated by the unfavorable effect on the working population of the deterioration of the demographic situation -- "the mathematical limit of the production of surplus value by social capital" (Marx)[11] -- manifested itself in a significant decline in the growth rate of labor resources. Table 4.3 shows the evolution of the resource situation over the recent years.

TABLE 4.3

PRODUCTIVE RESOURCES: AVERAGE ANNUAL RATES OF GROWTH IN PERCENTAGES (1960-1990)

	1960 1965	1965 1970	1970 1975	1975 1980	1980 1985	1986 1990
Electricity	14.7	9.2	8.0	4.9	3.9	2.2
Oil	12.8	9.0	7.8	4.5	-0.3	-0.8
Natural gas	36.5	10.9	9.2	10.1	9.5	4.7
Iron ore	8.8	5.7	3.8	0.8	0.2	-1.2
Coal	2.6	1.6	2.4	0.4	0.2	-0.4
Cement	11.8	6.2	5.6	0.5	0.9	0.8
Productive fixed investment	6.2	7.5	7.0	3.4	3.6	4.1
Labor in material production	2.2	1.7	1.3	1.0	0.5	-0.1

Sources: Growth rates of the first six items are computed from *Narkhoz* 1980: 154,156,157,158,178; *Narkhoz* 1987: 164,165,184; *Narkhoz* 1989: 378,381; and *Ekonomika SSSR* 1991: 11,12. Growth rates of investment are taken from U.N. *Economic Survey of Europe*, various issues, and *Economic Bulletin for Europe 1991*, vol. 43: 25. Growth rates of labor are taken or computed from Anchishkin 1973: 179; U.N. *Economic survey of Europe in 1982:* 201; *Narkhoz* 1987: 412; and *Ekonomika SSSR* 1991: 9.

A drastic reduction in the growth rates of the productive resources, implying their serious shortage in recent years compared to the early 1960s, is immediately clear. At the same time, if we look at the average annual growth rates of Soviet "net material product" during the same period, which were, respectively, 6.5, 7.8, 5.8, 4.3, 3.6, and 1.3 percent (*Narkhoz* 1985: 38; *Ekonomika SSSR* 1991: 9), we see, indeed, a case of what Kornai has called "resource -- constrained growth" within an over-all shortage in the economy (Kornai 1980, 1992). This, however, has nothing to do with *socialism* as such and, contrary to a widely held idea, this is simply a consequence of high quantitative accumulation of *capital* -- given the high growth targets -- in the *absence* of what Marx called "continuous revolutionization of the production methods."

It should be emphasized that unchanging or little changing method(s) of production here is not related to the *formal* subsumption of labor under capital. The case under consideration is certainly situated within the *real* subsumption of labor (under capital) where the old (pre-capitalist) method(s) of production have already been transformed. However, *once arrived at this stage*, there has taken place what Marx called "purely *quantitative* extension (of capital) on the *given technical basis*" (Marx 1962a: 473; italics added). As a well-known sovietologist has remarked, "there was a *one-shot infusion* of technological progress as advanced plant and equipment from Germany, the UK and the USA were imported, but there was little provision for on-going incremental innovation . . . . *Prevailing technology was being mastered*, but there was little innovation" (Hunter 1988: ix; italics added).

The functioning of the Soviet economy through time offers several indices of the *non-continuous revolutionization* of the technique of production. One index is the comparison of the growth of Gross Social Product (GSP) with that of Net Material Product (NMP) or National Income Produced (GSP is the sum of the newly created value *plus* the value of material inputs *plus* depreciation, while NMP is the newly created value, that is, the sum of the value of means of consumption and net investment). If we leave aside depreciation which seems to account for less than ten percent of Soviet NMP -- the proportion itself remaining stable over time -- the ratio of GSP to NMP over time would give us a good measure of "the material intensity of NMP" (UN 1984-85: 95), in other words, the degree of efficiency of material inputs in production and thereby the degree of metamorphosis in the method of production. This is illustrated in Table 4.4.

During only three Plan periods out of eight -- as given above -- did NMP grow slightly faster than GSP. During the rest of the time, NMP grew either at the same rate as GSP or at a rate even lower than GSP. Thus it seems that the record of Soviet capitalism was not particularly bright in regard to the efficiency of material inputs.[12]

Another index showing the degree of revolutionization of the method(s) of production is the traditional "factor-productivity" method. This has been the method used by the Western sovietologists to judge the Soviet economic efficiency. But not by them alone. It is interesting to note that the Soviet economists also used the same method while denouncing it as "originating from

TABLE 4.4

CHANGE IN MATERIAL INTENSITY OF PRODUCTION (1951-1990): AVERAGE ANNUAL PERCENTAGE

1951 1955	1956 1960	1961 1965	1966 1970	1971 1975	1976 1980	1981 1985	1986 1990
-0.3	0.0	0.0	-0.4	0.6	-0.1	0.0	0.6

Sources: Figures computed by us. Data for 1951-1960 as given from Soviet official sources in Becker 1972: 92; data for 1961-1985 as given in *Narkhoz* 1985: 38. Data for 1985-1990 as given in the U.N. *Economic survey of Europe* in 1990-91: 45; and *Economic Bulletin for Europe* 1991, vol 43: 25.

TABLE 4.5

AVERAGE ANNUAL RATES OF CHANGE (IN PERCENTAGE) 1951-1990

	1	2	3	4	5
	NMP Produced	Labor in Material Sphere	Fixed Productive Capital	Combined Inputs	Global Efficiency
1951-55	11.3	2.4	8.1	4.4	6.9
1956-60	9.2	2.6	9.4	4.9	4.3
1961-65	6.5	2.2	9.4	4.7	1.8
1966-70	7.8	1.7	8.3	4.0	3.8
1971-75	5.8	1.3	8.7	3.8	2.0
1976-80	4.3	1.0	7.2	3.2	1.1
1981-85	3.6	0.5	6.5	2.7	0.9
1986-90	1.3	-0.1	6.0	2.0	-0.7

Sources: Computed or taken from the following sources: for NMP 1951-60, *Narkhoz* 1967: 671; for NMP 1961-85, *Narkhoz* 1987: 51. For employment 1951-1970, Anchishkin 1973: 179; employment 1971-80, U.N. *Economic Survey of Europe in 1982*: 201; and employment 1981-85, *Narkhoz* 1987: 412. For fixed capital 1951-70, Anchishkin 1973: 129; and fixed capital 1971-85, *Narkhoz* 1975: 59, *Narkhoz* 1987: 101. For NMP, fixed capital and employment 1986-1990, *Ekonomika SSSR* 1991: 9. Figures for the last two columns are our computation with weights for labor force and fixed capital as in Anchishkin 1973:253, that is, 0.65 and 0.35 respectively.

the vulgar theory of production factors" [*iskhodit iz vulgarnoi teorii faktorov proizvodstva*] (Anchishkin 1973: 211). Following *their own* "factor model" method to measure what they called the "efficiency of social production"[13] -- which they, in perfect accord with the Western economists, took as the indicator of technical progress -- we obtain what is shown in Table 4.5 for the period 1951-1990.

From the table, it is not difficult to see that the productivity of labor had been consistently falling over the period, except for 1966-1970, and that capital productivity had been steadily negative, except for 1951-1955. Consequently the efficiency of social production, besides falling secularly, had grown consistently more slowly than the inputs since the Sixth Plan. Then again a decline in the growth rate of output had been closely associated with a slow down in the growth rate of inputs. It is clear that the major part of the output growth is explained by the *quantitative expansion* of inputs, the situation being particularly obvious for the more recent Plans. It is seen that for the period 1951-1990 as a whole, about 60 percent of the growth of the economy had been due to the expansion of the productive factors *quantitatively* speaking, and, leaving out the exceptionally unfavorable 12th Plan, the proportion rises around 70 percent during 1971-1985 our computation based on Table 4.5. In this respect, it may be noted, there seems not to have been much of a change compared to the earlier epoch. For the period 1928-1962, Moorsteen and Powell, in their thorough study of the question, concluded that "the share of increased inputs in total growth appears to have been significantly in excess of one-half and may well have amounted to three-quarters or better" (1966: 292).[14] This is a clear case of capital accumulation on the basis of an inadequately changing technology or largely on the given technical basis as Marx had envisaged.

The absence of what Marx called technical metamorphosis in the course of capital accumulation is also confirmed by the very low rates of retirement of Soviet fixed productive capital. Thus the annual rate of retirement of capital in Soviet industry, calculated as a percentage of the value of fixed capital stock at the beginning of the year -- which seems to have been already low by international standards (Cohn 1982: 180) -- went down further in recent years. It steadily declined from 2.1 percent in 1965 to 1.8 percent in 1970, to 1.6 percent in 1975, to 1.4 percent in 1980, to 1.3 percent in 1984, very slightly rose to 1.4 percent in 1985, reaching the 1970 rate of 1.8 percent in 1986 (*Narkhoz* 1970: 169; 1975: 225; 1980: 147; 1984: 157; 1985: 124; 1987: 151). A concomitant of the low retirement rate of fixed capital has been a deterioration in the age structure of the capital stock. The share of fixed capital under five years of age in industry's total productive equipment declined from 41.4 percent in 1970 to 31.5 percent in 1989 and the corresponding share of equipment over twenty years of age increased from 8 percent to 14 percent over the same period. The average period of equipment service remained very high -- 26 years, double the period of the official Soviet norm (*Narkhoz* 1989: 314). According to one unofficial estimate, the average service life of capital stock in the USSR was 47 years against 17 in the USA (Shmelev and Popov 1989: 119). In some industries like iron and steel, cost of capital repair was equal to the whole of their investments (Plyshevsky 1986: 23). In mid-1980s the Soviet repair industry had a stock of machine tools equal to that possessed by the entire engineering industry of Japan, and that the annual repairing cost of Soviet equipment was equivalent to the combined output of the Soviet coal, oil, and gas industries (Cooper 1986: 317). This is certainly *not* the situation where "scientific and technological progress allows the replacement of used instruments with more efficient ones" and where "a large portion of old tools is entirely renewed every year and thus becomes more productive" (Marx 1965: 1111; italics added).

Besides these, there are more direct indicators showing the absence of technical metamorphosis in the Soviet capital accumulation process. This is seen in the data concerning what has been called "invention, innovation, diffusion, of (new) technology and incremental improvements" in Soviet industry during the 1970s and early 1980s (Amann 1986). See Table 4.6, based on Soviet official data.

TABLE 4.6

**TECHNICAL PROGRESS IN SOVIET INDUSTRY:
AVERAGE ANNUAL GROWTH RATES
(IN PERCENTAGE) 1971-1983**

	1971 1975	1976 1980	1981 1983
Invention[a]	-1.19	-1.48	-1.42
Innovation[b]	9.36	4.89	2.32
Diffusion[c]	1.69	2.19	-1.40
Incremental improvements[d]	3.30	0.36	-0.65

[a] machines and equipment
[b] number of measures introduced
[c] modernization of industrial process
[d] number of inventions and rationalization measures utilized

Source: Amann 1986: 26-30.

It is seen that there is an absolute decline in the invention of (new) machines and equipment, a slowdown in the growth rate in the introduction of new technologies and their diffusion, and a fall in the growth rate of incremental improvements at the shop floor level. One cannot say (paraphrasing Marx) that the "basis" of Soviet industry "never considered and never treated as definitive the existing mode of a procedure", and was "revolutionary."

That the accumulation of Soviet capital -- euphemistically called "the growth of the Soviet economy" -- has been based not on the continuous *revolutionization* of the method(s) of production but on the *given* technical basis, began to be openly acknowledged by the Soviet spokespersons themselves toward the end of the regime. Thus Gorbachev declared that "the *structure of our production remained unchanged* and no longer corresponded to the exigencies of scientific and technological progress" (Gorbachev 1986b: 2; italics added).

A. Aganbegyan distinguished between revolutionary and evolutionary shifts [*sdivigi*] in scientific-technological progress. The first signified transition from the old to the mainly new technological systems, while the second signified technical non-transformation of the productive process, requiring only "more and more resources for successive improvement." He concluded that the "*evolutionary form . . .* has till recent times *prevailed* [*preobladala*] in our national economy" (Aganbegyan 1985: 7-8; italics added). It should be clear that the Soviet type of capital accumulation largely corresponds to Marx's second type of accumulation discussed earlier.

The Soviet accumulation process was marked, as is well-known, by the absolute priority of industry over agriculture and of the means of production over the means of (individual) consumption. Thus over the period of six decades (1922-1981) -- on official estimates -- while the "national income produced" grew by 167 times, the growth factors of industry and agriculture were, respectively, 514 and 5 (*Narkhoz* 1922-1982: 52). Over the more recent and shorter period (1940-1985), the three figures were, respectively 17, 25, and 3 (*Narkhoz* 1985: 34). On the other hand, the growth factors of the means of production -- the so-called Group A -- and of the means of (individual) consumption -- the so-called Group B -- over the first period were, respectively, 1400 and 150 (*Narkhoz* 1922-1982: 52), while the corresponding figures for the second period were 35 and 13 (*Narkhoz* 1985: 34). The priority of Group A over Group B in Soviet growth strategy[15] is seen in the breakdown of the shares of the two groups in total industrial output and total industrial investment over the last several decades as shown in Table 4.7.

On the other hand, the stock of productive fixed capital in the economy experienced a 22-fold growth between 1940 and 1985 (*Narkhoz* 1985: 34). This was accompanied by a high and rapid rate of proletarianization. First, labor force grew at a much faster rate than the population as a whole. Earlier we cited the relevant figures for the pre-war Plan period. As for the period 1940-1985, consistently with the earlier trend, the growth factors for the two were, respectively, 3.5 and 1.4 (*Narkhoz* 1985: 5, 34). Secondly, the share of independent producers (with their dependents) in the total population came down at an astonishing speed from three-quarters to less than three percent within the

TABLE 4.7

**TOTAL INDUSTRIAL OUTPUT AND
TOTAL INDUSTRIAL INVESTMENT:
PERCENTAGE SHARES OF GROUPS A AND B**

I. Industrial output

	1928	1940	1950	1960	1965	1970	1975	1980	1985	1990
Group A	39.5	61.0	68.8	72.5	74.1	73.4	73.7	73.8	74.8	73.0
Group B	60.5	39.0	31.2	27.5	25.9	26.6	26.3	26.2	25.2	27.0

II. Industrial Investment

	1928 1932	1932 1937	1937 1940	1946 1950	1951 1955	1956 1960	1961 1965	1966 1970	1971 1975	1976 1980	1981 1985	1986 1990
Percent	38.0	37.3	34.4	38.6	41.0	35.7	36.5	35.2	35.0	35.3	35.7	36.2
Group A	31.7	30.5	28.5	33.4	36.5	30.4	31.7	29.9	30.2	31.0	31.4	31.6
Group B	6.3	6.8	5.9	5.2	4.5	5.3	4.8	5.3	4.8	4.3	4.3	4.6

Sources: (1) Industrial output figures from *Narkhoz* 1922-1982: 152; *Narkhoz* 1987: 128; and Pervushin 1991: 4, except for figures for 1928 and 1950 which are from Notkin 1967: 53; (2) investment figures from *Narkhoz* 1922-1982: 369; *Narkhoz* 1987: 329; and *Narkhoz* 1990: 551.

first decade of planning and to around zero by 1950 (*Narkhoz* 1922-1982: 30). Also to be noticed are the high rates of conversion of surplus value into capital

TABLE 4.8

**NATIONAL INCOME UTILIZED FOR
CONSUMPTION AND ACCUMULATION
(IN PERCENTAGE) 1951-1989**

	1951 1955	1956 1960	1961 1965	1966 1970	1971 1975	1976 1980	1981 1985	1986 1989
Consumption	74.8	73.5	72.9	72.1	72.3	73.8	74.8	75.4
Accumulation and others	25.2	26.5	27.1	27.9	27.7	26.2	25.2	24.6

Sources: Figures for 1951-1965 computed from Becker 1972: Table 4.7 citing official data. Figures for 1966-1985 computed from *Narkhoz* 1985: 410-11; and for 1986-1989, *Narkhoz* 1989: 15.

as shown by the break down of "national income utilized" into consumption and "accumulation and others" over the post-war years (see Table 4.8). As is seen here, the accumulation's share consistently remained around a quarter of the national income.[16]

It is interesting to observe that associated with the over- accumulation of capital was an exceptionally high level of concentration of capital in the USSR. Soviet enterprises were considered to be the "largest in the world" (Shmelev and Popov 1989: 115). As a matter of fact (industrial) enterprises with 100 employees and less constituted less than two percent, those with 101 -- 1000 employees, 24 percent and those with more than 1000 employees, 74 percent of all Soviet enterprises in 1987, showing "an incomparably higher level of concentration of production in the USSR compared with the USA," where the corresponding figures for 1982 were 22, 47, and 31 percent respectively (Loginov 1992: 11). Comparable figures (in percentage) two decades earlier were 2.7, 35.5, and 61.8 for the USSR, and 27.9, 42.4, and 29.7, respectively, for the USA (Kvasha 1967: 27).

Let us note one or two other significant points in connection with the Soviet accumulation process. From the Soviet data, it appears that the means of production in the form of fixed and circulating capital have been growing at a much higher rate than the employment of living labor. Leaving aside the exceptionally unfavorable 12th Plan period and confining ourselves to the penultimate four plan periods (1966-1985), we see that their average annual rates of growth were 8.3, 8.1, 6.9, and 5.8 percent at comparable prices of 1973 on the one hand and 1.7, 1.3, 1.0, and 0.5 percent on the other constant capital growth rates are calculated from *Narkhoz* 1970: 61, *Narkhoz* 1975: 60, *Narkhoz* 1980: 51, and *Narkhoz* 1985: 50. Labor force growth rates are as in Table 4.5. However, with a consistently much higher rate of growth of constant capital compared to living labor there was no corresponding growth in the productivity of social labor. In fact, the ratio of the index of labor productivity to the index of fixed capital stock had been persistently declining over a twenty-five year period (1960-1985): from 100 in 1960, it came down to 46 in 1985 (*Narkhoz* 1985: 36-37). Perhaps no less significant in this regard is the fact that the rise in fixed capital intensity of labor had consistently exceeded the rise in labor productivity since the Sixth Plan (1956-1960). Their respective rates of growth (average annual) until the Eleventh Plan (1981-1985) were 6.8, 7.2, 6.6, 7.4, 6.2, and 6.0 percent on the one hand, and 6.6, 4.3, 6.1, 4.4, 3.3, and 3.1 percent on the other (calculated from Table 4.5).

Thus instead of seeing Soviet capitalism's "tendency and result" in the "constantly increasing productivity of labor" (Marx 1969: 101) due to the "continuous revolutions in the methods of production" (Marx 1964: 254) -- which happens in what we have called the first type of capital accumulation leading to its own type of over-accumulation -- we see here the very opposite. Now, a quantitative rise in the capital intensity of labor -- approximating the "technical composition of capital" -- unaccompanied by at least a corresponding rise in the productivity of living labor, would of course mean a rise in capital intensity of output -- designated in Soviet literature as the ratio of basically productive fixed capital to output.[17] Academician Khatchaturov has significantly qualified an "excessively prolonged development" [*slishkom prodolzhitel'noe razvitie*] of this kind -- which *is* the Soviet case -- as leading "to *over-accumulation*" [*k perenakopleniyu*] (Khatchaturov 1984: 22; italics added), which is, let us add, over-accumulation of capital of the second type, as we discussed earlier. In the face of this double decline, secularly speaking -- namely, decline in the growth rate of the productivity of living labor and the absolute decline in the productivity of materialized labor -- combined with the near-impossibility of steadily increasing the mass of labor power used, or given the *basically stationary* methods of production raising the rate of relative surplus value, we seem to be in the presence of a situation which largely -- if not in details -- corresponds to that of "absolute over-accumulation of capital" associated with the capital accumulation of the second type as analyzed by Marx. The result of course is underproduction -- as opposed to overproduction of commodities, an economy of shortage. As Gorbachev declared, "we lacked and we lack everything: metal, energy, cement, machines, consumption goods. Add to this the chronic shortage of labor and it will be clear that the economy finds itself in the impossibility of developing itself normally in these conditions" (Gorbachev 1987: 2).

We saw earlier that in a situation of (absolute) over-accumulation of capital, the means of production are effectively destroyed, that they cease to function as capital. An important indicator of the extent of Soviet capital "lying fallow" in the sense of Marx was the fall over time of the utilization coefficient of Soviet industrial capacity. First, beginning with the 1970s, in about three-quarters of the main lines of industrial production that were considered to be the sources of technological progress, as well as the "bottlenecks [*uzkie mesta*] in economic development," there was a distinct "tendency toward a decline in putting into operation of new capacities" (Val'tukh and Lavrovskii 1986: 21-22). Secondly, as Table 4.9 shows, incremental output -- capacity ratios in the important industrial branches had been falling over a longer period.[18]

TABLE 4.9

INCREMENTAL OUTPUT-CAPACITY RATIO
IN INDUSTRIAL BRANCHES
(IN PHYSICAL TERMS)

	1961-65	1966-70	1971-75	1976-80	1981-85
1 Electricity	4.46	4.28	5.10	4.70	4.90
2 Pig Iron	1.53	2.00	1.32	0.71	4.20
3 Steel	1.64	1.38	2.29	0.48	1.00
4 Finished Rolled Steel	1.97	1.32	1.47	0.58	0.67
5 Steel Pipes	1.30	1.38	1.51	1.20	1.50
6 Soda Ash	1.23	0.58	1.16	0.17	0.40
7 Coal	0.85	0.48	0.67	0.16	0.16
8 Plastic & Synthetic Res ins	0.89	1.20	1.19	0.53	1.14
9 Fibers & Chemical Fibers	0.88	1.43	0.95	0.96	0.66
10 Turbines	1.80	0.38	0.48	0.23	0.40
11 Machine Tools	0.85	0.74	1.14	-1.14	-7.20
12 Cement	0.95	1.30	1.29	0.27	1.00

Sources: Computed from data in *Narkhoz* 1922-1972: 136 and 319; and in *Narkhoz* 1985: 152,155,157 and 359-60.

As can be seen from the table, the trend of the incremental coefficients during 1961-1980 is, on the whole, downward. On the face of it, it looks as though there was some improvement in the majority of the branches between 1976 and 1985. However, a closer look at the data would put the situation in a somewhat less favorable light. Writing ΔQ and ΔM for increment, respectively, in output and capacity, we have the following data for the two recent sub-periods shown in Table 4.10.

It appears now that only in three branches there was real improvement: branches numbered 4, 6, and 10 in the table, where additional output and additional capacity grew at the same time. In 1 and 2, the growth of output went down while in 3 it remained stable. In all three cases additional capacity was reduced precisely because it was apparently considered excessive. For 5 additional output and additional capacity went down at the same time. In 8 and 12 additional output grew, but additional capacity creation was considerably reduced. In any case, the situation deteriorated in 1981-1985.

TABLE 4.10

INCREMENTS IN OUTPUT AND CAPACITY
IN INDUSTRIAL BRANCHES

		1976-1980		1981-1985	
		ΔQ	ΔM	ΔQ	ΔM
1	Electricity (milliard KW)	255	54.2	251	51.2
2	Pig Iron (million tons)	4	5.6	3	0.7
3	Steel (million tons)	7	14.3	7	7
4	Finished Rolled				
	Steel (million tons)	4.3	7.4	5	7.4
5	Steel Pipes (million tons)	2.2	1.8	1.1	0.7
6	Soda Ash (thousand tons)	88	505	248	619
7	Coal (million tons)	15	90.4	10	61.6
8	Plastics & synthetic				
	Resins (thousand tons)	799	1505	1383	327.6
9	Fibers & chemical				
	Fibers (thousand tons)	221	230.4	218	327.6
10	Turbines (million KW)	0.7	3.0	2	5
11	Machine Tools (thousand units)	-15.0	12.8	-34	4.7
12	Cement (million tons)	3.0	11.0	6	5.8

Sources: As in Table 4.9.

According to unofficial estimates "a correct evaluation of productive capacities will inevitably show that their *real level is much lower than reported*" (Medikov 1985: 153; italics added). Thus, toward the end of the 1980s, whereas the official estimate put the rate of capacity utilization in industry at about 90 percent, unofficial estimates put it at about 75 percent (Shmelev and Popov 1989: 142-45). A Soviet economist refuted the argument that the unutilized capacities in the USSR constituted some sort of reserves to meet unforeseen needs. He pointed out that, given the shortage of labor and raw materials, the unutilized capacities could not be considered as reserves. Their existence signifies "losses of capital investments," and "unutilized capacities are a straight loss of the country's national wealth" [*pryamoi vychet iz natsional'nogo bogatstva strany*] (Fal'tsman 1985: 47).

In other words, this signifies "effective destruction of the means of production" as *capital* in the sense of Marx.

NOTES

1. As the accumulation of capital in the USSR is our subject in this chapter, we shall not be concerned here with the growth (or development) of the Soviet economy as such, as it is usually understood. We shall refer only to those aspects of the development of the Soviet economy that are relevant for analyzing the accumulation process itself. Secondly, our analysis is limited mainly to the period of the so-called "administered economic system" that came to be established at the end of what is generally considered as the "reconstruction period" of 1921-1928, and continued, without basic changes, until the collapse of the regime itself. In what follows we have used mainly the Soviet (official) data. As we know, toward the end of the regime the Soviet economists themselves were questioning their official statistics (Seliunin and Khanin 1987; Khanin 1988; Aganbegyan 1988; Treml 1988; Shmelev and Popov 1989). However, the Soviet statistical service could not "carry out the kind of comprehensive adjustment necessary for a major revision of the official data on the economic growth of sixty years" (Shmelev and Popov 1989: 36). On the other hand, in order to put the Soviet case in the most favorable light we did not want to use, as far as we could help it, the non-Soviet (for example CIA) data. In Chapter 5, dealing with the specific manifestations of the crisis of the Soviet accumulation process, we shall, in order to have a better appreciation of its gravity, often have recourse to some alternative estimates of the Soviet economic dynamics that have appeared in recent years (Khanin 1988, 1991; Fal'tsman 1991, 1992).

2. A well-known authority has shown that, in terms of the mode of production, there was in fact a *regression* in the Russian countryside in the 1920s. The peasantry's percentage in the population was now greater than in Tsarist Russia. On the other hand, by taking over the land of the gentry, the peasants eliminated the results of the Stolypin reforms, and "got rid of whatever capitalist development they had experienced before" (Lewin 1985: 298). See also Danilov (1988) and Merl (1981). A historian has remarked that the 1917 revolution destroyed not only the ancient social order but also the "not yet sufficiently developed forms and functional mechanisms of developing industrial civilization" (Reiman 1987: 139-40).

3. To what extent the collectivization of agriculture contributed to the accumulation of capital at its initial stage in the USSR is well discussed in Nove and Morrison (1982: 47-62).

4. On the whole question, see Davies (1989: 84-86,252-56).

5. Population figure computed from the official data as given in Eason (1963: Table II.9) and laboring population figure computed from *Narkhoz* 1922-1972 (1972: 234).

6. It now seems that, contrary to the official claims, the rise in "productivity in the economy as a whole" was quite low for labor and negative for capital. The annual average rate of growth of productivity of labor was slightly above one percent and that of capital was *minus* 2.0 percent during 1929-1941 (Khanin 1988: 85).

7. Marx points out that "the capitalist relation develops at a particular stage of economic-social formation which is already the result of a series of earlier developments", so that "the productivity of labor is something that is created historically" (1976a: 226). True in general for the development of capitalism, this statement seems to have particular relevance for the development of Soviet capitalism which benefited from a series of earlier developments in the so-called classical capitalist countries though it could not take full advantage thereof. Before proceeding further and anticipating somewhat our later arguments, let us briefly consider here an objection against our position on the Soviet accumulation process raised in an interesting paper by P. Zarembka (1992). He holds that there had been *continuous* technological changes in the Soviet economy, and, as an index to this, he refers to the "increased productivity of labor" through time in the USSR. Now, our contention is not that technological changes did not occur in the USSR. We hold that the field of *continuous* technological changes had been rather limited outside of military and aerospace sectors (Berliner 1988: 219-20). Moreover, technological changes did not - - contrary to Zarembka's assertion -- "spread out" to the *rest of the economy*. In 1976 J. Berliner observed that unless the general level of Soviet domestic technology improved, the "contribution of the technological progress to overall economic growth is likely to be small" (1988: 251). As to the productivity of labor as an indicator of technological progress, it now appears that, for the economy as a whole, the rate of growth of productivity was at a fairly high level only for a very limited period, namely, during 1951-1960 when its average annual rate reached five percent. Before that period, between 1929 and 1950, it was only 1.3 percent, and, after the 1950s, and not simply in "mid-1980s," the growth rate had steadily declined reaching 1.9 percent in 1971-1975, 0.2 percent in 1976-1980, and 0.0 percent in 1981-1985 (Khanin 1988: 85).

8. During 1927/28-1940 real wages in the USSR *fell* at the average annual rate of 5.3 percent (Zaleski 1962: 266) or, on alternative estimates, at the rate of 2.1 percent (with 1937 weights) or 4.8 percent (with the given year weights) (Chapman 1963: 153).

9. According to unofficial estimates, the annual average rate of growth of national income was already moderate at the end of 1950s when it started to decline steadily (Khanin 1988).

10. Thus, the share of the population not employed or studying on a full time basis in the working age population was only 9.6 percent in 1970 and 6 percent in 1979 (Kotliar 1983: 112). In 1985, one-tenth of the labor force came from non-working age population, pensioners being the primary source (Rapawy 1987: 189).

11. Besides the demographic consequences of the Second World War, the rate of natural increase itself of the Soviet population was less than halved within two decades, coming down from 17.8 per 1000 in 1960 [it was around 29 per thousand in 1930s] to 8.0 per 1000 in 1980, only slightly rising to 8.8 per 1000 in 1985 (*Narkhoz* 1985: 31)

12. The change in the ratio of GSP to NMP could be seen as equivalent to the change in the ratio of constant capital to NMP (over time) where, to use Marx's symbols, c + v + m stands for GSP, v + m for NMP, c = constant capital or means of production used up, v = variable capital or the value of labor power, and m = surplus value or the value of surplus product, with c, v, m > 0. That is,

$$\frac{c+v+m}{v+m} = \frac{c}{v+m} + 1$$

The reciprocal of this ratio was considered by the Soviet economists as the "index of efficiency of the national economy," its decline over time indicating the existence of "negative [*neblagopryatnykh*] phenomena" (Khachaturov 1967: 46).

13. This is the application of the well-known neo-classical aggregate production function with first degree homogeneity, having labor and fixed capital as productive factors. See Anchishkin (1973: 248-60).

14. A later estimate by the authors, for the period 1928-1966, confirms this (Becker, Moorsteen, and Powell 1968: 3,11,26). Following an unofficial Soviet estimate, it is seen that the extensive factors accounted for 63 percent of the Soviet growth for the period 1929-1987 (Khanin 1988: 85). For the period 1971-1985, the corresponding share was estimated to be 66 percent by Aganbegyan (1988: 104) and 71 percent by Shatalin (1986: 60).

15. "The capitalist society," writes Marx, "employs more of its available annual labor in the production of the means of production" (1973a: 436).

16. Accumulation had maintained this share from the beginning of the planning period. See Vinogradov et al (1978: 22).

17. This is seen in the simple relation

$$\frac{K}{Q} = \frac{K}{L} \div \frac{Q}{L}$$

where K = fixed capital, Q = output, L = labor, and Q, K, L > 0.

18. Our computation here follows the method of G. Pavlov and L. Pchelkina (1981: 46).

Chapter 5

THE CRISIS OF ABSOLUTE OVER-ACCUMULATION OF CAPITAL

After having discussed in Chapter 4 the process as well as the specificity of the accumulation of capital in the USSR, leading to the over-accumulation of capital, the present chapter will show some consequences of that over-accumulation as manifested in different ways in the terminal crisis of Soviet capital.

SOME NEGATIVE INDICES

The ultimate economic consequence of the regime's inability either to prolong society's absolute labor time or extend its relative labor time is seen clearly in the behavior of the basic economic indicators during the final years of the regime, as summarily seen in the official Soviet data in Table 5.1.

It is seen that the slowdown in the rates of growth of these basic indicators ended in the indicators' absolute fall in the final year of the final Plan. The negative growth of the economy was associated with some other manifestations of the crisis. The deficit on state budget, which amounted to 2-3 percent of the GNP in the beginning of the 1980s, increased by five times during 1985-1989, running at 10 percent of the GNP by 1989, and reached 400 billion rubles, or more than 40 percent by 1990 (Khandruev 1991: 38). The population's money income increased by 13.1 percent in 1989 and 16.9 percent in 1990, thereby continuing to widen the gap between money incomes and the availability of goods and services in real terms (*Narkhoz* 1990: 7). This was seen in the volume of unsatisfied demand amounting to 55 billion rubles, and an increase in people's savings bank deposits by about 43 billion rubles in 1990, for which year the rate of inflation was calculated as running at 20 percent. (*Ekonomika SSSR* 1991: 10). At the same time, a much weakened ruble was leading to inter-enterprise exchanges in kind, making a return to the "primitive form of barter" (Ryzhkov 1990: 1).

TABLE 5.1

BASIC ECONOMIC INDICATORS (1986 - 1990)
RATES OF CHANGE OVER THE PREVIOUS YEAR
(IN PERCENTAGE)

Year	GNP	NIP	IP	AP	I	SLP
1986	3.3	2.3	4.4	5.3	8.3	3.8
1987	2.9	1.6	3.8	-0.6	5.7	2.4
1988	5.5	4.4	3.9	1.7	6.2	5.1
1989	3.0	2.5	1.7	1.3	4.7	2.3
1990	-2.3	-4.0	-1.2	-2.9	-4.3	-3.0

GNP = Gross National Product; NIP = National Income Produced; IP = Industrial Output; AP = Agricultural Output; I = Gross Investment; SLP = Social Labor Productivity.

Sources: *Narkhoz* 1990: 7; U.N. Economic Commission for Europe, *Economic Bulletin for Europe*, 1991, vol. 43, January: 25.

Toward the end of the Twelfth Plan, Gorbachev underlined that "there has been an evident disintegration [*yavnyi raspad*] of the consumer market, growth of budget deficit and state debt, disorganization of monetary circulation, revelry of speculation and shadow economy," and added that "all this is happening simultaneously with the downfall of contract discipline, breach of economic ties, complete stoppage of a series of vitally important production plants" (Gorbachev 1990: 2). Whereas in the initial phase of "restructuring," the Soviet rulers were still speaking of their society taking "pre-crisis forms" [*predkrizisnye formy*] (Gorbachev 1987: 1,3), now they openly acknowledged "society's *crisis*" [*krizis obshchestva*] (K gumannomu 1990: 1; italics added).[1] The absolute decline of the basic economic indicators would, indeed, suggest that the Soviet economy, following the erstwhile accumulation path, had reached a point where neither the absolute surplus value of the society could be raised nor its relative surplus value increased -- that is, a crisis of absolute over-accumulation of capital.

The crisis of the Soviet economy did not appear suddenly in the 1980s, nor is it even correct to say that it originated in the 1970s -- the "period of stagnation." The basic indicators of the crisis had manifested themselves at least since the beginning of the 1960s (Khanin 1988; Fal'tsman 1992). As a matter of fact, the accumulation crisis of Soviet capital manifested itself for the first time right in the initial years of planning when the economy failed to meet most of the planned targets. Contrary to Stalin's famous assertion in January, 1933, that the First Five Year Plan was "fulfilled" in four years and three months (1970: 245), the real rates of growth of the most important categories like national income, industry, and agriculture were lower, over the period 1929-1932, by 44 percent, 28 percent, and 69 percent, respectively, compared to their planned rates, and only in two out of the sixteen most important categories of industrial output were the planned targets in physical terms fulfilled according to the plan (Shmelev and Popov 1989: 52, 97). There was also another serious slowdown between 1937 and 1939 "when the ambitious targets outlined by the plans were rarely achieved" (Zaleski 1962: 257). On Zaleski's calculation, taking the basic economic categories into account, the mean absolute deviations from 100 percent plan fulfillment for the First Plan was 39 percent and for the Second Plan 35 percent (1984: 197).[2] Indeed, according to unofficial Soviet estimates, the annual average growth rate of national income *fell* from 14 percent in the NEP period to 8 percent over the 1929-1939 period (Shmelev and Popov 1989: 54). However, as Khanin has pointed out, even though the manifestations of crisis in the 1930s and those in the 1980s appeared in many respects similar, the crisis of the 1930s could be surmounted thanks to the enormous magnitude of available productive resources, including labor (1991: 30).[3]

A MOBILIZATION ECONOMY: HISTORICAL JUSTIFICATION

As mentioned in Chapter 4, the point of departure of the Soviet accumulation process (for the period we are considering in this book) was the officially adopted policy -- dictated both by the country's economic backwardness and by the perceived threat of outside military intervention -- of overtaking and surpassing the West in the shortest possible time. The pace of industrialization was the central issue requiring "maximum attention to the fastest development of those branches of the national economy in general and industry in particular on which will fall the role of ensuring the country's defense and economic stability in wartime" (*KPSS v resoliutsiakh* 1970: 507). In order to close the gap between the USSR and the West in a minimal historical period, a continuation of the NEP policy, under which economic mechanism was based on market principles, particularly in relation to the peasants (Davies 1989: 459; Shmelev and Popov 1989: 13), was considered inadequate. In fact, even with an impressive recovery of the economy under NEP, there remained significant lags in some major branches of industry in 1926/27 compared to 1913. Thus the production of pig iron, crude steel, and rolled steel (all in million tons) stood, respectively, for the earlier and the later date, at 4.2 and 3.0; 4.3 and 3.0; 3.5 and 2.8, while, for the same dates, the production of cement (million barrels), cotton fabrics (million meters), and sugar (thousand tons) stood, respectively, at 12.3 and 9.7; 2.6 and 2.3; 1290 and 870 (Carr and Davies 1974: 1008; Nove 1982: 94). In the same way, in the last years of NEP, the gap in production per capita between the USSR and the advanced countries was as wide as in 1913, and the technological gap had widened (Davies 1991: 25-26). As to the industrial sector in particular, whatever overall growth it had recorded by the end of the 1920s, was largely based on renovating the existing capacity and reabsorbing the available factory labor. Further progress, particularly in heavy industry, would need building newer and bigger plants and not merely repairing and renovating the old ones (Nove 1982: 117), which would mean rise in industrial investment far above the existing level. On the other hand, the food grains situation was extremely difficult where, besides a fall in production, a procurement crisis developed due to the increase in the peasants' internal consumption through a certain levelling-out process within the peasantry after October (1917). Thus "grain production was smaller than it had been before the war, the marketings less, and the requirements much greater" (Lewin 1985: 92-93). Even though alternative price policies might have mitigated or even eliminated the grain crisis, "the large further rise in industrial investment during 1928 and 1929 was not compatible with the market relations with the peasants, which was the cornerstone of NEP" (Davies 1974: 261).

Given the Soviet rulers' determination to close the fifty to one hundred year gap with the West in ten years -- to paraphrase Stalin's famous 1931 pronouncement (1970: 200) -- the Soviet development strategy had to be essentially a mobilization strategy following a "revised version of the civil war model" (Lewin 1985: 362) under an "administered" or "command" economy.[4] It was a policy of "growth at any cost" at the fastest possible rate and, as such, would necessarily emphasize maximizing *quantitative* mobilization of labor and material inputs, treating the efficiency of their use as secondary. This was "essentially an arrangement for resource mobilization rather than for efficient resource utilization" (Cohn 1987: 14). On the other hand, given the rulers' dominant aim of effecting rapid structural changes in the economy and, correspondingly, clearly defined priority sectors like basic and heavy industries including military production, a centralized administration would seem to be the most suitable mobilizing mechanism (Levine 1974: 47).[5]

The specific path of the enlarged reproduction of capital adopted by the Soviet authorities suited the initial resource position of the country. Given the shortage of cadres and skilled workers, availability of labor force with a low level of education, and largely underutilized natural wealth of the country, it was easier and, in a sense, more rational to expand industry on the basis of unexploited energy and raw materials rather than trying to increase the productivity of labor or of the existing fixed capital (Bobrowski 1956: 87). This strategy, later to be called by the Soviet economists the strategy of "extensive growth," was, as we know, only a specific type of capital accumulation as Marx had shown.

Indeed, far from being non-capitalist, the logic of command economy *is* the logic of capital in certain situations and at certain epochs of capital's development. A. Gerschenkron convincingly argued that the Soviet industrialization had all the "basic elements that were common to the industrialization of backward countries in the nineteenth century," and he justly emphasized that the "Marxian ideology . . . has had very remote, if any, relation to the great industrial transformation engineered by the Soviet government" (1966a: 28,149,150).[6] The Soviet rulers, it has been aptly said, were "really engaged in building the industrial base of a war economy in peacetime" (Nove 1982: 390). Under a command economy, given the worker's separation from the conditions of production, the Soviet economy did not cease to be capitalist any more than any other economy based on the workers' separation from the conditions of production ceases to be capitalist simply because it happens to be a war economy (necessarily) under a centralized administrative command. Thus O. Lange was very correct in characterizing the USSR as a "*sui generis* war economy" and in underlining that the policy of allocating resources according to administratively established priorities and concentrating them on one basic purpose under a centralized administration as in the USSR, "was the case in *all capitalist countries* during the war" (1969: 171-72; italics added).[7]

The structure of the Soviet economy, corresponding to the strategy of maximizing the rate of mobilization of labor and other productive resources for industrial production in conditions of backwardness, would of course conflict with the rationality of the so-called market mechanism, functioning on profit and loss calculation of individual enterprises. Given the initial backwardness of the economy, "the traditional profit-and-loss incentive system, not to speak of the private enterprise system, was incapable of generating the growth in heavy industry and military strength that Stalin and his supporters concluded they had to have . . . ." (Goldman 1987: 19). The authorities themselves were perfectly aware of the logic of pursuing a path of rapid industrialization in a backward country. As an official Plan document of the 1930s observed: "Our country makes the unprecedented experiment of tremendous capital construction carried out at the cost of current consumption, at the price of harsh regime of the economy and by sacrificing satisfaction of today's needs in the name of great historical aims" (Baykov 1970: 129). In Chapter 3 we have already referred to a pertinent observation by Stalin, namely, the need to consider global profitability of the national economy as a whole and for a long period as opposed to short-term profitability of the individual branches or enterprises. Marx had earlier noted the possibility of the "individual capitalist" being in "constant rebellion" against the "global interest of the capitalist class" (1976a: 162).

There is no denying the fact that, following the path of capital accumulation mainly based on the quantitative expansion of resources, and under a centralized command economy, the USSR did obtain highly impressive results within a short period. "In its speed and scale the Soviet industrial revolution has neither precedent nor successor anywhere in the world" (Davies 1980: xiii). It was widely agreed that by the mid-1950s, the USSR had become the world's second largest industrial power (Goldman 1970: 347). A present-day Soviet critic of this mode of accumulation has noted that during the period 1930-1950 "foundations of economic progress of the USSR were laid, a powerful investment basis was created that almost fully satisfied the requirements of the national economy, millions of qualified workers and engineer-technicians were formed, a powerful scientific potential was made and the present-day defense industry was created" (Khanin 1988: 86). However, after having attained that stage, this mode of accumulation seemed to have reached the limits of its "historic justification," perpetuated beyond which it would become an "obstacle to further economic progress" (Lange 1969: 172).[8]

It should be observed that even during the phase 1930-1950, which saw the impressive rise of the Soviet industrial power on the basis of an unprecedented mobilization of resources, the particular type of accumulation of capital contained within itself the elements of its own negation. This type of accumulation by its very nature would sooner or later be confronted with an insurmountable resource barrier. Also the centralized command system of economic administration, the promoter and executor of the particular type of accumulation, while "successfully solving the tasks of increasing the volume of productive resources," showed itself "incapable of securing a stable rise in the effectiveness of their utilization" and of preventing the "extravagant use of material resources" (Khanin 1988: 86,88). Khanin has argued that from the end of the 1950s a steady decline in the rate of growth of the economy conditioned by two factors was started: slowdown in the rate of growth of the productive resources and deterioration in their effective utilization -- a decisive role being played by the extraordinary decline in the growth rate of fixed capital from 33 percent for the period 1961-1965 to three percent for the period 1981-1985 and ceasing altogether toward its end (1988: 88).

It seems, indeed, that "the 1950s were the golden age of the administered economic system when it realized all its potential and gave the maximum of what, ideally, it was capable" (Shmelev and Popov 1989: 65). It is in the 1950s that national income, productivity of social labor, and productivity of capital reached their highest average annual rates for the entire planning period of the USSR with, respectively, 7.2, 5.0, and 1.6 percent. Beginning with the Seventh Plan (1961-1965), there was a steady slowdown of the growth-rate of these indicators until these became negative along with an absolute decline in the volume of national income in 1981-82 (Khanin 1988: 85; 1991: 29-30).

With declining rates of growth of labor force and fixed capital along with increasing difficulties of mobilizing natural resources, only a changeover to a new mode of accumulation of capital based on (continuous) revolutionization of the method of production or "technical metamorphosis" -- that is, the first and principal type of accumulation analyzed by Marx -- could have enabled the Soviet economy to continue to have high rates of growth. But the centralized administrative system of management -- so capable of effecting quantitative mobilization of resources when such mobilization was still possible -- proved itself incapable of inaugurating a new type of accumulation of capital and thus showed itself as a brake to further accumulation (Aganbegyan 1988: 166). Soviet capitalism continued to function as a mobilization economy and was unable to demobilize itself with corresponding changes in economic organization following the requirements of enlarged reproduction in the new situation. Without going into the question of why the necessary changeover to a new mode of accumulation could not take place, let us simply note that according to some longtime observers of the Soviet scene, on the one hand Party-State monopoly of power, expressed in centralized administration of the economy, could be compatible only with a high and quantitatively increasing rate of investment and, on the other hand, the centralized administration, comfortable only with increasing the scale of the *established* products and processes, would discourage all individual initiative and creativeness and thereby impede innovation and technological progress (Gerschenkron 1966a: 285,300; Berliner 1988: 253-62; Khanin 1988: 88; Fal'tsman 1992: 16).

ACCUMULATION AS A CONTRADICTORY PROCESS

A. Gerschenkron, after citing Marx's famous phrase about capitalist accumulation, "Accumulate, accumulate! This is Moses and the Prophets," added: "There is every reason to doubt that there has been any economy on modern historical record to which these words would apply with greater justification than the economy of the Union of the so-called *Socialist* Soviet Republic" (1966b: 285; italics in original). It is not difficult to see how this "hypertrophied thirst for accumulation" [*gipertrofirovannaya zhazhda nakopleniya*], this "production for production's sake" (Fal'tsman 1992: 17; Loginov 1992: 5), based on the "second type" of capital accumulation carried beyond its "historic justification," became a self-contradictory process and how the process of accumulation was negating itself.

We mentioned in Chapter 4 an important aspect of the logic of this hyper-accumulation, namely, the absolute priority of the means of production over the means of consumption in the Soviet accumulation process.[9] As the means of production comprised about three-fourths of the total industrial output (see Table 4.7), its growth was naturally closely related to the growth of the entire economy. In a study of this relation for the period 1951-1980, it was found that, on an (annual) average, the growth rate of national income amounted to about eighty percent of the growth rate of the means of production (Kossov 1984: 13). To what extent the rest of the economy bore the cost of Group A's growth could be seen in the long-term behavior of the "capital intensiveness" [*kapitaloemkost'*] of the development of Group A, defined as the ratio of the Group's share in the economy's total investment to the rate of growth of the Group's output (both in percentage) over time indicating what percentage of the economy's global investment went into one percent increase in Group A's output (Kossov 1984: 14-15). It is seen that this ratio, resulting from the superimposition of Group A's more or less stable investment share on the secularly declining growth rate of its output, monotonically increased from 1.2 during the First Plan to almost 9 during the penultimate Plan.[10] This seems to show how the Soviet accumulation process, based on non(continuous) revolutionization of the method of production, was steadily undermining the regime's priority sector itself, besides increasingly diverting society's production resources away from people's basic needs.

Given the "non-susceptibility [*nevospriimchivost'*] of the Soviet economy to technical progress," the regime, in order to maintain the tempo of accumulation, increasingly tried to compensate for this lacuna by "redundant [quantitative] growth of investment and excessive consumption of natural resources" which amounted to the "eating away" [*proedaniiu*] of the natural wealth and the national wealth as a whole (Fal'tsman 1992: 15,16,17).

We saw in Chapter 4 that even in Soviet official estimates, the rates of growth of the natural resources -- along with those of investment and labor force -- had been steadily falling over the years. However, recent alternative estimates, corrected for inflationary and other distortions in the official data, show that the situation was far worse. As regards the basic natural resources, the stocks of all of them show absolute decline over the period 1960-1988. Thus, in physical terms, oil, natural gas, coal, iron ore, forest, and land (tillage) resources were down, respectively to 24.3, 79.2, 90.2, 88.2, 65.2, and 91.2 percent of their initial stocks.[11] Taking account of the other elements of national wealth -- such as fixed capital, commodity-materials stock, unfinished construction and peoples' residential property -- we have an idea of the dynamics of the USSR's national wealth over three decades as shown in Table 5.2.

The table clearly shows -- thanks to the particular type of capital accumulation we have been discussing -- that, during the ultimate three decades of the regime, material national wealth of the country did not only not increase even at a falling rate; on the contrary, it absolutely declined by 25 percent. This contradicts what appears in the official statistics of the period which, not taking into account the decline of accessible natural wealth, the inflationary process, and the accumulation of "fictitious property," showed an eight-fold increase of national wealth (Fal'tsman 1991: 242). In the same way, in terms of the alternative (unofficial) estimates, national wealth per capita shows an absolute decline by 1.8 times over the same period indicating what has been called the "process of absolute impoverishment of the population" [*absoliutnogo obnishchaniya naseleniya*] (Fal'tsman 1992: 19). Particularly during the last decade of the regime, on Khanin's estimate, there was an absolute decline in the volume of national income by two percent and, taking the growth of the population into account, the absolute decline in per capital income was of the order of 12 percent (1991: 28-29). Per capita (real) income growth, "the most general indicator reflecting the dynamics of people's level of living" (Shatalin 1986: 60), seemed to have virtually stopped in the 1970s (Fal'tsman 1992: 16).

A necessary aspect of the enlarged reproduction of Soviet capital -- based on the ambition of overtaking and surpassing the advanced capitalist countries -- and, at the same time, negating the reproduction process itself was the increasing military burden of the Soviet economy. The share of defense expenditure in the Soviet national income steadily rose from two percent in 1928 to about 20 percent in the 1980s.[12] The defense share of national income for the USSR seemed to have been two to three times higher than for the European OECD countries as well as the USA, and with only about 50 percent of the per capita income level of the USA, the country's defense burden was extremely heavy and could be sustained only at the cost of the vital social needs of the people (Ofer 1987: 1788; Shmelev and Popov 1989: 183).[13]

The military-industrial complex occupied a vast area of the Soviet industry. According to F. Kushnirsky, the complex comprised branches of machine-building and other industries which produced, in part or in whole, military hardware or raw materials, energy and semi-finished parts as inputs for such production. Among them would be the industries for arms production proper, and aircraft, electronics, radio, general machinery, shipbuilding, precision instruments, and those which meet "special orders" for the military. "With all this investment in military production and heavy industry," it would be "impossible to develop sufficient capacities for producing consumer goods" (Kushnirsky 1982: 92). The military-industrial complex, the "kernel of the Soviet industry," it has been observed, made "the economy bloodless [*obeskrovlivaet*]" not only by consuming huge volumes of all kinds of raw materials and equipment but also by "swallowing labor, investment, innovation and other resources of the highest quality" (Fal'tsman 1992: 17-18). That is also precisely the reason why a continuous slowdown of the growth rate of expenditure for Soviet defense -- the regime's highest priority sector -- appeared, in the context of the general slowdown of the economy, as a sure sign of the regime's crisis. It came down steadily from 7.6 percent in 1961-1965 to minus one percent in 1986-1990, actually reaching *minus* 6 percent for the final year of the Twelfth Plan, 1990 (Fal'tsman 1992: 16). This rapidly decelerating trend could certainly not be seen as a trade-off against a corresponding secular rise in the rate of growth of the Soviet people's welfare, as we shall see in the following section.

TABLE 5.2

MATERIAL WEALTH OF THE USSR (1960-1988)
(IN COMPARABLE PRICES, BILLION RUBLES, END OF YEAR)

	Elements of National Wealth	Years			
		1960	1970	1980	1988
	Total	11884	11196	10159	9046
I	Property, Total of which	583	951	1868	2861
	Fixed Productive Capital	247	320	620	973
	Fixed Non-productive Capital	172	279	503	755
	Stocks of Commodity -Materials Values	43	81	136	192
	Unfinished Construction	21	41	109	151
	Population's Residential Property	100	230	500	790
II	Natural Wealth, Total of which	11301	10245	8291	6185
	oil	4815	4062	2606	1170
	gas	4444	4318	4015	3528
	coal	532	516	496	480
	iron ore	1046	911	765	639
	forest resources	214	194	174	140
	land (tillage)	250	244	235	228

Source: Fal'tsman 1991: 254.

PEOPLE'S NEEDS AS A RESIDUAL

As a matter of fact, people's level of living served only as a constraint in this system of production for production's sake where "party's objective function" was predominantly "the maximization of the growth of the capital stock" (Berliner 1972: 349). Secular decline in people's living standard was a consequence of following the so-called "remainder principle" of allocating resources. According to this principle only what remained of the resources after the needs of productive investment, including those of the (heavy) industrial and defense sectors, were met would be allocated to the social sphere related to people's living conditions (Aganbegyan 1988: 67). Thus, as respects housing, where the inadequacies had been persistently acute, the official data show that its share in the total investment after rising from 18.4 percent during 1918-1940 to 23.5 percent in 1956-1960 gradually fell for twenty years to reach 14.2 percent in 1976-1980, rising only slightly to 16.4 percent in the final Plan (*Narkhoz* 1987: 328-29; *Narkhoz* 1990: 551). In fact, speaking more generally, it appears even from the official data that the share of total investment allocated to people's living conditions, in one way or another, decreased over time, coming down from 71 percent in 1940 to 64 percent in 1986 (Loginov 1992: 7).

In Chapter 4 we mentioned that the Soviet regime with its "hypertrophied thirst for accumulation" had successfully repressed the Soviet workers' real wages for a considerable length of time. In fact the average real wage level of the Soviet workers after steadily declining until the early 1950s would exceed the 1928 level by a mere 14 percent only some four decades later (Pavlevski 1969: 360).[14] More generally, "investment interest of the government" was "constantly opposed to the consumption interest of the population" (Gerschenkron 1966b: 285). In the event, the "long run" in which people's consumption was supposed to increase substantially due to an earlier lengthy period of investment would never come. "Investments became not deferred consumption but *deferred further investments*" (Winiecki 1988: 26; italics in original). The share of consumption -- household plus communal -- in Soviet GNP was estimated to have come down from 84 percent in 1928 to 63 percent in 1937 and then further down to 58 percent in the 1950s, the proportion remaining about the same in later years (Kuznets 1963: 359; Cohn 1974: 257; Schroeder 1983a: 312-13). According to one Soviet estimate, consumption constituted less than fifty percent of the national income in the final years of the regime (Shmelev and Popov 1989: 183). In the same way, the annual average rate of growth of per capita consumption (household and communal) was estimated to have slowed down steadily from 4.3 percent (1951-1960) to 3.9 percent (1961-1970) and then to 2.4 percent (1971-1981) (Schroeder 1983a: 312; 1983b: 370).

The over-accumulation of capital took a heavy toll on the Soviet people's health. Over a period of two and a half decades starting with the 1960s the mortality rate went up from about 7 to about 11 per thousand people -- a unique record of decline in life expectancy for an industrialized country during peacetime (Aganbegyan 1989: 228; Shmelev and Popov 1989: 104). Taking the share of health care in the Soviet national income -- about 4 percent -- the USSR was considered to occupy between seventieth and eightieth place among the countries of the world (Shmelev and Popov 1989: 104). In recent years, the share of the enfeebled and those predisposed to illness in the total Soviet population was calculated as ranging between 53 and 60 percent while this share among the children and young people ranged between 53 and 70 percent. Such a sharp deterioration in people's health resulted from the high level of environmental pollution, malnutrition, and the low quality of medical service (Khanin 1991: 26). Considering the general conditions of people's lives in the USSR, A. Aganbegyan wrote: ". . . when we look at housing, infant mortality rates, the development of the service industry, the supply of consumer durables and a number of other indices, we have to admit that we trail behind somewhere among the last of the top fifty countries" (1989: 230). We could only remind ourselves that all this was happening during the time when Soviet socialism was claimed to have reached a higher stage -- the period of "developed socialism." Such social consequences of over-accumulation with their immediate repercussions on the working people's lives naturally put a brake on the accumulation process itself. "The widespread characteristics of many [Soviet] workers are low labor -- and production -- discipline, an indifferent attitude to the work performed and its low quality, social passivity, a low value attached to labor as a means to self-realization, an intense consumer orientation and a rather low level of moral discipline" (Zaslavskaya 1984: 106).

OVER-ACCUMULATION AND AGRICULTURE

Agriculture, like people's consumption and services, was, for a long time, considered, in the Soviet accumulation process, a low priority sector for allocating resources. However, agriculture was taken to be a prime sector for generating capital and, as we saw in Chapter 4, every attempt was made to squeeze the sector to the maximum via collectivization. The attempted oversqueezing proved to be counterproductive. Along with the destruction of much of agriculture's productive potential, the volume of agricultural production in the First Five Year Plan declined by one-fifth and was restored only at the beginning of the 1940s, whereas grain harvest and meat production exceeded the 1913 level only in the 1950s (Shmelev and Popov 1989: 54, 302). As respects the farm population's per capita real income, it was down by 40 percent between 1928 and 1940 (Jasny 1961: 447).

An important means of financing the USSR's super-industrialization was the practice of "scissors" policy, that is, very low procurement prices for farm products compared to their retail prices, the difference finding its way into the state budget via turnover tax. As a result of the low price that the collective farms received against compulsory delivery of their products to the state, the collective farm laborers were paid a remuneration well below the average wage in the rest of the economy (Wädekin 1989: 2386). Due to the systematic expropriation of the agricultural output and its producers, "for a quarter of a century, from 1929 to 1953, the countryside lived on the edge of starvation" (Shmelev and Popov 1989: 59). In fact, because of the stagnation, if not diminution, in its output until the beginning of the 1950s, as well as very low income of the farm laborers -- reduced to forced labor -- agriculture increasingly appeared as an important obstacle to the further accumulation of capital in the USSR (Pavlevski 1969: 380). Conscious of this problem, the Soviet authorities in the post-Stalin period tried to introduce positive measures to redress the situation. Beginning with the mid-1950s procurement prices paid to the collective farms by the state rose, the supply of industrially produced inputs increased, and the level of remuneration of all collective farm laborers went up. However, a rise in the remuneration level of the farm laborers unaccompanied by any significant reduction in their number -- due mainly to the continuing low level of the productivity of agricultural labor as a result of the non-revolutionization of the method of production -- meant higher labor costs; on the other hand, for political reasons, consumer food prices were kept stable. This naturally led to an increase in state subsidies. Thus from 1.5 billion rubles in 1960, the agricultural subsidies went up to a huge sum of about 58 billion rubles in 1986. If one adds to this sum the subsidies for farm inputs, donations to state farms, etc., one finds that, toward the end of the 1980s, agricultural subsidies amounted to nearly one-fifth of the Soviet national income or, alternatively speaking, were annually equivalent to roughly two average monthly wages of the Soviet non-agricultural workers and employees (Wädekin 1989: 2388). In this way "from being a source of accumulation of capital for investment in industry, agriculture became a net burden on the rest of the economy" (Nove 1982: 371).

At the same time, with the relative rise in the population's standard of living in the post-Stalin period, there was a higher demand for better foods, such as meat, milk, fruits, and vegetables as well as better quality of the basic foods. On the other hand, agriculture was expected to release labor for the non-agricultural sectors, particularly in the context of the Soviet population's declining natural growth rate, which had come down from 17.9 per thousand of the population in 1960 to 8.0 per thousand in 1980 (*Narkhoz* 1985: 31). The main response to these exigencies was sought, as in the industrial sector of the economy, in raising the quantitative stock of capital in agriculture without any fundamental change in the method of production or any marked improvement in the infrastructure. Thus agriculture doubled its share of total investment from a little more than one-tenth during 1918-1940 to a full one-fifth in the beginning of the 1980s before declining a little in the end. Similarly, fixed productive capital in agriculture increased by almost six times between 1960 and 1985 (in "comparable prices") (*Narkhoz* 1985: 50; *Narkhoz* 1987: 328-329; *Narkhoz* 1990: 551). At the same time, with a relatively low level of productivity of labor -- being one-fifth or less of the US level (*Narkhoz* 1988: 680) -- Soviet agriculture did not release labor for the non-agricultural sectors as expected. Its share in total employment declined slowly from a little over one-half to one-fifth over a forty year period (1940-1980) and remained at that level until the end (*Narkhoz* 1989: 45). The growth of the agricultural output, in its turn, was inconspicuous, its rise amounting only to 1.7 times over the period 1960-1985 (*Narkhoz* 1987: 8). In fact, along with most of the economic indicators, agriculture showed its best performance in the 1950s with an average annual rate of growth exceeding 4 percent. But afterward the growth rate steadily declined -- except for a brief period (1966-1970) -- remaining between 1 and 2 percent most of the time (*Narkhoz* 1972: 56; *Narkhoz* 1990: 8).[15]

To maintain the consumption level, the regime had to increasingly import foodstuffs. Between 1960 and 1980, the share of "foodstuffs and raw materials for their production" in Soviet imports increased from 13 percent to 24 percent and then declined only to 16 percent toward the end. On the other hand, this foodstuff, with the associated raw materials, had to be bought abroad mainly by increasing the export of fuel and electric power. Thus, the latter's share in Soviet exports increased by more than three times in twenty-five years (1960-1985). Though the share came down later, it still constituted more than two-fifths of the total exports toward the end (*Narkhoz* 1990: 660-61). "Thus the foreign trade in the USSR today," wrote two Soviet economists, "is largely the sale of non-renewable natural resources in order to maintain the present level of consumption. This is literally eating away our future, living on borrowed time" (Shmelev and Popov 1989: 223). The increasing share of fuel and energy in Soviet export with the simultaneous doubling of the share of machinery and equipment in Soviet imports between 1950 and 1990 -- from 22 percent to 45 percent (*Narkhoz* 1990: 661) -- could be seen as leaving the country to a position of what a Soviet economist called a "raw materials appendage [*syrevoi pridatok*]" of the West (Loginov 1992: 8).[16]

FALLING BEHIND THE WEST

In an important essay, Moses Abramovitz, on the basis of a study by A. Madison on the long-term trends in comparative economic development of sixteen leading industrialized countries, has held that in comparison across countries growth-rates of productivity in any long-term period tended to be inversely related to the initial levels of productivity, that is, differences among countries in productivity levels created a strong potentiality for subsequent convergence of levels (Abramovitz 1986: 386,405). Abramovitz's analysis appears to be pertinent for the Soviet case inasmuch as the Soviet development strategy was expressly aimed at "catching up with and surpassing" those countries which were far ahead of it in economic development. Let us try to see how the Soviet economy, in its "ravenous appetite for surplus labor" (Marx), fared vis-à-vis its "competitors" with respect to the development of some leading indicators.

As respects technological progress (outside of the military sphere), considering one of the Soviet priority sectors, that is, metallurgy, if we take two important indices of up-to-date metallurgical process, namely, first, the share of electric and basic oxygen process and, secondly, the share of continuous casting, in total steel production (both in percentage), we find, on the basis of the Soviet official data, that, for the years 1970 and 1987, the figures for the two for the USSR were, respectively 26 and 4 for the first date and 47 and 16 for the second date, whereas the corresponding figures for the two dates were 40 and 1 (1970), 100 and 93 (1987) for France; 72 and 4 (1970), 100 and 90 (1987) for Italy; 96 and 6 (1970), 100 and 93 (1987) for Japan; 66 and 8 (1970), 100 and 88 (1987) for West Germany; 52 and 27 (1970), 100 and 65 (1987) for the UK; 63 and 20 (1970), 96 and 58 (1987) for the USA.[17] It appears from these data that the USSR was away from and falling behind its international competitors in one of the priority sectors of technical progress.

Let us turn to more synthetic economic indicators. As regards national income -- perhaps the most important single indicator for an economy -- while we have long period GNP data for the advanced capitalist countries, we do not have comparable Soviet data for the USSR, at least not freed from statistical distortions. We have, of course, the CIA's reconstruction of the Soviet GNP which, as we now know, were found by a number of Soviet economists to be rather overvalued. Taking GNP thus understood, its annual average growth rate for the USSR over the period 1960-1989 was estimated at 3.1 percent, about the same as that for the USA for the same period. On the other hand, both were lower than the average 3.6 percent for the eleven major OECD countries over the same period (Pitzer and Baukol 1991: 51). The growth-rate for the Soviet national income as such -- freed from inflation and other statistical distortions -- for more or less the same period was, of course, much lower: 2.5 percent for 1961-1987.[18] Again, the Soviet economy's "global efficiency" grew at an average annual rate of 0.8 percent during 1961-1987, while the "total factor productivity" -- the Western equivalent of the Soviet global efficiency -- grew at 0.9 percent for the USA, 2 percent (on an average) for the European OECD countries, and 4.1 percent for Japan during 1960-1961 to 1988-1989.[19]

How did the USSR perform in relation to its main rival, the USA, particularly with regard to two basic indicators of the economy, namely, national income and consumption? First, as regards national income, we find, on official Soviet estimates, that the Soviet national income starting at 31 percent of the U.S. national income, increased its share (in percentage) to 58 in 1960, 65 in 1970 and 67 in 1980 until it came down to 64 at the end of the 1980s (*Narkhoz* 1972: 64; *Narkhoz* 1988: 880). In other words, first there was a gradual slowdown in the rate of growth of the relative share and then the relative share itself declined.

However, toward the end of the Soviet regime, the Soviet statisticians themselves pointed out that if one leaves aside the erstwhile Soviet computations of international comparison of economic indicators, which were "not objective," and which always ended up in overvaluing the Soviet indicators, particularly in relation to the U.S. indicators, and if one follows the standard UN methodology toward international comparison, it appears that the Soviet GNP per capita was a mere 37 percent of the U.S. GNP per capita in 1985 -- the "level of development" of the Soviet economy being only 43 percent of the U.S. level (Kirichenko and Pogosov 1991: 96,98). As to the population's final consumption per capita (including household and communal), the corresponding Soviet share was below 30 percent of the USA in 1985 and came down rapidly to 20 percent in 1988 (Kirichenko and Pogosov 1991: 98-99). Thus, here again it appears that the gap regarding the level of economic development between the USSR and the USA was considerable and increasing even at a time when the U.S. economy itself was in a poor shape.

In effect, toward the end of the regime, the Soviet people themselves, it seems, were considering their country to be among the "developing countries," deserving UN economic aid. In the light of the UN data on comparative development in 1985 (concerning 58 countries), some Soviet statisticians, on their part, while refusing to consider their country as a developing one, nevertheless did place it, in terms of per capita indicator, at 21st rank as regards gross domestic product, at 27th rank in terms of final consumption, and at 8th rank in terms of gross capital formation (Kirichenko and Pogosov 1991: 99).

In terms of our brief review of the Soviet performance over time in relation to the advanced capitalist countries, it seems that, at a time when the "Western world had been in a mess," far from "catching up with and surpassing" the West economically, which had been "fundamental to the Soviet official view of the Soviet role in world history" (Hanson 1992: 7,43), the USSR was in fact falling behind the West. Thus it might appear at first blush that Abramovitz's proposition about convergence of the developmental levels between countries, with which we started the section, has not been confirmed in the Soviet case. However, Abramovitz had added a rider to his proposition: only a country having "a social capability adequate to absorb more advanced technologies" would be able to effect the convergence (1986: 405). Clearly, the persistence of what we have called the second (Marxian) type of capital accumulation in the USSR shows that the system largely failed to "absorb more advanced technologies" (outside of the military and related spheres).

NOTES

1. For a critical overall review of the Twelfth Plan's performance see Schroeder (1991: 31-45).

2. According to the alternative estimates, the respective figures are 54 percent and 39 percent (Shmelev and Popov 1989: 98).

3. C. Bettelheim was one of the first to show the relevance of the Marxian category of "overaccumulation of capital" for the Soviet economy of the 1930s (1982: 289-98).

4. We cannot discuss here the question of the possibility of an alternative development path as argued by some Soviet economists (Shmelev and Popov 1989: 46-47,55-56,68-69; Khanin 1988: 87-88). However, like (Hegelian) Minerva's owl, opening its wings only after sundown, we can only reflect, retrospectively, on the consequences of the path that was in fact pursued.

5. On "mobilization" as a distinguishing character of the Soviet economy, see Hanson (1971: 328,332).

6. Basically the same point was made by J. Berliner in an illuminating paper (1966).

7. In his turn J. Berliner, comparing the Soviet economy with the wartime U.S. economy, mentions "overfull employment, total immersion of government into economic life with a great burgeoning of materials allocation, price fixing, cost-plus contracting and shortage of supply" in the USA and then, speaking of the U.S. wartime rate of growth of production, comparable to the (peacetime) Soviet rate, observes that the U.S. economy "could grow as rapidly as the Soviet economy" if the Americans "would consent to being pushed around as totally as the Soviet people are" (1962: 372-73). Nobody would suggest that the wartime U.S. economy ceased to be a capitalist economy.

8. On the other hand, by continuing to use extra-economic constraints for capital accumulation, the Soviet system seemed clearly to violate one of the important laws of capitalist development: once the "capitalist organization of production develops,...the extra economic direct force" of the state, perfectly natural at an earlier stage of capital's existence, becomes unnecessary for the continuous subsumption of labor under capital which, "in the ordinary course of things," is "left to the natural laws of production" (Marx 1962a: 765).

9. The relative shares of means of production and means of consumption in the total industrial output rose from 39.5:60.5 in 1928 to 73:27 in 1990, and the ratio of investment in the first to that in the second (in industry) rose from 4.5:1 during 1918-1940 to 7.3:1 in the final Plan (See Table 4.7, and Loginov 1992: 7). We may recall that according to Lenin the priority in question was the "principal conclusion" [*glavnyi vyvod*] from Marx's theory of realization under *capitalism* (Lenin 1958:41).

10. Computed from data on Group A's share in total investment and the annual rates of growth of the Group's output in *Narodnoe khoziaistvo SSSR*, various years. Computation follows Kossov (1984: 15).

11. Computed from the data in Fal'tsman (1991: 249-52).

12. The 1928 figure is the official Soviet figure as given in Ofer (1987: 1788-89), while the second figure is taken from Shmelev and Popov (1989: 183).

13. In this connection, see the article "A Survey of the Soviet Economy" in *The Economist* April 9, 1988: 3.

14. It is worth noting that the gap between the real wage level of the Soviet workers and that of the workers of the Western capitalist countries increased between 1928 and 1936-1938, and again between this latter date and 1950. It is particularly interesting to note that whereas in 1928, the German level was about 1.4 times higher than the Soviet level, it was more than two times higher a decade later under a different variety of "socialism". The level was nearly three times higher in 1950 (Pavlevski 1969: 385, Table 16).

15. For an estimate of slowdown of the global efficiency of Soviet agriculture for the period 1951-1979, see Diamond, Bettis and Ramsson (1983: 146).

16. For a perceptive analysis of the contradictions in the agricultural situation of the USSR within the general crisis of the economy toward the end of the regime, see K.E. Wädekin (1990: 405-17).

17. Figures for continuous casting for 1970 are as given in Kornai (1992: 296), citing Soviet data; all other figures for both 1970 and 1987 are taken from *Narkhoz* 1988: 684.

18. Calculated from Khanin (1988: 85).

19. The Soviet figure is calculated from Khanin (1988: 85) and the rest from Pitzer and Baukol (1991: 69) who cite J. Kendrick's data for Western Europe and Japan.

Chapter 6

THE SOVIET ECONOMY AS A
NON-CAPITALIST ECONOMY:
THEORETICAL CONSIDERATIONS

After having argued the capitalist character of the Soviet economy, we now propose to encounter the opposite point of view, namely, the one which holds that this economy was non-capitalist. In this chapter we consider the latter point of view theoretically, reserving for the next an examination of the Soviet economic reality as it appears in this representation.

Behind the point of view under consideration there are two distinct positions: the first holding the Soviet economy to be socialist, the second viewing it to be neither socialist nor capitalist (NSNC for short). Below we consider these two positions. We shall be concerned here basically with the left radicals.

THE SOCIALIST ARGUMENT

The victory of socialism in the Soviet Union was proclaimed on the basis of the fulfillment of the Second Five Year Plan (1933-1937): 98.7 percent of the means of production, including 99.6 percent of fixed capital, was under the state or cooperative-collective farm ownership generating 99.1 percent of national income, 99.8 percent of industrial production, 98.5 percent of agricultural production, and 100 percent of commodity circulation (Vinogradov et al. 1978: 512). On this basis, it was declared at the end of the 1930s that there was now "definite liquidation of all exploiting classes and total destruction of the causes giving rise to the exploitation of person by person," and that "in our country … the first phase of communism, socialism, has been basically realized" (*KPSS v resoliutsiakh* 1971: 335). Underlying this conclusion was a specific concept of the socialist economy, expressed in the Stalinist "political economy of socialism," elaborated over a period between late 1930s and early 1950s.[1] Until almost the end of the Soviet regime, this concept of socialism -- without any basic modification over the years -- was used to characterize the USSR as "socialist." Let us analyze the economic content of this "socialism."

The point of departure for characterizing the Soviet economy as "socialist" is the character of the new ownership form of the means of production. Since "social ownership" forms the basis of *production relations* of the USSR, the regime is claimed to be socialist (Stalin 1980: 505). The transfer to the state of the means of production from the private capitalist is identified with socialist ownership and, on this basis, Soviet socialism is identified with Marx's first phase of communism (Stalin 1970: 383,386).

As respects distribution of the means of consumption under socialism, though labor power has ceased to be a commodity, laborers still have to be paid in wage form, thus reflecting the need for material incentives according to the quantity and quality of labor (*Manuel* 1956: 472,499). Against the "leftist" wage equalization principle Marx's *Gothakritik* is invoked in order to assert socialism's principle of distribution according to one's labor (and not according to one's needs) (Stalin 1970: 345 386-87).

Similarly, as regards exchange relations, Stalin was the first in the Soviet tradition to assert the existence of commodity production and the law of value under *socialism*. When the earlier theoreticians had discussed commodity production they had confined its existence at most to the "transitional period" *preceding* socialism. The existence of commodity production under socialism follows, according to the "political economy of socialism," from the duality of property form over the means of production: state property and collective farm property, and the necessity of circulation between them (*Manuel* 1956: 485-87; Stalin 1980: 581-82). On the other hand, under a single ownership of the means of production, commodity production would cease to exist (Stalin 1980: 582). However, one should not, according to Stalin, confuse commodity production with capitalism. Commodity production is older than capitalism, and under socialism, too, commodity production is without the capitalists and, given the absence of private ownership, cannot lead to capitalism (1980: 579-80). Under socialism commodity production is limited to consumption goods in order to compensate for the expenditure of labor power in production. The means of production under the state ownership have no commodity character, they are only transferred from one enterprise to another. Here "cost of production" or "sales price" of the means of production are nevertheless used for two reasons: first, the necessity of accounting and control of the enterprise activities and, secondly, the existence of foreign trade. Really speaking, the means of production are commodities only in *appearance*, not in *essence*. Only the old form persists, the content is new, socialist. The same is basically the case with the old categories like money and the banks which are only utilized by socialism to serve its own interests (Stalin 1980: 584, 610-11).

The economic content of socialism -- claimed to be seen in its manifestation in the Soviet economy -- as developed by Stalin and his associates, remained basically the same throughout the Soviet period almost until the regime's demise. Soviet socialism continued to be considered as based on public (state) ownership of the means of production, associated with central planning and including the law of value, with the differentiated wage system of distribution following the principle of remuneration according to one's ability. However, in the post-Stalin period, the operation of the law of value under socialism was conceived in its generalized form, and not simply restricted to the consumption goods or to the transactions between the state and the collective farm sectors (Zaostrovtsev 1959; Rumyantsev and Bunich 1968). Of course, the socialist law of value is of a different kind compared to the law of value under capitalism, and, given the absence of private ownership in the means of production, cannot give rise to capitalism (Aganbegyan 1988: 185-86). Particularly, the operation of the law of value within the state sector was connected with the low level of productive forces -- insufficient for need-based distribution of material wealth among individuals -- non-homogeneous character of labor, and the need for material incentives for labor -- not yet perceived as a "prime necessity of life" -- capable of being satisfied only through equivalent exchange (Kozlov 1977: 120-22).

It is essentially on the specific characterization of socialism as given above that the Soviet economy was considered -- outside the USSR -- as "socialist" also by most students of the Soviet economy and bulk of the radicals including members and sympathizers of the traditional communist parties. Thus M. Lavigne defines socialist system as an "economic system based on social ownership of the means of production" where the latter is represented by "state and cooperative ownership." She justifies this socialist label by the concerned regimes' identical self-characterization, adding that this definition has been "verified by history" (Lavigne 1979: 12,16). Similarly, A. Bergson, following the "customary usage," considers the USSR as socialist on the basis of the "predominance of public ownership of the means of production" (Bergson 1944: 3; 1984: 1053). The characterization of the USSR as socialist was also made on similar grounds by, among others, Nove and Nuti (1972), Nuti (1981), Wilczynski (1970). Recently J. Kornai identified the USSR as socialist on the basis of its rule by the communist party and the latter's claim that the system was socialist (1992: 10-11).

On the left, a systematic defense of the Soviet economy as socialist has recently been advanced by D. Laibman (1992). Not only Laibman's conceptualization of socialism, but also his arguments in defense of the Soviet system, are basically the same as those that used to be offered by the Soviet spokespersons, at least in the pre-*perestroika* period, though Laibman's presentation is more academic.

According to him, a socialist society is one where the state power is under the working class rule, and where the role of commodity-money relations is regulated by comprehensive planning. Like the Soviet spokespersons, and unlike Marx, Laibman makes a distinction between the "communist mode of production" and "socialism as a period of transition," and citing Stalin's "famous pamphlet" of 1952, posits commodity relations between the socialist sector and other sectors of the economy.[2] However, like the post-Stalin Soviet economists he also postulates commodity relations within the state sector, dismissing, as "Rousseauian collective utopia," the non-commodity image of socialism. Finally, Laibman also posits in socialism "capital stock" and, for the workers, "money wages less than the value added by labor." Specifically Laibman writes about "labor value of Marx's *Capital*, vol. 1" as the optimal prices for the socialist society, and mentions Marx's *Gothakritik* as a rationale for differential "distribution of income in money form" under socialism (1992: 315,328-29,330,332,335-36,350,354).

"SOCIALISM" IN THE SOCIALIST ARGUMENT

Reserving for later consideration the question of the extent to which the Soviet reality was in accord with what was claimed on its behalf by its defenders, let us first examine here to what extent Soviet socialism's theoretical -- conceptual framework would be compatible with Marxian socialism conceived as a "society of free and associated producers," even in its first phase, to which Soviet socialism was claimed to correspond.

We first note a general point. Determining a society's character mainly on the basis of its specific *ownership form* -- as was the case with the Soviet spokespersons -- is a complete inversion of the Marxian materialist point of view. In Marx it is the specificity of the social relations of production which characterizes a particular social formation. Taking a particular form of ownership in the means of production -- and not the specificity of society's production relations -- as an independent variable, and trying to derive from this ownership the character of a social formation, would be an exercise in "juridical or metaphysical illusion" (Marx 1965: 118). Thus a formal-juridical act of the state abolishing private ownership in the means of production was thought to be sufficient for a change in the old relations of production. That would be like trying to "enact away" the old society, in Marx's famous phrase (1962a: 16). Moreover, it is denaturing Marx to equate the proletarian state's expropriation of the individual capitalists, which is only the *beginning* of the revolutionary process, as the *Communist Manifesto* asserts, with the collective appropriation of the conditions of production by *society* -- where the state has ceased to exist along with the proletariat -- which can only be the outcome of a long-drawn out temporal process as a prelude to the humanity's entry into "history."

It should be stressed that right from the start of the first phase of the Association there is no *state* (not even a state under the "working class rule"), and hence no state ownership either, which was taken as the basis of socialism by the Soviet spokespersons and their sympathizers, simply because this "deadening incubus," this "organized force of suppression" (Marx 1971: 150,153) cannot be, as Marx shows convincingly, a means of workers' self-emancipation which is what socialism really is.[3] True, immediately on establishing itself as the ruling class, the working class "centralizes all instruments of production in the hands of the state." But that is only a *beginning* measure "to revolutionize the whole mode of production," and, in course of the movement, "all production is concentrated in the hands of the associated individuals," thereby inaugurating the new society, and "political power properly speaking," that is, the state, along with the ruling class itself, ceases to exist (Marx 1965: 136; 1966b: 76-77).

Now, coming to society's exchange relations, it should be observed that there is a total incompatibility between a society based on the union of producers with the conditions of production -- for that is what the Marxian socialism is -- and the commodity-money categories, however plan-regulated, thought to be essential for socialism, inasmuch as the products of human labor in the free union need not and are not mediated by value form in order to be recognized as social. In the "union of free individuals," even at its first or lower phase with still insufficient development of the productive forces, "producers do not exchange their products" (Marx 1966b: 178). It is, indeed, surprising that labor value of *Capital*, Volume 1 -- exclusively relevant for a commodity society -- are thought to be applicable to a society where labor, by definition, has become directly social (at the level of society). Marx shows precisely in the same book (as elsewhere) that exchange value is only a *particular* way of counting and measuring labor corresponding to a particular society. It is "a *particular social manner* of counting the labor employed in the production of an object" (1965: 617; italics added).[4] Indeed, value, as a specific social form, "belongs to a social formation in which the process of production dominates individuals, individuals do not dominate the process of production" (1962a: 95). Marx faulted Proudhon for not understanding that the "economic categories are only the theoretical expressions of the social relations of production" (1965: 78).

In the same way, it is strange that Marx's "Marginal Notes" of 1875 are invoked by those professing Marxism in order to justify the particular form of distribution of consumer goods in Soviet socialism. In that writing, the principle of distribution of the means of consumption is set in the context of the first phase of the new society from which the *wage form* of remuneration, "the value or price of labor power," has already disappeared together with wage labor and capital, even as "stock" (along with the state), simply because under society's direct appropriation of the conditions of production labor power has ceased to be a commodity. In the same text Marx qualifies wage labor as slavery, and his explicit recognition of "unequal individual endowment" and of labor being not yet perceived as the "first necessity of life," does not lead him to accept wage as a form of labor remuneration even in the first phase of the Association.

Secondly, the Marxian socialist principle of differentiated remuneration, based on individuals' unequal contributions to total social labor, is set in a situation of freely associated individuals whose mutual relations are unmediated by commodity-money categories. Thus it is an unfaithful representation of Marx's position to say that "following Marx . . . income is distributed (in socialism) in money form . . . and the net output is distributed in consumer markets by means of money prices" (Laibman 1992: 327). Contrariwise, under commodity-money relations, the labor bestowed on production by the individual receives its social recognition only indirectly, only through the market, and it is impossible to determine how much an individual has contributed to the total social labor. Hence rewarding a working person according to the person's own labor under commodity-money relations -- a running theme in the Soviet doctrine until the end[5] -- is an empty phrase. It is only under society's direct appropriation of the conditions of labor that Marx's phrase has its full meaning. In such a situation only the contribution of each individual laborer is recognizable and directly countable inasmuch as the social relations of individuals in regard to their labor as well as to the products of labor are here "simple and transparent" (Marx 1962a: 93). Thus even when "just for a parallel" Marx brings in commodity production to illustrate the principle of equivalence of exchange of one form of labor against another form of labor, he stresses that under commodity exchange this equivalence is established "only on average but not for each individual case" which is what it is in the first phase of communism (1962a: 93; 1966b: 179).[6]

We conclude that the conceptual-theoretical framework of Soviet socialism was a complete inversion of Marx's concept of the emancipated union of producers[7]. On the contrary, the Soviet "political economy of socialism" turns out to be a vast exercise in rationalizing as Marxian socialism the policies of the Soviet regime pursued at different periods. Thus, the objective existence of value categories -- commodity, money, bank, credit -- in the USSR could be ideologically accepted for a transitional, pre-socialist period, as under NEP, while still reiterating the well-known Marxian position on their eventual elimination in (future) socialism. However, once the "victory of socialism" was proclaimed, the continuation of these categories in socialism had to be rationalized -- given the regime's Marxist pretensions -- as socialist categories, different from the capitalist categories, and the earlier position on their elimination in socialism had to be abandoned.[8] Similarly, the wage form of labor remuneration could be accepted for the transitional period ruled by the *proletariat* when socialism as a classless society had still not arrived. With the society supposed to have already entered the first phase of communism, however, the objective existence of wage labor had to be rationalized as socialist by simply connecting wage form of remuneration and its considerable differentiation -- dictated by the needs of rapid accumulation -- with

Marx's socialist distribution principle.[9] The same attempt at rationalizing the Soviet practice as Marxian socialism is seen in the last days of the Soviet regime which ultimately tended to renounce the Stalinist heritage. Faced with society's generalized crisis, the Soviet rulers proposed a "new model of socialism" which was still claimed to be "a legacy of Marx, Engels and Lenin" even when the model involved an "essential role of private ownership" and a "full-blooded market" (Gorbachev 1990a: 4, 1990b: 2; Osnovnye napravleniya 1990: 3).

It is, indeed, the logic of accumulation of capital that had all along dictated the Soviet economic policies and correspondingly shaped the concept of Soviet socialism. Long ago discerning non-Marxist students of the Soviet economy like A. Gerschenkron (1966a: 150) and J. Berliner (1966: 23) very correctly concluded that, propelled by the "catching up and surpassing" strategy, the Soviet regime had little to do with Marxism, just as the eminent historian E.H. Carr had observed that (since a certain point in NEP) "it was no longer true that the class analysis determined policy, but that policy determined what form of class analysis was appropriate to the given situation" (1958: 99).

THE NSNC ARGUMENT

A series of radical thinkers have argued that the Soviet society is neither socialist nor capitalist. This non-socialist-non-capitalist (NSNC) approach appears basically in two versions. According to the first, the Soviet society is an exploiting society *sui generis*, and it is ruled by a new class -- often termed bureaucracy -- which derives its exploiting power through its control of the state which owns the means of production. The second version denies the existence of a new (ruling) class in this society, holding that it is a "transitional society between capitalism and socialism," albeit under a "bureaucratic degeneration." Below we treat successively the two versions of the NSNC thesis.

NSNC THESIS: FIRST VARIANT

Confronted with the monstrous presence of bureaucracy in the USSR, a whole series of Marxists came to reject the USSR as socialist, though they were not prepared to view it as capitalist either, at least not in the usual -- the so-called Western -- sense of the term. A number of Marxists came to hold a more specific point of view regarding the Soviet regime. According to them, bureaucracy constituted the new (ruling) class based on the "collective" (state) ownership of the means of production.[10] This new trend within Marxism develops from the 1920s onward.[11] Bruno Rizzi seems to be the first to develop systematically (within Marxism) the thesis of bureaucracy as a class (in his polemic with

Trotsky) in 1939 (Rizzi 1976). According to him, the USSR represents a new type of society led by a new social class, the bureaucrats, who collectively own the nationalized means of production, thereby resolving the capitalist antagonism between collective production and private appropriation. It is no longer the bourgeoisie that is the exploiting class. Exploitation has changed from individual to a collective form. The bureaucracy has the monopoly of labor power which is no longer bought by the capitalists (1976: 60,72). Initially maintaining that the bureaucratic class replacing the bourgeoisie extracts surplus value from the Soviet proletariat, Rizzi later comes to hold that, under state's monopoly of the means of production and labor power, there was neither commodity production nor a market for labor power and that consequently, there was no surplus value either (1977: 151, 154, 129). Thus there has emerged a new type of production relation in the USSR, neither socialist nor capitalist. The new system is more appropriately called "bureaucratic collectivism" which he thinks is part of the emerging universal phenomenon: the "bureaucratization of the world." It is essentially the Rizzian thesis that was later upheld by M. Shachtman in his theory of "bureaucratic collectivism" and by M. Djilas in his popular theory of "new class."

Perhaps the most eminent contemporary partisan of the theoretical tendency in question is P.M. Sweezy (1980, 1985). The "post revolutionary" or the "Soviet type" society, he holds, is a "self-reproducing system of antagonistic classes". It is a new social formation in its own right. Neither socialist nor capitalist, it is an authoritarian class society with the state ownership of the main means of production and central planning. Even though the "basic class relation of exploitation is capital-labor relation," we are not, he holds, dealing with a capitalist society. The new ruling class -- the "huge bureaucracy" -- derives its power and privileges from the unmediated control of the state and its multiform apparatuses of coercion, and not from the ownership and control of capital. This means that the utilization of society's surplus product is "no longer governed by the laws of value and capital accumulation." There is the "politicization of (social) surplus utilization." In capitalist society, the state is the servant of the economy, in this new society under the new ruling class, the "state is the master." While Rizzi stresses the bureaucratic part of the thesis, Sweezy emphasizes its non-capitalist part. We first examine the bureaucratic position in the light of Marx's ideas on the organization of capitalist production, reserving our examination of the non-capitalist position later.

BUREAUCRACY AND CAPITALISM

To get a proper perspective, we are not taking bureaucracy as signifying only *political* bureaucracy (in the usual sense of the term), confined to state administration. We are taking it as a *general* form of administration under functionaries nominated and hierarchically organized from top downward and accountable only to the superiors in the hierarchy.

Though Marx himself limits his *explicit* discussion of bureaucracy (within capitalism) only to its political aspect, that is, as an integral part of the bourgeois state apparatus, it is quite consistent with the Marxian framework to extend the sphere of bureaucracy outside the limits of state administration. Indeed, Marx seems to have been the first to discern the inherently bureaucratic character of the organizational form of capitalist production, even though he does not use the *term* bureaucracy in this connection. As he observes, "the capitalist mode of production itself engenders a relation of hierarchy [*Über und Unterordnung*] [which is] objective, purely economic" (1969: 54). Inherent in the capitalist mode of production, this type of organization manifests itself at least since the stage of "simple cooperation", the initial stage of what Marx calls the "real subsumption of labor under capital" (1976a: 235,237; 1962a: 350). All labor done in common on a large scale requires a direction for harmonizing the individual activities and for performing the general functions which originate from the distinction between the movement of the collective body and its independent organs, and "this function of direction, supervision and mediation becomes the function of capital the moment labor subordinated to it becomes cooperative labor" (1962a: 350). This specific type of hierarchy -- involving the "process of valorization" of capital -- is necessarily "despotic" -- though, contrary to the pre-capitalist forms, impersonal and "objective" -- and corresponding to the development of collective labor, "this despotism develops its own forms" (1962a: 351). Thus, when the stage of simple cooperation is superseded by the division of labor in manufacture, the "hierarchical gradation" involves the workers themselves (1962a: 381,389). With the ultimate stage of real subsumption of labor under capital reached in (machine operated) "big industry," under a completely elaborated "barrack discipline" in the factory, the "work of supervision" as well as the "division of laborers into common soldiers of industry and industrial sub officers" -- already initiated earlier -- is "fully developed" (1962a: 447). This essentially bureaucratic form of organization of production becomes more and more palpable as the accumulation of capital progresses through the increasing concentration and centralization of capital. We referred earlier to what Marx calls "directly social capital" (DSC) as the form of capital that corresponds to the exigencies of capital at a higher stage of its accumulation where, as we saw, the non-owning "functionary of capital" is a simple "administrator of alien capital" receiving a "wage" or a "salary" for a "special kind of labor," that of extracting surplus value from the immediate producers. With the change in capital's property form and with the control of the process of production by the (non-owning) salaried functionaries of capital, the capitalist organization of production shows its bureaucratic character at its starkest form. It is clear that the "administrators of capital," hierarchically organized as "higher officers (managers) and lower officers (foremen, overlookers) commanding in the name of capital" (1962a: 351),[12] are simply *bureaucrats* of the capitalist process of production. The highest stage in the bureaucratization process of capitalist production is reached when the state itself becomes a capitalist producer, as Marx explicitly envisages. (This has been discussed earlier).

Thus although Marx does not use the particular term bureaucracy in his critique of capitalist production, the specific form of organization of this production underlined by him is certainly bureaucratic in the proper sense of the term.

It is interesting to note that bureaucracy as a general form of organization of activities under modern capitalism began to be stressed by the non-Marxist social scientists long after Marx had discerned its essence in the organization of capitalist production. Thus, what an avowedly anti-Marxist like Max Weber wrote on this question basically confirms what Marx had observed much earlier. Weber noted that bureaucracy in the sense of the "principle of hierarchy of functions and of different levels of authority," implying a "well-ordered system of domination and subordination [*Über und Unterordnung*]," "fully developed" -- outside of the state apparatus -- "only in the most advanced institutions of capitalism," and that the "huge modern capitalist enterprises are themselves the unrivalled model of rigid bureaucratic organization." (1925: 650, 661). J. Schumpeter, in his turn, from a different point of view, while analyzing the process of demise of capitalism, spoke of the "bureaucratized giant industrial unit" as a part of the "bureaucratization of economic life in general" with the remuneration of the "industrial bourgeoisie" being reduced to "wages for current administration" (using practically Marx's words cited earlier) (1950: 124, 206). Similar ideas on bureaucracy have been expressed by the students of modern business organization. Thus, as one could see, already in traditional capitalism, in the sectors under DSC -- including the state sector -- the "functionaries of capital" can discharge their exploiting function only as bureaucrats (in the so-called public sector the functionaries of capital are at the same time state functionaries).

It is logical that in the USSR, with the juridical abolition of private ownership in the means of production, the real non-ownership of the means of production by the immediate producers -- a consequence of separation between the two -- would necessarily mean bureaucratic organization of production in the units of production as well as at the level of the national economy, and the exploiters of wage labor would present themselves as bureaucrats. The mode of production -- by the fact of the separation of the conditions of production from the commodity producing wage laborers -- was capitalist even though capital was no longer "private" but directly social (statist) and the capitalist was no longer the private owner of capital but simply a functionary of capital and, as such, a salaried state (party) bureaucrat. Those who extracted and appropriated the unpaid surplus labor of the proletariat were not bureaucrats *qua* bureaucrats. They exploited the proletariat as the salaried "functionaries of capital" which was state property, juridically speaking, and they were thus, at the same time, the state (party) functionaries. This was not the bureaucratic organization of production giving rise to a new (bureaucratic) mode of production. On the contrary, the mode of production and the organization of production corresponding to it continued to be capitalist, but, arrived at a certain stage of the accumulation of capital, the capitalist organization of production assumed the *bureaucratic form*. Just as the state sector of the economy in traditional capitalism is *capitalist* not because of the capitalist character of the state *as such*, but because of the capitalist character of the *relations of production* (in the immediate process of production), in the same way the economy in the USSR was *capitalist* precisely for the same basic reason -- the enlarged reproduction by the commodity producing wage laborers of their separation from the conditions of production (now under a single ownership, juridically speaking).[13]

Rizzi saw the growing state intervention in different spheres along with increasing bureaucratization in modern society. Overwhelmed by the *phenomenal* trait, he failed, however, to see that the increasing bureaucratic character of modern capitalism -- "bureaucratization of the world," as he called it -- is only a manifestation of the superstructural exigency of *capital* arrived at its directly social stage, reaching its highest form -- logically, not necessarily chronologically -- in the statist social capital.

"CAPITALISM" AND "SOCIALISM" IN THE NSNC ARGUMENT

We now turn to the concepts of capitalism and socialism as they appear in the NSNC thesis. Here we choose to consider the relevant ideas of Paul Sweezy, inasmuch as Sweezy, more than anybody else in the NSNC tradition, to our knowledge, has offered, explicitly as a Marxist, the most cogent and lucid reasoning for his particular characterization of the Soviet economy by rigorously presenting his central concepts. However, the non-capitalism of the Soviet economy being his principal focus, he elaborates his concept of capitalism at a much greater length than his concept of socialism. Quite appropriately, we first discuss his concept of capitalism and later briefly note his concept of socialism.

For Sweezy the "determining characteristics of the economic foundation of capitalism" are (1) private capitalist ownership of the means of production; (2) competing character of separately existing units of social total capital; and (3) propertyless wage laborers producing bulk of the commodities (1980: 139-40). Sweezy further emphasizes that "capital-labor relation, while a basic and necessary feature of capitalism, is not by itself sufficient to define the capitalist system in its full historically developed form," and that "for such a definition it is necessary to add that capital exists not as a single entity, . . . but as many capitals organized separately and acting independently of one another" (1985: 100-101).

When Sweezy's conceptualization of capitalism is considered in the light of

Marx's, of the three characteristics that Sweezy ascribes to capitalism, the first refers to a *specific* (juridical) *form* of ownership of the means of production, it does not refer to the capitalist ownership *relations* as such which, as we know from Marx, are the juridical expression of the capitalist production relations themselves; the second refers to the reciprocal behaviour of the fragments of social total capital (STC) that appear, in Marx's familiar expression, "on the surface of the bourgeois society" as participants in pure exchange relations with one another in order to realize each one's share of the social surplus value; only the third refers to the production relations under capitalism. Thus, from a Marxian point of view, the three determining characteristics of capitalism as Sweezy conceives them to be, cannot have equal weights. Really, of the three characteristics it is only the third that *defines* capital as a specific (social) relation of production and, as such, is the *unique* determining characteristic for the other two (which are *determined* by it).

Somewhat reversing Sweezy's order of presentation we first consider capital's economic property (including the exchange relation) and then pass on to its juridical property as they appear in Sweezy's discourse.

For Marx "*capital*" is "the separation of the laborer from the conditions of production" (Marx 1962b: 419; italics in original). This characteristic of separation, as we saw earlier, distinguishes capitalism from all other modes of production. Now Sweezy, in his characterization of capitalism -- given above -- does not mention this separation. The nearest he comes to it is when he mentions his third characteristic which is non-ownership of the means of production by the laborers. However, separation and non-ownership are not equivalent terms. While the first implies the second, the converse is not necessarily true. An immediate and necessary consequence of this separation is wage labor which Sweezy considers as only one of the determining characteristics of capitalism. In this, we submit, Sweezy is radically departing from the Marxian concept of capital, inasmuch as for Marx wage labor relation is *the* determining characteristic of capitalism. As Marx emphasizes, capital is capital "only in regard to the negation of capital; the effective [*wirkliche*] non-capital is labor" (1953: 185). Similarly, "the consumption process of the labor power, . . . this very special [*eigentümlichen*] commodity, . . . is, at the same time, the production process of commodity and surplus value" (1962a: 189). We saw earlier that for Marx wage labor was the alternative designation for capitalist production.

Sweezy writes: "I do not believe that the fragmentation of the social capital . . . necessarily derives from wage relation and/or separation of the workers from the means of production" (1985: 104). The "separation" in question is of course the very concept of capital from which the wage labor relation necessarily follows. Now, this "separation" -- or double freedom -- of the laborer cannot be, as we emphasized earlier, with respect to STC of which the laborer is, in Marx's words, an "accessory." This separation is only in relation to *individual* capitals with respect to which the laborer is free, hence we submit that the existence of separation/wage labor would necessarily imply "fragmentation of the social capital." On the other hand, the fragmentation of the social capital would imply wage labor because that would mean that the laborers are doubly free with respect to individual capitals which is what makes labor wage labor. Of course, if there were no (social) *capital* then each unit of production could be run on cooperative principles *without wage labor*, that is, where "the antagonism between capital and labor is overcome," and, consequently, where these cooperatives, as fragments of total social non-capitalist production, could "use the means of production to valorize their own labor" (Marx 1964: 456) and exchange products as *simple commodity producers*. That would be a totally different situation.

Firmly holding on to the totality -- singularity configuration of capital, and knowing that wage labor relation is equivalent to generalized commodity production, it is not difficult to show that all the particular features of capitalism follow from this single relation.

As to Sweezy's second characteristic -- competition of capitals -- he, as it appears in a different text, seems to be using Marx's competition of capitals in the same sense as the classical economists' free competition (1981). However, these are two very different concepts. Unlike the classics, Marx does not consider individual capitals as *absolutely* independent entities inasmuch as they are the fragments of, and hence determined by STC -- a concept foreign to the classics. For Marx it is the *reciprocal* independence of the units of capitalist production mutually exchanging their commodities, thereby each one striving to realize its share of total (social) surplus value, produced by the STC collectively, that constitutes the competition of capitals (1953: 323; 1973a: 351-352; 1959: 20-21). This is, moreover, completely independent of any specific form of ownership over individual capitals. On the other hand, competition of capitals, "appearing on the surface of the bourgeois society," is the necessary "exoteric" aspect of capital, not its "esoteric" aspect -- as Marx would call it -- and cannot be a *determining* characteristic of capitalism. As a necessary manifestation of capital's essence, it is *determined* by capital-wage labor relation constituting the essence of capital.

Coming to capital's juridical property, it is private (capitalist) ownership of the means of production that Sweezy presents as a determining characteristic of capitalism. It seems that Sweezy is using the concept of private ownership in its traditionally (commonly) accepted sense -- that is, private property as it is *juridically recognized*, in other words, in what we earlier called Marx's second sense of private property, not in Marx's first and (what we consider as) fundamental sense, in the sense of *class property* (equivalent to the *non-property* of the laborers), irrespective of its specific juridically recognized configuration. Individual private property in the means of production is only a particular historical form of property in which capital manifests itself juridically at the initial stage of accumulation (of capital). It is the "old form in which the means of production appears" (Marx 1964: 456). As we know, Marx already speaks of abolition (sublimation) of individual private ownership of the means of production *within* capitalism itself at a certain stage of its development -- as a part of the process of capital's self-negation -- when it becomes a hindrance to further accumulation of capital, the consequence of the process being "directly social capital." When, in his discussion of changes in the forms of competition of capitals, Sweezy (1981: 4-5) quite correctly refers to chapter 27 of *Capital*, volume 3 (where Marx writes about the ownership-function separation within capital), he, unfortunately, does not seem to mention what appears to us to be one of the revolutionary conclusions of Marx's analysis -- repeated elsewhere in his writings -- namely, the existence of the individual capitalist as a pure functionary of capital *without* being its (juridical) private owner (See earlier discussion in Chapter 1). He also does not mention that what appears on the "surface of the bourgeois society" as concentration and centralization of capital (affecting the earlier forms of competition) only indicates the deeper process at work -- (direct) *socialization* of capital as a necessary transitional stage toward the "associated mode of production." Hence Sweezy's characterization of the juridical property of capital remains partial and incomplete. Thus, it seems, on the whole, that Sweezy's concept of capitalism is not quite the same as Marx's.

While conceptualizing capitalism, Sweezy also lays down his concept of socialism. According to him "a socialist society" is one "in which classes would necessarily persist for a long time, classlessness being a characteristic not of socialism, but of the higher stage of communism" (1980: 116). Then he adds, more categorically, that "the essence of socialism, running like a red thread through all of Marx and Engels's writings, is the replacement of the bourgeoisie as the ruling class by the proletariat" (1985: 98). Returning to the subject later, Sweezy affirms that "as an antithesis of capitalism, . . . socialism, from the Marxist perspective, is . . . an economic system of state ownership and planning" plus a "political system of workers' democracy" (1991: 2-3).

The first thing that strikes one here is the basic similarity between Sweezy's concept of socialism and the traditional Soviet *concept* of socialism (which we analyzed above) -- abstracted from its *practice* -- at least in so far as the economic core of this socialism is concerned. In both cases, socialism is conceived basically in terms of state ownership of the means of production and planning, which is supposed to be a negation of capitalism. Socialism is conceived in neither case in terms of a set of new (emancipatory) social relations of production -- essentially the relation between the immediate producers and their conditions of production -- or, more specifically, in terms of *society's appropriation* of the conditions of production. We already argued why Marxian socialism -- assumed by Marx to be the same as communism -- conceived as a classless association of free individuals (going through a lower and a higher phase), has little in common with this "socialism." We shall not repeat the arguments here. The fundamental difference between the two concepts remains, even when, as with Sweezy, "workers' political democracy" is added to the state ownership in order to complete the concept. The reason is simple. In the Marxian framework politics -- along with the state -- disappears already with the establishment of socialism after the end of the "revolutionary transformation period" (1965: 126; 1966b: 77; 1976b: 409). As we mentioned earlier, in 1871 Marx admires the Communards for their "Revolution against the State itself." We have to add that Sweezy's assertion, that the establishment of the proletariat as the ruling class is the essence of *socialism*, has no textual basis in Marx (and Engels). This is, of course, as it should be, because in the Marxian framework, socialism has no ruling class, not even the *proletariat* -- the class of *wage laborers* by definition. Socialism is already a *classless* society even if we accept it as the first phase of communism (in Lenin's revisionist sense). In Marx (and Engels) the proletarian rule *precedes* socialism.

On the other hand, it is difficult to imagine that when capital is conceived basically as a specific (social) relation of production, given by wage labor -- as in Marx -- and not a thing, a socialist society, very correctly supposed to be the exact opposite, the "antithesis of capitalism," is conceptualized by abstracting from the question of *production relations*.[14]

We conclude that Sweezy's concept of socialism, like his concept of capitalism analyzed above, is his own and, in terms of Marx's own texts, cannot strictly be considered Marxian.

NSNC THESIS: SECOND VARIANT

Originally elaborated by L. Trotsky, the "transitional society" thesis has E. Mandel as its most important spokesperson today. According to Mandel, just as there was a transitional society between feudalism and capitalism, in the same way there is a "transitional society between capitalism and socialism," and the same method of analysis is valid for both the cases (1974). This transitional society is characterized by a specific set of production relations different from the other sets of production relations corresponding to other societies appearing in history. Though Mandel affirms that there is no mature transitional society yet, this affirmation does not prevent him from finding, in societies "from the USSR through Yugoslavia to China and Cuba" -- with their "conditions of under-development" -- elements constituting a general theory of a "post capitalist society" transitional between capitalism and socialism.

In the transitional society between capitalism and socialism there is a "socialized planned economy" where, however, the law of value continues to operate mainly in the sphere of consumption goods. The society is governed by the antagonism between the logic of plan and the logic of market. In this society we have simultaneously non-capitalist relations of production and "bourgeois distribution relations," expressed mainly in the wage form of remuneration for the expenditure of labor power. The transitional society is thus a "hybrid combination" of these two contradictory sets of relations (1974: 7-9; 1981: 35-36). It is a "post-capitalist economy with elements of the market" (1990: 47). This transitional society is ruled by "a form of proletarian dictatorship," but with "bureaucratic degeneration." Given the "deformation," it will require a "political revolution," but not a social revolution, by the working class in a transitional society to arrive at socialism (1978: 41-42; 1974: 15).

CONCEPT OF "TRANSITIONAL SOCIETY"

Let us examine Mandel's concept of a transitional post-capitalist society in relation to Marx's ideas concerning the transition between capitalism and communism) alternatively and equivalently, socialism) even though, in Mandel's terms, Marx was presumably dealing with mature conditions of transition. When we analyze them closely, it appears that Mandel's transitional society has little in common with Marx's image of the transition. Unlike Mandel, Marx speaks not of a transitional "society" but of a transitional "period" between capitalism and communism. The difference is *basic* inasmuch as, according to Marx, there is no new society that comes into existence immediately with the establishment of political power by the proletariat. After establishing its own rule, the proletariat starts to transform the old relations of production, and the society corresponding to them, toward communism. Of course, Mandel's two-transition proposition -- first to socialism and then to communism (1974:7) -- has no textual basis in Marx. There is only a single post-capitalist society in Marx -- socialism or communism, also called Association or Union -- that comes into existence at the *end* of the "political transitional period." Only to this society will correspond the new relations of production, the basis of the "associated mode of production."

The difference between the two conceptions of the transitional society lies in the difference between the two approaches to the proletarian revolution. For Mandel the installation of the proletarian dictatorship signifies the simultaneous collapse of the bourgeois state *and* the bourgeois society (1974: 7). That is why he can so lightly speak of the "victory" of the socialist revolution in October, 1917 (1981: 35), which was supposed to have inaugurated a post-capitalist society in Russia. On the contrary, in Marx, a social revolution, like the socialist revolution, is not a momentary event in history, it corresponds to a whole *period* of time. The establishment of political power by the proletariat far from signifying an instantaneous victory of the socialist revolution, is only the starting point of the latter, it only inaugurates the "epoch of social revolution" -- the period of "prolonged birth pangs" -- which would ultimately usher in socialism (1958: 13;

1966b: 179). For, unlike what happened with the pre-proletarian revolutions, the process of consciously abolishing the old relations of production starts, for the proletariat, only *after* it becomes the ruling class. Consequently, on the morrow of the installation of the proletarian political power, there is, by definition, no bourgeois state, but the old *society* only starts to be revolutionized consciously (Marx 1966b: 68). It is still within the "womb of the old society" -- in Marx's vivid image (1966b: 178) -- that the new society is struggling to be born. Needless to add, there is nothing in the Marxian concept of proletarian dictatorship that would correspond to the very original Mandelian position on the need for a second "political revolution" by the proletariat against a part of itself under its own dictatorship. Indeed, by definition, a proletarian dictatorship in the profoundly self-emancipatory sense of Marx would exclude the possibility of an "upper stratum" of the proletariat to dominate it. The Mandelian case would rather mean that there is no proletarian dictatorship to start with in the supposed to be post-capitalist society (we are still at a *theoretical* level).

Similarly, Mandel's method of identifying the transitional society with post-capitalist society has little in common with Marx's method. Mandel derives social relations of production from society's (juridical) forms of ownership and exchange. The state ownership of the means of production, together with central planning, and state monopoly of foreign trade, are supposed to have eliminated "generalized commodity production" and, consequently, capitalist relations of production (1981: 35). In Marx, on the contrary, it is the type of production that determines the types of ownership and exchange. In other words, the point of departure in the latter case is the inquiry into the *mode of production* which forms the basis for the specific ownership and exchange forms. Thus a social order cannot be simply "enacted away" (Marx 1962a: 16), not even by a proletarian state. In the same way, it is absurd to postulate the elimination of commodity production -- at least most of it -- on the basis of the juridical acts of the proletarian state, the *beginning* measures, as the *Communist Manifesto* emphasizes, on the long way to the workers' self-emancipation. The Mandelian position would simply mean that the above-mentioned measures are adequate to eliminate the "universal alienation" [*allseitige Entäusserung*] represented by commodity production (Marx 1958: 37,38). On the contrary, commodity production is eliminated only with the direct appropriation of the conditions of production by *society* itself, that is, only under communism.

Mandel's non-Marxian approach is, again, clearly seen in his juxtaposing non-capitalist relations of production with bourgeois relations of distribution. We could only recall Marx's statement that it is "from the bourgeois economists" that "vulgar socialism has learnt to consider and treat distribution *independently* of the mode of production" (1966b: 180; italics added). Strangely, Mandel refers to Marx's "Marginal Notes" of 1875 to support his juxtaposition (referred to above) in connection with his discussion of the Soviet transitional society (1986a: 548).

One wonders how Marx's case of "bourgeois rights" -- still remaining in the realm of distribution in the first phase of *communism* -- would correspond to the Mandelian case of bourgeois *relations* of distribution in a *transitional* society. Similarly, Mandel's originality -- again nowhere encountered in Marx -- lies in his treatment of the laborer's wage remuneration, or "sale of labor power against money wage," as he calls it, as a "bourgeois form of distribution" within the non-capitalist transitional society (Mandel 1981: 35-36; 1986a: 637), in other words, *separating wage labor from the capitalist production relations.*[15]

We conclude our discussion of Mandel's theoretical position by noting that, if we abstract from the difference between the two labels applied to the USSR, namely, "transitional society" and "socialist society" -- and the underlying differences in the respective political standpoints -- Mandel's *theoretical* position does not appear to be basically different from Stalin's, in so far as they concern the post-capitalist characterization of the Soviet economy. The assertion of the abolition of capitalist relations of production on the basis of a specific property form of the means of production, namely, the state or "socialized" ownership -- associated with central planning -- is common to both Stalin and Mandel. In the same way the assertion of the absence of generalized commodity production on the basis of the limited operation of the law of value, confined to exchanges between the state sector and the collective farm sector as well as to the consumption goods and foreign trade sectors -- itself the result of the state's juridical act -- are also common to both. Interestingly, again, both evoke Marx's "Marginal Notes" of 1875 in support of each one's respective position on the distribution of means of consumption in the post-capitalist society.[16]

NOTES

1. For a comprehensive critique of Stalin's "political economy of socialism," see B. Chavance (1980).

2. Laibman of course denounces the "Stalin era authoritarianism and illegality" (1992: 354), but does in no way reject the theoretical model of the socialist economy that was, in all its essentials, developed in the Stalin era.

3. In fact, Marx praised the Parisian workers for their "Revolution against the *State* itself" (Marx 1971: 152; italics in original).

4. The term "counting" [*compter*] was substituted in the French version for the term "expressing" [*auszudrücken*] of the original version (Marx 1962a: 97).

5. Thus the eminent Soviet social scientist T. Zaslavskaya, while emphasizing the "human factor" -- so long supposedly neglected -- textually cites Marx's "Marginal Notes" on the individual remuneration based on labor contribution in the first phase of communism, and then adds that labor is represented here by "wage" [*zarabotnaya plata*], and goods and social benefits are represented by "prices" [*tseny*] (1986: 71). See also Aganbegyan (1989: 66).

6. The logical inconsistency between commodity production and distribution according to labor has been lucidly brought out by the (ex) Yugoslav economist A.M. Vacic (1977).

7. Thus, even assuming Soviet social formation's full conformity to Laibman's criteria of socialism, we would not have in the Soviet Union socialism in the sense of Marx, for the simple reason that, Laibman's claim notwithstanding (1992: 315), all those criteria would still belong to what Marx would call the "pre-history of human society," *preceding* the "socialist constitution of mankind" (Marx 1958: 14; 1976a: 327. The last phrase appears in English in the original).

8. The problem was explicitly recognized by the Stalinist ideology: "The mistakes of the former teaching in denying the law of value in socialism created innumerable difficulties in explaining the existence under socialism of such categories as money, banks, credit" (*Teaching* 1944: 523).

9. See on this question the interesting analysis by Yanowitch (1966).

10. For a good introduction to the debate on this question, see B. Bongiovanni (1975: 259-69).

11. Perhaps the most notable among the Marxists of this trend initially are B. Souvarine, A. Treint, S. Weil, and A. Ciliga. Their views are conveniently summarized in R. Tacchinardi, and A. Peregalli (1990: chapters 3 and 5).

12. The words "managers", "foremen", and "overlookers" appear in the original.

13. Herbert Marcuse wondered "what Weber would have said if he had seen that it is not the West but the East that has deployed, in the name of socialism, the most extreme form of Western rationality" (where "rationality" is understood to include bureaucracy as a necessary form of domination) (1965: 107, 120). He seemed not to have fully appreciated the necessary correspondence between the degree of bureaucratization and the degree of capitalist development, given his neglect of the *essentially* capitalist character of the Soviet social formation. See Marcuse (1958).

14. We have to say that Sweezy's very concept of "post-revolutionary society" as a new society — neither capitalist nor socialist — raises problems from the point of view of the materialist conception of history. He emphasizes that in the new society "capital-labor relations" is maintained and "social surplus continues to be produced by propertyless wage earners" (1985: 100). In other words, compared to capitalism, which the new society replaces, there is no change in the social relations of production (in the Marxian sense). Could we then say that the "post-revolutionary society" is a new social formation based on the old social relations of production, its very foundation?

15. Referring to Rossi, Marx writes about the "stupidity of recognizing wage labor but not [*wegzudemonstriren*] the relation of this labor to capital which it [wage labor] constitutes" (1976a: 126).

16. The surprising closeness of the Stalinist and the Trotskyist points of view on the Soviet question has been well brought out by Buick and Crump (1986:67-101).

Chapter 7

THE "NON-CAPITALIST" POSITION AND THE SOVIET REALITY

After having analyzed the theoretical premises of the adherents of the "non-capitalist" (including the "socialist") tendency (concerning the Soviet economy), we propose to examine in this chapter their representation of the reality of the Soviet economy. It goes without saying, just as there are differences in the theoretical positions of the adherents of the tendency in question, in the same way there is no unique representation of the Soviet economy that comes out of their writings. For example, NSNC's first variant is much more critical than its second variant in this regard, while the "socialist" variant of "non-capitalism" is an unvarnished exercise in apology. In the discussion, we shall not neglect these differences. However, given the space-limitation, the emphasis will be on the elements that unite the different adherents in their representation of the Soviet economy as "non" or "post capitalist." As the existence of capital, its extended reproduction, and its crisis in the USSR have already been argued (in Chapters 3, 4 and 5), what remains for examination, in the light of the appropriate Marxian categories, is the specific arguments that have been advanced to establish the non-capitalist character of the Soviet economy. In this chapter, again, the concern, basically, is with the views of the left radicals.

Let us first summarize the alleged non-capitalist features of the Soviet economy. All the proponents of non-capitalism emphasize the dominant role of central planning based on state ownership of the means of production. While some have denied the commodity character of the greater part of the products of labor, others, not denying the (quasi) generality of commodity production, have stressed the non-spontaneous character of price formation. All deny the competition of capitals. While recognizing the wage form of labor remuneration, all deny the existence of labor market, because the Soviet wage is not the result of spontaneous forces of the labor market and because there is job security and full-employment. Again, while recognizing the high rate of accumulation they deny the capitalist character of this accumulation. Finally, all of them hold, explicitly or implicitly, that, succeeding capitalism, as it does, the Soviet economy is a more progressive economy compared to capitalism in several aspects, positive -- such as planning and job security together with social benefits -- as well as negative -- such as non-existence of the crisis of overproduction and reserve army of labor, and of inflation. Let us examine these arguments. In the first four sections that follow, we successively analyze the arguments on commodity production, competition of capitals, the accumulation of capital, and the character of labor power. In the fifth section, we examine the arguments on the alleged superiority of the Soviet economy compared to capitalism.

COMMODITY PRODUCTION

On commodity production, the non-capitalist argument holds either that the greater part of the Soviet economy's products -- including the means of production -- has no commodity character due to the absence of juridical private property in the means of production, or that commodity production exists, but in a non-spontaneous, planned, hence non-capitalist, form. An immediate consequence of this argument is, of course, that there is no inter-enterprise competition, at least not in the capitalist sense of the term. Interestingly, some proponents of the "state capitalist" thesis share this argument with their opponents to a considerable extent. Thus T. Cliff denies the existence of the law of value and hence competition of capitals *inside* Russia's state capitalist economy on the strength of the absence of juridical private ownership in the means of production (Cliff 1964: 203,209). Similarly R. Dunayevskaya, while holding that the law of value operates in the Russian economy, denies the existence of the competition of capitals due to the absence of individual legal titles to property in the means of production (Dunayevskaya, 1992: 72,73,74). In short, commodity production (particularly the competition of capitals) is posited by these writers on the existence of juridically recognized private ownership in the means of production.

Taking Marx's well-known formulation -- "the objects of utility become commodities only because they are the products of private labors executed independently of one another" (Marx 1962a: 87) -- we do not see any necessary one-to-one correspondence between private labor and juridical private property in the means of production in order for the products to appear as commodities, particularly when the latter have ceased to be "simple" commodities and become "capitalist" commodities (in the sense of Marx). "Private labor" here basically signifies *non-immediately social* labor irrespective of the specific form of property.

True, Marx does say that commodity producers "must recognize one another as private proprietor" (1962a: 99,102). However, the chapter where this sentence occurs is exclusively devoted to the simple "exchange process" where capital has not yet appeared as a category. In (simple) exchange process, corresponding to simple commodity production, private labor of course coincides with the ownership of private individuals/households over the means of production, labor power itself being not yet a commodity.[1] When simple commodity production changes into capitalist commodity production -- within which itself juridical private property undergoes increasing transformation responding to the exigencies of accumulation, as Marx shows in detail -- "juridical relations corresponding to [simple] commodity production" would naturally be as little "everlasting" (Marx 1962a: 99) as the simple commodity production itself.

The rule that "labor time represented in the exchange value is the labor time of the individual" (Marx 1958: 245) -- where labor of the individual becomes social only through exchange -- is strictly valid only in the case of simple commodity production; it is only then that the labor of the individual/private laborer and individual/private labor coincide. This rule and this coincidence are no longer valid under capitalist commodity production where each commodity is the product of *combined labor* of individuals, and "with the progress of centralization [of capital] . . . production loses its private character and becomes a social process" (Marx 1962b: 445).[2] This social process Marx calls "real" as opposed to "formal" as in the case of simple commodity production. However, this real social process does not, in capitalism, still have an immediately social character at *the level of society* in the precise sense of being "the offspring of the association which distributes labor among its members" (Marx 1953: 76). Even at the stage of directly social capital, with the abolition/sublimation of capitalist private property, the social process is "real" *within* each capitalist collective, that is, within each fragment of STC, but at the level of society labor remains individual (private), that is, non-immediately social, in the sense that social total labor remains fragmented. Even in the extreme case of a single national capital, clearly envisaged by Marx as a tendency, this remains true in so far as this capital as a totality remains *functionally* fragmented into reciprocally separate and independent individual capitals competing with one another (in the sense of Marx). Thus, as long as commodity production prevails -- either in its simple or in its capitalist form -- Marx's definition of commodities as "products of private labors executed independently of one another" remains valid. What is fundamental from the point of view of Marx is that private labor is the basis of commodity-production (simple or capitalist) only in so far as it is the "opposite" [*Gegenteil*] of "immediately social labor" (Marx 1962a: 73,109), irrespective of the specific juridical form of ownership involved. An acute internal observer of the so-called Soviet-type societies has offered what he calls the "general definition" of "market" which largely corresponds to Marx's concept of commodity production (and exchange). According to this definition, market is "a system in which isolated producers and consumers are functioning as actors, [and] products are exchanged between them for money," including the "firm manufacturing the means of production and the firm using the means as seller and buyer," the definition covering "the market which is centrally planned and controlled in full detail, the one that is only influenced by the centre, as well as the one that is totally decentralized and free" (Kornai 1983: 153).

On the other hand, a mere *juridical* abolition of private ownership and the institution of juridical public (state) ownership in the means of production does not eliminate commodity production (or market) simply because private labor does not become immediately social labor (society-wise) merely through these juridical -- constitutional changes. It is only under the direct collective appropriation of the conditions of production by *society* itself -- and not through any juridically proclaimed public ownership over the means of production -- that labor ceases to be private and becomes immediately social. Marx refers to only two alternatives to "private exchanges": either a hierarchy-regulated society, or a society of "free exchange" of activities among "social individuals," that is, Association. "The private exchange of products of labor, wealth and activities stands in opposition both to the distribution based on domination and subordination of individuals by other individuals, and to the free exchange of individuals who are associated on the foundation of common appropriation and control of the means of production" (Marx 1953: 76-77). Needless to add, this "common appropriation and control" -- corresponding to socialism -- and state ownership and control (even under a proletarian regime) are neither identical nor equivalent.[3]

Thus, even if the Soviet society were ruled by the proletariat (which of course it never was) which had juridically eliminated private (individual) bourgeois ownership in the means of production, commodity production, showing private exchange, would thereby not be eliminated. The latter would cease to exist only under Association, with production assuming a collective character (Marx 1953: 88). This is, of course, as it should be, inasmuch as even with the "proletariat's governmental power" -- necessarily *preceding* socialism -- the "old organization of society has still not disappeared" (Marx 1973c: 630). Contrary to Mandel's absurd assertion, no "*fiat* of the proletariat's power" can "make possible the *immediately social* character of labor" (1974: 11; italics in original), which would be tantamount to "enacting away" the old order, as Marx would say, whereas the "Association is in no way arbitrary [*Willkürliches*]" (Marx 1962a: 16; 1953: 77).

Even in the simplest case of "simple reproduction," which "always forms a part, a real factor of accumulation" (Marx 1973a: 354), it is hard to imagine, following the Stalin-Mandel argument, that the means of consumption (in the Soviet economy) assume value form and could be exchanged against the means of production without the latter taking value form. Recognizing the value form of the means of consumption and not of the means of production would mean, for the economy as a whole, an artificial dissociation of consumption from production. After the demise of Stalin, the Soviet economists started to point out that a considerable part of the machines and equipment manufactured in "Department I" entered into the enterprises in "Department II" as well as agriculture in order to produce raw materials and consumption goods, and that the production costs of the machines and equipment ultimately had repercussions on the consumption goods.[4] Impelled by the accumulation imperative and yielding before the reality of non-immediately social character of labor at the level of society, the Soviet regime, at a particular stage of its existence, had to accept the general character of commodity production in the economy, though, for purely ideological reasons, it continued to rationalize the reality of the commodity production under the absurd appellation of "socialist commodity production."

A dominant strand within the non-capitalist tendency opposes "spontaneous market process" -- supposed to be a feature of capitalism -- to "plan regulated market process," supposed to characterize a non-capitalist (if not socialist) economy like that of the ex-USSR. The particular approach, we submit, appears to be empiricist-positivist. Simply because the form of exchange of products of labor in the Soviet economy appears to be different from the one encountered in the actually existing capitalist economies the conclusion is drawn that the Soviet economy, to that extent, is non-capitalist. We hold that a less superficial and more fruitful approach, particularly for those professing Marxism, would have been to ask why at all the products of labor continue to take *commodity form* in the USSR. The question is never posed, as if commodity is an eternal, ahistorical category, equally valid for societies that have supposedly transgressed the capitalist limits. Speaking of the (post-capitalist) transitional society, E. Mandel writes: "The mass of the big means of production in industry, transport, communications, trade, etc., has no commodity character, [because] they cannot be *freely bought and sold*" (1974: 13; italics added). On the other hand, speaking about the "advanced capitalist countries today," he comes to the "startling conclusion" that "bulk of both consumer and producer goods are not produced in response to market signals," and that "they are largely, if not completely, *independent of the market*" (Mandel 1986b: 11; italics added). We hold that proposition-wise the two statements are basically equivalent and that, to that extent, Mandel's argument on the distinction between the two systems, based on forms of exchange, falls apart.

Now, regarding the so-called spontaneous market process, supposed to distinguish capitalism from the non-capitalist Soviet economy (marked by its absence), let us first note that there are economists -- Marxists and non-Marxists -- who would deny the relevance of this spontaneous process for actually existing *capitalism*. Thus according to J.K. Galbraith, right in the midst of the capitalist society, over a vast area governed by large corporations with their most exacting advanced technology -- constituting the most significant part of the economy (in effect where capital is already directly social) -- there has arisen a "planning system" which has "most completely replaced the market by an authoritarian determination of price and the amounts to be sold or bought at these prices" (1978: 24). This sea-change in the so-called classical capitalism -- dictated by the exigencies of the accumulation of capital at its directly social stage -- is invisible only to those who are still obstinately clinging to the traditional folklore of capitalism being necessarily associated with planlessness and market spontaneity. In his turn, the eminent German Marxist economist W. Hofmann had associated the law of value uniquely with free competition, and emphasized that this law was "incompatible" [*unverträglich*] with both socialism and modern capitalism, dominated by "monopolistic competition" (1968: 121,122).

It was argued in Chapter 5 that the Soviet economy was a mobilization economy, given its initial backwardness and perceived military threat from outside, and that accumulation of capital at an extraordinarily rapid rate was taking place within this war economy in peacetime. Keen non-Marxist observers of the Soviet economy have found the Soviets' apparent rejection of the so-called market rationality to be quite consistent with the logic of accumulation, given the historical context. Thus J. Berliner has pointed out that, in the situation of relative economic underdevelopment, it is not the "Marxian influence on the Soviet economic practice" but the "widely-used slogan of 'overtaking and surpassing' the advanced capitalist countries," that is the "most fruitful basis available for explaining the actual policy of (Soviet) economic development" (1966: 26-27).[5] Similarly, A. Nove has remarked that "the rational way of organizing the rapid development of a backward country" is "surely not the achievement of a purely economic optimum which, in any country, is rendered impossible by considerations of political feasibility and social circumstances," just as observing the "war economies of the Western states" one cannot conclude that "wars should have been run on free-market principles" (1982: 389-90). Referring particularly to the immense Ural-Kuznets combine, "a long term project par excellence" with its "vast external effects in the long run," including military usefulness, Nove emphasizes that the investment choice in this case "could not be justified by rate-of-return calculations" inasmuch as, among other things, it would "lock up a great deal of capital" (1982: 133). The existence of a single national capital under a single ownership -- as Marx would call it -- immensely facilitated this process of extended reproduction of capital.[6]

That the absence of the spontaneous market process in an economy does not necessarily signify that economy's non-capitalist character is clearly seen not only in the case of wartime economies of the so-called classical capitalism (earlier we cited Berliner on the wartime US economy), but also in the case of another "war economy in peacetime" -- the (pre-war) German economy of the late 1930s. Here the existence of juridical private property in the means of production did not prevent a peacetime capitalist economy from showing -- though for a short period

-- striking similarities with the peacetime Soviet economy in the mode of its functioning. In an unduly neglected brilliant work on the post-1936 "centrally administered" German economy, where the "fixing of needs and the direction of production" were (in a single hand), W. Eucken wrote:

The political authority (was) able to shape developments in economic life in accordance with its political objectives, regardless of cost calculations . . . . For the economic process as a whole it was not the plans and actions of individual businesses and households that were decisive, but the plans and orders of central authorities . . . . Huge investment projects were undertaken, stretching ahead for very long periods into the future. The amortization period and the rate of interest were not taken into account . . . . The checks on investment, effective in the commercial economy, [were] lacking . . . . The process of investment was very simple, and could not fail because of insufficient liquidity . . . . The central administration decided about the investment (1969: 130,139,150,151).[7]

COMPETITION OF CAPITALS

In Chapter 3 the existence of competition of capitals in the Soviet economy on the basis of the relative isolation of the Soviet enterprises -- based on wage labor -- and consequent reciprocal exchange of the means of production taking commodity form were asserted. The Soviet spokespersons themselves recognized the relative isolation, as well as the inter-enterprise commodity exchange of the means of production. These conditions, automatically containing reciprocal "repulsion of capitals," are, as we know, necessary and sufficient for the existence of competition of capitals in the sense of Marx. However, while accepting the reality of these conditions in the Soviet economy, its spokespersons would not like to mention competition of capitals almost until the end. Thus the late distinguished Soviet economist R.G. Karagedov went so far as to underline the "organizational separateness of the branches of industry," and of "centres of decision making on the development of industry" with "differences in the economic interests," giving rise to "collisions" and "striving [*stremlenie*] for the priority of one's own branch" (1983: 52, 54), but would not qualify this as competition. Similarly, A. Aganbegyan observed that in the Soviet economy, given the conditions of division of labor and the "relative isolation of the producers," there arose commodity production and commodity-money relations. "Within the framework of public, state ownership (of the means of production), which prevails in the national economy, there arises relative isolation [*otnositel' noe obosoblenie*] of separate enterprises . . . ." (1988: 184). In plain Marxian terms, Aganbegyan is here referring to the division of the STC into relatively autonomous fragments exchanging commodities, which are all that is required (given wage labor) for the competition of capitals to exist. Of course, he would have none of the latter, and to signify the inter-enterprise relations in "socialism" he uses, as he says, a different expression, namely, "economic emulation [*sorevnovanie*] to designate this specific (original) type of competition [*svoeobraznuiu konkurentsiu*] between enterprises in socialism" (1988: 191). In their refusal to recognize the existence of competition of capitals in their economy, the Soviet economists followed basically the same logic as the one followed by the adherents of the non-capitalist tendency, namely, the existence of public ownership of the means of production. In their society, as they said, "based on the principle of public property," competition between units "based on private property in the means of production" does not and cannot exist (Budarin 1978: 28-29).

The economists of the other Soviet type societies of the epoch, however, seemed less inhibited by private-public ownership dogma, and straightaway referred to the reality of competition in their economies while, ritualistically, continuing to call the latter socialist. Thus a Czechoslovak economist wrote about the "commodity base of the socialist economy" giving rise to "mutual conflict of interests among enterprises," and "*competition among producers* of various products" (Kodet 1966: 35; italics added). The eminent Hungarian economist J. Kornai discussed what he called competition in the Soviet type economies at both "vertical" and "horizontal" levels. At the vertical level, several firms as claimants "compete with each other for investment resources at the disposal of the allocator," and each firm director "fights for more investment for *our* team, *our* firm, *our* ministry." Horizontally the buying firms are faced with selling firms creating a market relation in which buying firms "continue to compete with each other" (1980: 202-203; italics in original). Earlier we cited Karagedov on the struggle for the "priority of one's own branch" occasioned by the differences in economic interests of the separately organized branches of Soviet industry.[8]

As we mentioned earlier, some proponents of the (state) capitalist thesis also believe in the absence of competition of capitals in the Soviet economy basically for the same reason as that advanced by their opponents, namely, the absence of juridical private property in the means of production. Thus for T. Cliff, as the ownership of all the enterprises in Russia belongs to the state which regulates the economy through planning, there is no exchanges of commodities, that is, the law of value has ceased to exist. By the same token, there is no competition of capitals within the Soviet economy. It has to be and is introduced from outside. Russia's state owned single enterprise competes with the capitalist enterprises in the world economy. The state as the sole owner of the means of production is, of course, the sole employer of labor power in the Soviet economy (Cliff 1964). True to the Second Internationalist-Bolshevik tradition, Cliff ignores the double meaning of capitalist private property (as well as capital's totality-singularity configuration) in Marx -- private property as *class* property and private property as *individual* property (as well as capital as a social totality facing singular capitals). It was argued earlier (Chapter 1) that as long as the conditions of production remain separated from the immediate producers, and hence remain their *non-property*, those conditions remain private property in the first and fundamental sense of Marx, even when the state is the only proprietor. This private property ends with capital itself (including state capital) only with the direct social appropriation of the conditions of production under Association. However, in the Soviet economy the conditions of production remained private property under the juridical single ownership by the state. Needless to add, private property in the first sense is unknown to jurisprudence. Again, as previously mentioned, private ownership and private production are not necessarily identical. For the existence of commodities what counts is private production in the sense of *non-immediately social* production, executed independently (of each other) in the different units of production. And if that production is based on wage labor, we have all the conditions for the existence of competition of capitals. In other words, neither commodity production nor competition of capitals as its specific form of existence depends necessarily on the juridical private ownership of the means of production, however paradoxical that might sound to the habitual mode of thought. Hence Cliff's argument on this score is untenable. It could be added that the single employer concept of the Soviet state would exclude the existence of wage labor in the Soviet economy by definition, and the introduction of the world market as the creator of competition could not transform the Russian laborer into a wage laborer in the absence of freedom to travel abroad in search of employment. In a word, the Soviet economy could even then not be characterized as capitalist. (Indeed, Cliff's position would amount to conceptualizing capital by abstracting from the relations of production).

In her turn R. Dunayevskaya, as mentioned earlier, holds that both the law of value and wage labor exist in Russia but not competition of capitals in the absence of "legal titles to the means of production." This argument, too, is not acceptable. Contrariwise, we would submit that the existence of wage labor and the law of value (the latter necessarily associated with the former) would automatically signify the existence of the competition of capitals, irrespective of the juridical form of ownership in the means of production. As we have been arguing, for competition of capitals to exist -- and capital cannot exist without confronting another capital, as Marx would say -- all that is required is the *functional* fragmentation of the STC into reciprocally isolated units of production exchanging products of wage labor, even when we have Marx's extreme case of one national capital under one ownership.[9] As a contemporary Hungarian economist, when still under a Soviet type society, correctly observed, enterprises as "bearers of partial tasks connected with the material transformation," and "separated from each other" are in a "competitive position," and the "actions and behaviors . . . connected with the elementary acts of realization, with buying and selling" through which the enterprises "try to enforce and improve their position against other enterprises" constitute "*forms of competition*" (Lanyi 1980: 112, 116; italics in original).

Those who deny the existence of competition of capitals in the Soviet economy seem to be considering certain historically determined forms of competition, as they appear in the so-called classical capitalist society, as identical with competition (of capitals) as such. The concept of competition underlying such a view is really that of the classical political economy and its followers -- the proponents of free competition -- and *not* of Marx, which is very different (see Chapter 2 above). As we know, contrary to Marx, the classical view ignores the social totality of capital as an entity in its own right and holds each singular capital -- the fragment of this societal totality -- to be absolutely independent, based on juridical private property in the means of production. Thereby this view fails to see what Marx calls the inner interconnection of capital (which he claims to have first discovered), and remains superficial, confined to what appears on the "surface of the capitalist society" at a particular period of its history. After Marx's discovery of the inner interconnection why go back?

Finally we submit that, rather than inferring capital's existence from the nature of inter-enterprise relations (whether the latter amounted to competition, that is), it would be more in accord with the Marxian method to *start* with the question of the existence of capital as such, that is, whether capital exists at all (as a specific social relation of production) before examining the reciprocal relations between the units of production. "The examination of capital as such is different from that of capital in relation to another capital," and "the relation of capitals in their reciprocity is explained *after* the examination of what they have in common: [that is] being *capital*" (Marx 1953: 576,416; italics added), because "the scientific analysis of competition is possible only after the inner nature of *capital* is understood" (Marx 1962a: 335; italics added).

In the contemporary discussion on the nature of the Soviet economy, Paul Sweezy, more than anybody else, has the merit of justly emphasizing the relevance of the category of competition of capitals. In fact, his main reason for characterizing the Soviet economy as non-capitalist is his denial of the existence of competition of capitals in that economy. Sweezy's position, characterizing the Soviet economy as non-capitalist, can be summed up as follows: (1) total social capital exists; (2) wage labor producing the great bulk of commodities exists, but modified by job security; (3) capital-labor relation exists; however, capitalism does not exist mainly because separate capitals do not exist due to the non-existence of juridical private property in the means of production (Sweezy 1980, 1985, 1991).

First, let us note that the dichotomy between total social capital and capitalism exists in Sweezy because he rejects what we consider to be the logical connection between the existence of wage labor and the existence of separate units of production. We already argued earlier that wage labor, involving laborer's double freedom, *necessarily* implies reciprocal separation of production units -- that is, singular capitals -- in other words, competition of capitals. Secondly, it is difficult to accept the contention that total social capital exists but that there are no separate capitals. If there is total social capital then it must *appear* as separate capitals inasmuch as capital cannot exist without confronting other capitals. "The repulsion of itself [*sich von sich Repellierendes*]" is within the "essence of capital" (Marx 1953: 323).[10] In this connection, let us recall that when Marx speaks of society wide one single capital under one ownership (see Chapter 1 above), he is still referring to this tendency *within* the capitalist society itself (where, of course, this "one capital" has to be *functionally* divided into a plurality of reciprocally autonomous units of production).

Total social capital, the existence of which Sweezy affirms for the Soviet economy, is, as we know, a central Marxian category (see Chapter 1). The category in question stands for the capitalist class (as a whole). Now, if the USSR is a "class exploitative society," with labor appearing as wage labor, and capital labor relation as the "basic relation of exploitation" -- as Sweezy maintains -- then, given the Marxian sense of total social capital (as well as of the other categories), only the capitalist class can be that exploiting class, and the USSR, based on exploitation (by assumption), *is* a capitalist society.[11]

ACCUMULATION OF CAPITAL

One of the arguments advanced to prove the non-capitalist character of the Soviet economy has been that the Soviet accumulation was not really the accumulation of capital for the same reason which accounted for the alleged absence of the competition of capitals, namely, the non-existence of individual capitalists with their profit motive based on private ownership of the means of production. It is clear that here again, as in the case of competition of capitals, the argument is essentially based on the existence of a historically specific form of property in the means of production at a specific stage of capitalist production and not on capital as a relation of production. Necessarily associated with this argument is the failure to consider the individual capitalist simply as a functionary of capital, not necessarily the latter's juridical owner.

After the earlier somewhat prolonged discussion of the process of capital accumulation in the Soviet economy (in Chapters 4 and 5), we would simply recall here that the accumulation of capital is basically the extended reproduction of the capitalist *relation* of production, that is, the laborers' separation from the conditions of production, and that (alternatively speaking) the accumulation of capital is simply the increase of the proletariat (Marx 1962a: 641-42). Here again Sweezy's position on the Soviet economy is worth considering. As seen above, Sweezy holds that the basic relation of exploitation was the capital labor relation and that total social capital existed in the Soviet economy. He also correctly speaks of an "extremely high rate of accumulation" in that economy, but adds that this was only "in response to external danger," not due to any "internal imperative." He emphasizes that contrary to the "capitalist countries," which are "narrowly constrained by the accumulation imperative which operates under all circumstances and regardless of the external environment, in the Soviet situation the only comparable imperative is to maintain the basic capital-labor relation" (1985: 110).[12]

First of all, what is the accumulation imperative of the capitalist countries? Is it not the imperative to reproduce the capital-labor relation at an enlarged scale? If this is true, does not the Soviet "imperative to maintain the basic capital-labor relation" (as Sweezy holds) amount to the imperative to accumulate *capital* (where the expression "to maintain" obviously includes reproduction at an enlarged scale and not simply to maintain the relation at the same scale). Thus -- to start with -- irrespective of the origin of this imperative, that is, whether it is internal or external, the existence of the imperative itself based on *capital-labor relation* is sufficient to establish the existence of the accumulation of capital in the Soviet economy. However, to say that this imperative was purely external to the Soviet economy is, we submit, an oversimplification. Although one of the factors behind the accumulation imperative was undoubtedly the perceived danger of external military intervention, it cannot adequately explain the Soviet regime's extraordinary accumulation drive. We think that the basic factor behind the Soviet accumulation drive was the economic backwardness of the country and the determination of its rulers to build "socialism in one country" which, of course, had to demonstrate its superiority in every sphere.[13] In fact, even before the seizure of power Lenin had emphasized, referring to the unfolding revolutionary movement in Russia, that though the country was advanced politically, it remained backward "economically," compared to the advanced capitalist countries, and that the country must "catch up with and surpass" the capitalist countries "*economically too*" [*takzhe i ekonomicheski*] (1982b: 206; italics in original).

Lenin's phrase became the oft-repeated slogan of the Soviet regime and summed up the imperative of the Soviet accumulation process. Several years before the First Plan had started, the Soviet authorities emphasized the country's industrialization as an essential prerequisite for building socialism in a single country. In the 14th Party Congress (1925), "the famous 'general line' of the Party was adopted: it demanded the maximum development of industry, the 'transformation of our country from an agrarian into an industrial one, capable by its own means of producing the necessary equipment'." (Baykov 1970: 127). The perceived danger of external military intervention was explicitly added as a factor behind the accumulation strategy only later, in 1927, and of course gave a certain urgency to the accumulation process (Baykov 1970: 129). This imperative to industrialize an economically backward country at the fastest possible rate is the key to the understanding of the Soviet accumulation process as has been very correctly emphasized by some of the best students of the Soviet economic history like, among others, Gerschenkron, Nove and Berliner (whom we referred to earlier). It is precisely this imperative -- rapid accumulation in a situation of backwardness effected under a "war economy in peacetime" -- that explains many of the basic traits of the Soviet accumulation process, apparently so different from the accumulation process of peacetime *advanced* Western capitalist countries, as A. Gerschenkron had so pertinently shown (1966a). In Chapters 4 and 5, we have argued that the Soviet accumulation process, given this historical context, did not at all contradict the logic of *capital*, even though this process operated under a single national capital with a single ownership.[14]

Catching up with and surpassing became the point of departure of the Soviet economy's "persistent expansion drive" and the associated "insatiable investment hunger," in the much used words of J. Kornai (1980, 1982, 1992). To "fulfill the [production] plan at any price [*liuboi tsenoi*]" (Manevich 1985b: 29), the Soviet enterprises' behavioral regularity showed itself precisely -- contrary to what Sweezy thinks -- in "accumulation for the sake of accumulation," or, alternatively speaking, in "production for the sake of production" (Loginov 1992: 5). The absence of juridical private property in the means of production -- with capital-(wage) labor relation remaining intact, as Sweezy, more than anybody else of the NSNC tendency, has justly noted -- instead of hindering the accumulation process, in fact, immensely helped it. In the interest of what Stalin had called long term "higher profitability" (of STC), short term profits of singular capitals in the particular lines of production could be foregone. As we have argued in Chapter 3, profitability of particular units of production was not of much importance for maximizing total social surplus value from the economy as a whole. In the event, as is well-known, unhindered by any political or trade union opposition, untrammelled by calculations of private profit, and constrained only by the physical limit of productive resources and minimum living needs of the population (the political tolerance limits), the Soviet regime did catch up with and surpass the Western capitalist countries in accumulation's share in national income as well as in its speed. We earlier cited (Chapter 4) official data showing the extraordinary rapidity of *proletarianization* of the Soviet population. As we know from Marx, the proletarianization of the population (starting with original expropriation) is the very essence of the accumulation of capital. "The shift of labor force out of agriculture of the magnitude that occurred in the USSR between 1928 and 1940 took from thirty to fifty years in other countries" (Kuznets 1963: 345). Labor force participation ratio (employed population divided by working age population) rose from 57 percent to 70 percent in less than a decade (1928-1937), and, by the early 1970s, it already went beyond 80 percent. "No other economy has remotely matched the Soviet labor influx rate at comparable stages of development" (Cohn 1974: 252,253). Even if this astounding rate of proletarianization is due to the perceived "external danger," does it mean that this proletarianization is not the accumulation of *capital*?

Let us reiterate that as long as the Soviet total social capital along with the capital-labor relation as the basic relation of exploitation was reproducing itself at an enlarged scale, the accumulation of capital was taking place in the Soviet economy (by definition), whatever might have been the specific motive or "imperative" behind this "hypertrophied thirst for accumulation" (Fal'tsman 1992: 17).[15] In fact, the regime could manage the accumulation of capital so well that an estimated "four-fifths of the productive potential of industry served the needs of production [*obsluzhivaet nuzhdy proizvodstva*]" leaving the rest for directly satisfying people's needs (Pervushin 1991: 4).[16] Is this not precisely accumulation for the sake of accumulation, facilitated by the juridical elimination of private property in the means of production?

Naturally, given this accumulation momentum, it is not surprising that in the Soviet economy, not less than in any (other) capitalist economy, the accumulation process "operated under all circumstances and regardless of the external environment" (Sweezy, 1985), particularly when we know that the Soviet economy was following the extensive path of accumulation. Liberated from their earlier constraints, the Soviet economists themselves, toward the end of the regime, openly spoke of the "extravagant use of the material resources," "ecological catastrophe," and "eating away of the natural wealth" (Khanin 1988: 88; Pervushin 1991: 7; Fal'tsman, 1992: 15). The fact of absolute decline in the stocks of natural resources, continuously for almost three decades preceding the collapse of the regime (see Chapter 5), speaks volumes in this regard.

CHARACTER OF LABOR POWER

The adherents of the non-capitalist tendency deny the capitalist character of the Soviet labor (power) on two grounds: the alleged absence of a labor market, and the existence of job security with full employment.

Now, if there is no labor market, labor power is certainly not a commodity. In that case there is naturally no capital. However, the same persons according to whom there was no labor market in the USSR, hold that in that country wage existed as remuneration for labor power. Here again Mandel makes statements where it is difficult to find consistency. While speaking of the Soviet economy he says that "labor power has ceased to be a commodity" (1981: 35). On the other hand, while referring to the post-capitalist, transitional society in general -- where he, of course, includes the USSR -- he writes about the "sale of labor power against money wage" [*vente de la force de travail contre un salaire en argent*] (Mandel 1986a: 637). These two statements cannot be equivalent. Even sticking to the first statement, he speaks freely of "wage form of retribution of labor power" (1981: 36), and, as we saw earlier, he identifies this form, by inverting Marx à la Stalin, with the lingering bourgeois rights in distribution in the first phase of the Association.

When Sweezy speaks of the existence of total social capital and the state replacing the private capitalists as the owner of this totality as well as the *sole employer* of labor, this would imply that laborers are not free, and are no longer wage laborers in the Marxian sense. Now, this unfreedom of laborers is always true in relation to the capitalist class (as a whole) representing the total social capital (see Chapter 1), where the capitalist class is simply a "set of employers of labor power" (Marx 1968: 208; 1969: 30; 1973d: 401). However, in order to be wage laborers, these laborers must be free in relation to *individual* capitals such that they are free to choose their master. Otherwise we have to admit that the particular laborer is a slave who, "together with his labor power is sold once and for all to his owner," and that "he is himself a commodity but the labor power is not a commodity" (Marx 1973d: 401). In such a case in what sense can we talk of "wage labor," or "wage form of retribution of labor power?"

Labor power as a commodity exists -- hence the labor market exists -- whenever labor power is sold by the laborer to an individual employer of labor power irrespective of the particular way its price is determined, administratively or spontaneously. We have already argued in Chapter 3, the commodity character of labor power in the USSR. Labor power as a commodity in the Soviet economy, in spite of its absurd denial by the Soviet spokespersons (almost until the end) as well as by some outside Marxists (like Mandel), had been clear to the external observers of the Soviet economy for a long time. According to them, even under the Stalinist conditions in the 1930s, "the labor market was free (with the exception of forced labor), and managers raided each other for bidding up wages. True, wages were set by the state; but these scales presented no obstacles to wage inflation because of the widespread upgrading and other devices" (Holzman 1962: 176). The insight concerning the reality of the market for labor power in the (European) Soviet type economies -- certainly applicable to the Soviet economy as well -- we also find among the non-Soviet economists belonging to those societies during the epoch of "real socialism." Some Hungarian economists of the time first of all questioned the very premise of the noncapitalist argument -- qualifying it as "liberal," namely, that the "self-regulated market is the only form of market" instead of being (historically) only a specific form of market. Then they pointed out that under [what they called] socialism, the "laborer enters into a contract not with the state but with the *enterprise* . . . [which] can compete for labor [with other enterprises] even if the central regulation is very rigid, inasmuch as it is only the basic wage which can be determined by the planner . . . . Wage formation is the consequence of wage bargaining between the workers and the enterprise management" (Galasi and Sik 1982: 1089, 1090,1093, 1094; italics in original). As we saw earlier, an indicator of the freedom of the Soviet laborers to sell labor power was the fairly high rate of job changes by laborers. As A. Aganbegyan wrote, "Every worker in the USSR can leave his job at two weeks' notice. He then has the *unrestricted right to compete* for other jobs." (1989: 46; italics added).

It should also be noted that this change of jobs was effected mostly through what the Soviet economists called "hiring by the (individual) enterprises themselves" [*priem samimi predpriyatiami*]; the rate of this hiring in relation to the total job placement was nearly 80 percent in 1980. Secondly, such change of jobs was not at all favored by the authorities who considered it as a weakening of labor discipline, and emphasized the "necessity of *decisive struggle* for reducing personnel turnover" (Kotliar 1984: 53,54; italics added). Thus the reality of the Soviet economy not only showed the commodity character of labor power but also conformed to the Marxian concept of total social capital being a set of employers of labor power, rather than to the image of the Soviet state being the single employer of the Soviet labor -- even though total social capital had a single juridical owner.[17]

An essential argument to prove the post-capitalist character of the Soviet economy is that, unlike capitalism, this economy provided job rights and full employment to the laborers. Let us, first, take the Soviet definition of full-employment (as summarized by an American sovietologist) It is a situation where there is a job for everybody who wants it, where labor is allocated rationally across the economy, and where it is efficiently utilized at the work place (Bornstein 1978: 35). It should be clear that the Soviet economy did not fulfill these conditions. First of all, even job rights could not prevent admitted existence of unemployment at a non-negligible level in the Soviet Union's eastern republics. For example, at the end of the 1970s, it was estimated that between a quarter and a fifth of the working age population was unemployed in Azerbaidzhan and Armenia, and that in Tadzhikistan the percentage of working age people without a job was two and a half times the national average.[18] For the economy as a whole there was no full employment; there was, particularly beginning with the 1970s, labor shortage accompanied by unutilized or hoarded labor at the level of the production unit (Manevich, 1985a: 59-60). If full employment of labor would signify at least a balance of the demand for labor with the existing labor resources, that balance was never attained in the USSR, where the failure to reach full employment was seen in the "*opposite feature* [*protivopolozhnaya cherta*] -- a systematic shortage of labor power" (Manevich 1985b: 21; italics added). On the other hand, this overall macroeconomic over-full employment went hand in hand with inefficient utilization of labor power in the economy. Within the production units, fulfilling the plan at any cost, coupled with low labor productivity, resulted in surplus or hoarded labor, a kind of disguised unemployment where laborers' earnings would really amount to unemployment benefits.

It is, indeed, odd that job security and full employment of the *hired wage laborers* should be qualified as non-capitalist, if not socialist, by Marxists (For Marx post-capitalist labor cannot be hired (wage) labor, it can only be associated labor). This would imply that in wartime capitalism, with (over) full employment of wage labor, there is an interruption in the process of extraction of surplus value, and that, to that extent, capital ceases to exist (at least for the war period). And not only in wartime capitalism. In peacetime (national) "socialist" Germany, based on juridical private ownership in the means of production, there was over-full employment of labor beginning with 1937-1938, and labor being "a scarce commodity" (as in the USSR), "competition for workers led to firms making wage offers which ran counter to the basic Nazi economic policy" (Grunberger 1983: 245).

From the elementary truth (emphasized by Marx in different places) that it is the means of production that employ *wage labor* (by definition), it follows that the level of employment of such labor is determined by the needs of capital accumulation, the latter being the "independent variable." Marx shows that in capitalism there could be phases of capital accumulation when the needs of accumulation would exceed the existing labor supply, which obviously would mean more than full employment. This would be particularly true in a situation of extensive accumulation, as was indeed the case in *capitalist* England in the whole of the first half of the eighteenth century and over a longer period earlier (Marx 1962a: 641). On the other hand, high unemployment of labor continued in the USSR for more than a decade after October 1917 -- with all the commanding heights of the economy in the Party-State hands -- in spite of the famous right to work guarantee to all able bodied citizens by the RSFSR (Russian Soviet Federated Socialist Republic) "Labor Codex" (1918).[19]

It is interesting to observe that full and over-full employment was reached in the Soviet economy only after the "bureaucracy" had consolidated its power. Thus full-employment was finally realized (and carried to the hilt) precisely under a power that had otherwise distanced itself increasingly from the revolutionary heritage of 1917 according to many on the left. In the same way full employment was realized in peacetime Nazi Germany and not under a superior bourgeois democracy in peacetime Germany. This only shows that employment responded to the needs of extended reproduction of capital.

Following our discussion in Chapter 4 above, it could be said that the Soviet economy's labor shortage -- inappropriately called (post-capitalist) full employment -- was basically the result of following, at an extraordinary rate, a specific type of accumulation of capital with insufficient metamorphosis of the method(s) of production. "Full employment [was] not the automatically guaranteed attribute" of the Soviet economy, as was emphasized by a Soviet economist, according to whom it "[was] maintained to a significant extent by the extensive tendency of economic growth" (Mikul'skii 1989: 54). It was the "serious defects in the Soviet economic mechanism (itself) which impeded technical progress, the introduction of new technology," that contributed to the "shortage of labor resources" (Manevich 1985b: 22, 26). J. Kornai has summed up very well the rationale of full employment in the so-called Soviet type societies (of Europe):

One cannot say that this is simply the result of a wise employment policy. It is rooted much deeper . . . . If you have expansion-drive, investment hunger and quantity signals reporting the scarcity of capital and abundance of labor, and if you have the usual European type of demographic circumstances . . . you get, as a consequence, the absorption of labor reserves (1981: 967).[20]

That the Soviet job situation was really not a case of full employment (because of job rights), but a case of labor shortage for the economy as a whole -- a rather unwholesome phenomenon -- is seen clearly in the regime's persistent efforts to recruit workers from outside the range of the working age population, that is, pensioners, students, holders of more than one job, and individuals working at home. According to some estimates, in the middle 1980s, such supplementary labor resources supplied (at an annual average) about 14 percent of the total employment in RSFSR's so-called socialized sector where the overwhelming majority was constituted by the pensioners who were offered special inducements to continue working instead of really retiring (Rapawy 1987: 190, 192).

In a remarkably self-critical piece, the doyen of Russia's labor economics has underlined that

The state ownership was neither public nor socialist. Surplus labor and the corresponding surplus value belonged not at all either to the people or to those who generated them. Profit was appropriated by the state, . . . the directors (administrators) of the enterprises hired labor power in the name of the state. *Wage*, in these conditions, was, *as in any capitalist society*, the transformed *form of the value of labor power as a commodity* [*prevrashchennoi formoi stoimosti tovara rabochaya sila*] (Manevich 1991: 139; italics added).[21]

A MORE ADVANCED ECONOMY?

Considering the Soviet economy as an economy that came after capitalism, the adherents of the non-capitalist tendency have viewed it as a superior type of economy compared to the capitalist economy, and have mentioned a number of its positive elements allegedly absent from capitalism, along side the latter's negative elements supposed to be absent from this post-capitalist economy.

In the sense given above, the positives mainly are (a) planned economy, (b) full employment and social benefits, and (c) higher rates of growth (compared to capitalism); while the negatives (supposed to be absent) mainly are: (a) crisis of overproduction, including cyclical fluctuation, and (b) inflation. After our analysis of the Soviet economy in Chapters 3, 4, and 5, our discussion can be brief here. Considering their interrelation, we shall take account of some of these features together.

To what extent could one say that the Soviet economy was a planned economy? E. Zaleski, on the basis of his thorough study of all the available documents concerning planning during the most classical, that is, Stalinist period of this "post-capitalist" economy, showed that the different plans of this period were mutually inconsistent, and that, in general, there was no conformity of the plans' results with their objectives. After remarking that our perception of Soviet (Stalinist) planning was "too much influenced by our observation of plans in the market economies," he concluded that "in the face of the moving and ephemeral character of the [Stalinist] plans the power of administration is the sole reality that emerges. The pre-eminence of the power of administration over that of planning is the dominant trait of the Stalinist Soviet economy." Thus he preferred to call this economy a "centrally administered economy" [*économie centralement gérée*] rather than a "planned economy" (Zaleski 1984: 616).[22] In general, the claim of the conformity of the Soviet plans (Laibman 1992) is refuted by the Soviet data which show that as regards the growth rates of the key economic indicators, namely, national income, gross industrial and agricultural output, labor productivity in industry, agriculture and construction, per capita real income, and retail trade, the mean deviation of the actual from the planned growth rates as percentages of planned growth had been in the range of an average of 14-56 over the planning period (Shmelev and Popov 1989: 95,98-99).

Just as the Soviet economy could not really be characterized as a planned economy, in the same way that economy was not at all free from periodic fluctuations. First, for the period 1928-1940, Zaleski found that "a fluctuating movement of varying amplitude" applied to the series he studied, namely, industrial production, agricultural production and grain harvests, employment and real wages in industry, and railroad freight traffic (1962: 258,262-63,265). Speaking of the same period, a well-known German historian noted the "spasmodic and unequal development of (Soviet) industrial production which largely was similar to the cyclical development of capitalism" (Lorenz 1976: 235-36). Similarly, a distinguished student of comparative economic systems, on the basis of his research for the period 1950-1979/80 concluded that patterns of aggregate growth of GDP as well as the growth of the major sectors of the economy did not differ significantly as between the OECD countries and those of Eastern Europe (including the USSR), that there was not much difference between the two systems as regards the "retardation of aggregate growth of GDP," and that "*fluctuations* of aggregate production *in east and west appear quite similar* (excepting perhaps agriculture)" (Pryor 1985: 205; italics added). Even when we include cyclical fluctuations within (economic) fluctuations, they too do not seem to have failed the Soviet "post-capitalist" economy. Thus, regarding what he called the capitalist and the socialist systems, the well-known Hungarian Marxist economist A. Brody wrote: "In both systems the *same pattern of cycles* in time series of production and investment is found. Just by looking at the graphs traced by respective economies there is no way of making a distinction between market and plan-control" (1983: 431; italics added). Finally, in one of the best recent accounts of the Soviet cyclical process we read: "The stability of cycles, affecting investment, employment, consumption and productivity (of labor) has been regular since the end of the war" (Sapir 1989: 217).[23] As regards the much-proclaimed full employment in the Soviet economy, we saw in the last section that, even according to the definition of the term given by the Soviet economists themselves, there was no full employment in the system and that, on the contrary, macroeconomic *labor shortage* was combined with the most inefficient use of labor power -- a consequence, basically, of the regime's inability to revolutionize its methods of production. In the same way, the extension and quality of social benefits of the Soviet people appear to have been exaggerated. In our analysis of the Soviet accumulation process, we saw earlier how people's needs only served as a constraint to the hypertrophied thirst for accumulation, and how the allocation of resources to the social sphere followed the so-called remainder principle, with the result that the living conditions of the population including consumption, housing and health gradually deteriorated. We mentioned earlier that in view of the absolute decline in per capita national wealth during three decades preceding the regime's collapse the Soviet economists talked about the "absolute impoverishment of the Soviet people." As regards the services the regime bestowed on the Soviet people, we simply recall here Aganbegyan's placing of the USSR, in this regard, among the last of the top fifty countries of the world. A. Sakharov wrote that "the much acclaimed free medical care [getting] steadily worse . . . is 'free' because wages of most workers are kept so low and because one must pay for expensive medicines" (Sakharov 1982: 234).

Now, coming to the negatives (from capitalism) -- supposed to be absent from the post-capitalist economy -- it is of course true that there was no overproduction crisis here, simply because this economy was incapable of achieving it. The elementary point, which should be clear to any student of Marx, is that the crisis of overproduction is uniquely associated with the so-called intensive accumulation of capital under which there is "continuous revolutionization of the method of production," as Marx would say. It does not occur under the second type of accumulation of capital -- the so-called extensive type -- where, by and large, this technical metamorphosis is not the rule. For a long time capitalism existed without the crisis of overproduction and the reserve army of labor. In fact Marx points out that the overproduction crisis, necessarily associated with the reserve army of labor, did not exist at an epoch when "technical progress was slow and progress of capital accumulation was constrained by the natural limits of the exploitable laboring population which only the state power could remove" (1962a: 661-62; 1965: 1148). The Soviet economy, with its "non-susceptibility to technical progress" (in the opinion of the Soviet economists themselves), naturally could not experience a crisis of overproduction. Its specific crisis corresponding to its specific path of accumulation (and over-accumulation) of capital was a crisis precisely of under-production -- a generalized "economy of shortage."[24]

As to inflation, its "absence" (like the "absence" of crisis in general) in the Soviet economy was another carefully nurtured myth. Though inflation was considered "incompatible with the nature of socialism" and there was a taboo on the very use of the term, "even centralized price fixing [did] not prevent it" (Khandruev 1991: 35; Aganbegyan 1989: 49). Inflation existed for most of the planning period, the decade of the 1950s being, in fact, the only period when there was a deflationary process (Khandruev 1991: 36). There was rampant inflation in the 1930s. "The focal point of inflation was the labor market in which excess demand for workers found full and free expression in rising wage rates as managers competed vigorously for their services" to fulfill the unreachable plan targets (Holzman 1962: 173,187). Rising wages and reducing enterprise profit margins led to pressure for higher wholesale prices which added to production costs and the "wholesale prices began to spiral upward in typical inflationary fashion" (Berliner 1988: 227).[25] Indeed, the authorities tried to exercise price control in regard to the wholesale prices of industrial commodities. Prices were allowed to rise at different rates. Some enterprises were allowed to raise prices to generate the normal rate of profit while the prices of others were kept constant or allowed to rise at a slower rate such that the enterprises of the latter type were paid subsidies from the state budget to fill the cost-price gap (Berliner 1988: 227). Chapter 3 showed that this differential pricing was an ingenious way of the Soviet planners to realize the maximum surplus value from the Soviet immediate producers.[26]

Inflation for most of the post-war period had been basically of the hidden and suppressed type. Hidden inflation mainly took place through the constant process of cheaper goods "melting away" to be replaced by more expensive goods. This type of inflation was estimated to be annually 3-4 percent on an average (Aganbegyan 1989: 229). Given the official price control, the dominant type of inflation in the USSR was, however, the suppressed inflation manifesting itself in rationing, queues, systematic shortages of goods, and forced saving. Needless to add, one would have no idea of any inflationary pressure from the official price statistics. Thus for the period 1960-1970, while the officially reported annual average rate of inflation was 0.1 percent, one Western estimate put it at 8.6 percent (compared to about 4 percent in some Western European countries) (Culbertson and Amachar 1978: 393). Again, for 1981-1985, while one gets 1.6 percent rise on an average for the consumer goods from the official statistics, the Soviet statisticians themselves came up with a figure of about 6 percent (including the suppressed part), the corresponding figures for 1986-1988 being, respectively, 3.4 percent and 7 percent.[27] A telling example of the reality of inflation in the "planned", "post-capitalist" Soviet economy was the way in which, by systematically underestimating price rises, fantastic claims were made about the growth of the economy over the planning period. Shortly before the collapse of the regime, the Soviet economists themselves blew the cover and showed that the true increase in the Soviet national income over the period 1929-1987 was overstated in the official estimate by a factor of almost 13, that is, instead of claimed 89.5 times, the increase was in fact only 6.9 times (Seliunin and Khanin 1987; Khanin 1988).

A definite indication of suppressed inflation via forced saving was the dramatic growth in the savings bank deposits of the Soviet population. Between 1950 and 1960 these deposits increased annually (on average) by 905 million rubles, in the next decade it rose by 3, 569 million annually, and between 1970 and 1980, the corresponding figure was 10,990 million rubles. In the last decade of the regime the figure was 22,420 million rubles (*Narkhoz*, various years; *Ekonomika SSSR* 1990: 10). The basic reason for the accumulation of free money lies in the scarcity of goods, not in any precautionary or speculative desire for liquidity. It was observed that the ratio of the total inventories of consumer goods to the sum of savings bank deposits had been steadily decreasing. This ratio was estimated to have come down from 530 percent in 1950 to 98 percent in 1970 and to 37 percent in 1987 (Katsenelinboigen 1990: 263-64). Finally, the Soviet growth record. This does not require much discussion after what we have seen in Chapters 4 and 5 (on the basis of the very revealing latter day Soviet data). We simply recall the following: (1) the rate of growth of national income had *always* been falling excepting for the decade of the 1950s; (2) material national wealth absolutely declined over the regime's final three decades by 25 percent; (3) per capita national wealth absolutely declined by 1.8 times over the same period, leading to the absolute impoverishment of the population; (4) per capita national income absolutely declined by 12 percent over the final decade, having reached a (near) zero rate of growth toward the end of the 1970s. In view of the fact that the CIA growth indices of the Soviet economy -- until recently denounced as belittling socialist achievement -- have proved to be generous compared to the latter day data of the Soviet economists themselves, it is superfluous to go into the question of comparative growth rates of the USSR and the "capitalist" countries. Let us simply note that on Western estimates there were about half a dozen capitalist countries whose rates of growth of GDP were superior to the corresponding Soviet rate during 1950-1979 (Pryor 1985: 209-10).[28]

NOTES

1. It is not without significance that, in the same chapter we are referring to, the term "owner" [*Eigentümer*] is used equivalently with "holder" [*Hüter*] and "possessor" [*Besitzer*], where owner is used only a couple of times and possessor is used innumerable times. Significantly, again, the French version uses often "*échangiste*." In the standard Moore-

Aveling English translation, owner is used almost all the time, even invariably being the rendering of *"Besitzer"* which, of course, is not strictly correct.

2. Marx observes that with the development of big industries "product ceases to be the product of individual, immediate labour; it is the social activity's *combination* that appears as the producer," and then cites the English economist Hodgskin: "There is nothing on which the laborer can seize: this is my produce, this I will keep to myself." (Marx 1953: 596-97; italics in original). See also Marx (1962a: 354).

3. It should be observed that Marx's reference to "private labor" as the unique basis for transforming useful objects into commodities is precisely set in a context where he explicitly opposes this private labor as indirectly social labor not to any public (state) ownership of the means of production but to the "immediately social relations among individuals in their labor itself" (1962a: 87).

4. For a good account of the post-Stalin Soviet views on the whole question, see Lavigne (1960).

5. In his illuminating work on nineteenth century capitalist development of the then backward European countries, A. Gerschenkron found features most of which reappeared in the Soviet accumulation process, such as greater stress on producers' goods as against consumers' goods, bigness of plant and enterprises in industry, pressure on people's level of consumption, major role of coerciveness, and comprehensiveness of institutional factors for increasing the supply of capital, discontinuity, and great spurt in the industrial process with a high rate of growth of manufacturing output (Gerschenkron 1966a: 353-54). Another backward country with a perceived military threat from outside but under no public ownership of the means of production, was Japan which also demonstrated capitalist development not exactly following the path of spontaneous market process. As a distinguished student of Japanese history pointed out, because of the country's "concern with strategic industries a *normal order* of the starting point and the succeeding stages of capitalist production was *reversed.*" From the first, the "strategic military industries" were favored by the government, and "technologically they were soon on a level with most advanced Western countries," while industries "without strategic value" were "left in their primitive stage of development" (Norman 1975: 232-33; italics added). Obviously (individual) profitability did not count in this choice.

6. "The central control of the country's resources," writes an American sovietologist, "was a particularly effective way of building up not only the Soviet Union's heavy industry but a powerful military force as well. Indeed the Soviet Union was able to commandeer resources for the military much more effectively than could any market economy" (Goldman 1987: 9-10).

7. A leading American sovietologist, M. Bornstein, in his editorial note on Eucken's paper, remarked that "almost all his analysis applies as well to centrally planned socialist economies" (Eucken 1969: 128).

8. Referring to the post-1936 Germany, Eucken speaks of the struggle between the "control offices" for factors of production, and particularly for labor supplies, and adds: "Each control would be using every means it could to procure factors of production or labor supplies. This collision between sectional controls was a characteristic of the centrally administered economy. A sort of group anarchy seemed to be inherent in the system." (1969: 145).

9. C. Bettelheim is one of the few within the capitalist tendency to have correctly affirmed the existence of competition of capitals in the Soviet economy (Bettelheim 1983: 295-301; 1985b: 45-47). In this connection, he rightly denies the absence of all autonomy of the Soviet enterprises in relation to the centre. However, in our opinion, for competition of capitals to exist the enterprise's relation to the centre is much less important than its relation to another enterprise. If this relation is *reciprocally* autonomous, as manifested in the exchange of the products of wage labor in *value form*, then the necessary and sufficient conditions for competition of capitals exist (in the sense of Marx) independently of the question of single/multiple ownership.

10. Regarding Plato's deduction of "many" from "one," Hegel observes that "this truth of one and many" has to be "grasped as 'becoming,' as a process, as repulsion and attraction, not as 'being,'. . . not as 'one' at rest [*als ruhige Einheit*]" (1963a: 163).

11. Sweezy says that the "new ruling class...derives its power and privileges not from the ownership and/or control of capital but from the unmediated control of the state" (1980: 9). Considering that total social capital continues to exist, but now under the state ownership replacing the private ownership, one might be permitted to ask, paraphrasing what Marx said about the antiquity (supposed to be dominated by politics): on what did this ruling class live (and reproduce itself)? See Marx (1962a: 96).

12. It is curious to note that, to emphasize the capitalist countries' "accumulation imperative," Sweezy cites Marx's famous sentence, "Accumulate, accumulate! That is Moses and the Prophets," precisely the same as that which A. Gerschenkron cited to underline the Soviet regime's superiority in the level and speed of accumulation (of capital) compared to these capitalist countries.

13. See the analysis in Kornai (1992: 160-61).

14. E. Mandel's attempted explanation of the Soviet over-accumulation process as turning, for its major part at least, on the consumption goods of the bureaucrats, we may be excused for saying, is so superficial as to border on the ridiculous (Mandel 1990: 56-57). Indeed, in the analysis of the accumulation process of what Mandel calls post-capitalist societies, a non-Marxist like J. Kornai appears to be infinitely superior to a Marxist like Mandel.

15. Let us note that there is no unambiguous answer among the economists to the problem of motivation behind accumulation even in Western capitalism. In fact, a distinguished body of economists (Marris 1964; Baumol 1967; Galbraith 1978), observing the working of the modern industrial corporations -- where, precisely, under directly social capital, the separation between capital's juridical existence and economic existence has been carried to great lengths -- has concluded that it is no longer the (individual) profit maximization motive, as usually understood, that impels the accumulation of capital. The corporate directors, the "salaried functionaries of capital" (as Marx would call them), but not necessarily capital's individual owners, appear to be motivated in their business behavior rather by the growth of the corporation itself, which, based on workers' ongoing separation from the conditions of production, is, of course, identical with the enlarged reproduction of capital.

16. In the same article, Pervushin cites Gorbachev to the effect that in his country only 6 to 8 percent of capital worked to produce consumer goods (1991: 4).

17. Cf. "Support of the appropriateness of the labor market notion in application to the Soviet Union's practice stems primarily from two well-documented phenomena: (1) the high rate at which individual workers leave state enterprises through quitting, (2) the low production of job vacancies that are filled through any form of planned hiring" (Granick 1987: 12).

18. The French sovietologist F. Seurot cites these estimates from different (including the Soviet official) sources (1989: 248).

19. At a later period, other "post-capitalist" countries like China and Viet Nam also showed the coexistence of right to work and considerable unemployment of labor. Thus the "abolition of private property" in the means of production is neither necessary nor sufficient for ensuring "full employment" of wage labor, contrary to Mandel's claim (1990: 58).

20. In his immensely insightful work on the laws of motion of the Soviet type economies (in Europe), Kornai did not originally include the Soviet economy explicitly. However, the Soviet economists themselves underlined the work's relevance for their economy (Karagedov 1987; Aganbegyan 1988: 197). Later Kornai himself included explicitly the Soviet economy in his analytical framework (1992).

21. In her highly interesting recent work on the Soviet employment planning, the Italian sovietologist S. Malle cites Aganbegyan to the effect that in the Soviet approach "workers [were] considered as a factor of production in the same way as equipment, energy and raw materials," and she adds, "Soviet history and practice show that the output approach in economic planning, of which *employment is a subsidiary element*, has always prevailed. This has meant that output growth is *not designed to bring about full employment*, but eventually faces a constraint in the amount of available labor" (1990: 17, 289; italics added).

22. We may note in passing that this is exactly the appellation [*Zentral-verwaltungswirtschaft*] used for the "national socialist" German economy earlier by W. Eucken whom we cited before.

23. Cf. "In a totalitarian-capitalist economy such as pre-war German economy, it was widely proclaimed that cycles were eliminated" (Zaleski 1962: 270). On the whole question of economic cycles in the East European "post-capitalist" economies, see the interesting work by B. Dallago (1982).

24. Zaleski wondered why a slow-down of growth under the Tsarist regime due to lack of effective demand without, however, affecting the level of real wages, was called a "crisis," "yet a slow-down (in the USSR in the 1930's) resulting from excess demand triggered by government investment and reducing the living standard of the population to the barest necessities is not considered a 'crisis'" (1962: 278).

25. Between 1928 and 1940 wage rates rose six times, consumer goods prices in state sector twelve times, those in collective farm markets twenty times, and prices of basic industrial goods two and a half times (Holzman 1962: 172-73). The price behavior of wholesale prices, referred to above, it should be noted, contradicts Stalin-Mandel thesis of partial commodity production (confined to consumer products) as well as the widely accepted idea of the dichotomy between "passive" and "active" money in the Soviet economy.

26. Referring to the *price control*, one of the proponents of the passive money thesis posed the significant question: "If prices in the state sector perform almost entirely 'passive' functions, as is often stated, why should the avoidance of open inflation in this sector be of such importance to the authorities?" Then he almost grudgingly added that "wholesale prices are passive, but not altogether so. . . . Price changes have both allocative and distributive effects" (Grossman 1977: 132-33; italics in original).

27. The figures, estimated by A. Shmarov and N. Kirichenko, are cited by Hanson (1992: 179). On the question of inflation and monetary disequilibrium in the last decade of the Soviet regime, see Ellman (1992).

28. Given the Soviet economists' own established data, Mandel's claim -- absolutely unsubstantiated -- that the growth of the Soviet economy since 1928 "really was regular and uninterrupted," that "for more than sixty years there was no absolute fall in production," and that the rate of growth began to fall only "20 years ago" (1990: 50), is really strange.

Chapter 8

FROM NON-PROLETARIAN REGIME TO NON-RESTORATION OF CAPITALISM

With the analysis of the Marxian category of capital as a point of departure, we have, in course of the earlier chapters in the book, argued the capitalist character of the Soviet economy viewed both statically and dynamically. We thus conclude that the disintegration of the Soviet economy signifies the collapse of a specific mode of capital accumulation "carried beyond its historic justification," in Lange's previously cited phrase, bringing down with it the corresponding regime itself. It follows that logically there could be no restoration of capitalism on the ruins of the Soviet economy. It is only by a process of singular inversion of categories that one could equate this breakdown with the end of socialism, as conceived by Marx, and the triumph of capitalism. On the contrary, we would hold -- however paradoxical that might appear -- that the Soviet case, on the whole, validates Marx.

The present chapter is divided into two sections. The first questions the *idée fixe* on the left that the Bolshevik seizure of power in 1917 constituted, or at least inaugurated, a socialist revolution in Russia. The second section deals with the question of meaningfulness of the idea of restoration of capitalism in the Soviet Union.

A NON-PROLETARIAN REGIME

The contention here is that the regime issued from the Bolshevik seizure of power in 1917 was not a proletarian regime and that, in general, the seizure of power did not inaugurate a *socialist* revolution in Russia (in the sense of Marx). Indeed, a socialist revolution -- which the Bolsheviks thought was embodied in the act of seizure of power in October, 1917 -- is very differently conceived by Marx and Lenin as regards both the instrument of the revolution and the content of the revolution.

For Marx, the instrument of the socialist revolution is "the working class constituting itself into a political party" (*General Council* 1964b: 445), while for Lenin it is a group of professional revolutionaries, a self-appointed vanguard, completely outside the control of the laboring masses, bringing revolutionary consciousness to the working class from outside and guiding it in the struggle for socialism. Here we find it useful to examine an argument advanced in this connection by the eminent historian E.H. Carr. Carr discerned a difference between the "earlier Marx" of the Communist League and the "mature Marx" of the First International, and held that Lenin, in this respect, was "a disciple of the earlier rather than of the later Marx." Carr was here referring to Lenin's doctrine of the party "as a repository of revolutionary theory and revolutionary consciousness leading and guiding" the workers (Carr 1964: 19). Carr's contention, we submit, is based on rather a superficial reading of Marx's texts.

It is of course true that the Leninist position of a vanguard party bringing revolutionary consciousness to the proletariat from outside and guiding it -- given the proletariat's supposed incapacity to go beyond "trade union consciousness" -- is the exact opposite of the principle enshrined in the opening lines of the First International's "Provisional Rules," drafted by Marx: "The emancipation of the working classes must be conquered by the working classes themselves" (*General Council* 1964a: 288).[1] Does this late Marxian position contradict the early Marxian position on the question under consideration? According to the *Communist Manifesto* -- commissioned by the Communist League -- the communists, far from being a party formed outside the working class (and beyond its control), are "a part of the working class parties of all countries," and only as such are their "most driving and resolute part." At the same time, "the communists have no special principles after which they like to model the proletarian movement" (Marx 1966b: 70). On the other hand, Marx had emphasized the self-liberating role of the proletariat even earlier. "The proletariat can and must liberate itself," and it is "from this class [itself] that the communist consciousness, the consciousness of the necessity for a profound revolution arises," he had stressed a few years earlier (1972a: 38; 1973b: 69). It is clear that what Marx expresses here is perfectly in line with his thinking twenty years later.[2] It is also clear that there is an unbridgeable gulf between Marx's concept of the party of the working class corresponding exactly to the task of workers' self-liberation and Lenin's concept of the revolutionary vanguard corresponding to the workers' guided liberation.[3]

We now come to the issue of the socialist revolution itself. It is for the first time in April, 1917, upon his arrival in Petrograd from exile, that Lenin called for a socialist revolution in Russia. In support of his call, Lenin advanced the argument that "the state power in Russia has passed into the hands of a new class, namely, the bourgeoisie and the landlords turned bourgeois. *To this extent* the bourgeois democratic revolution in Russia is completed" (1982b: 19; italics in original). Lenin and the other Bolsheviks following him always claimed that the October seizure of power had inaugurated a socialist revolution in Russia, and that the state, resulting from that act, embodied the dictatorship of the proletariat. Now, what they called socialist revolution, had occurred -- it was clear to the Bolsheviks -- in circumstances which apparently differed from the circumstances under which Marx had thought it would occur. The Bolsheviks argued that this could happen in Russia precisely because it was a backward capitalist country where European capitalism was at its weakest -- a situation resulting from the uneven development of capitalism accelerated by imperialism, not quite foreseen by Marx (and Engels) writing in the pre-imperialist stage of capitalism. Two years before the seizure of power, Lenin had emphasized that "uneven economic and political development is an unconditional law of capitalism" and that, consequently, the "victory of socialism" could be possible "in several or even in one capitalist country taken separately" (1982a: 636). Shortly after the seizure of power he observed that it was easier for "the [socialist] movement to start" in a backward capitalist country like Russia, and that "things had worked differently from what Marx and Engels had expected" (1982b: 509,510).

To paraphrase Keynes's famous statement about Ricardo, Lenin conquered not only the subsequent (Marxist) revolutionary movement, but also many scholars, almost as completely as the Inquisition had conquered Spain. Among the scholars we refer to three outstanding cases. According to E.H. Carr, "Marxist scheme of revolution was bound to break down when the proletarian revolution occurred in the most backward capitalist country," which thus showed "an error of prognostication in the original Marxist scheme" (1964: 43-44). Carr is here joined by I. Deutscher who opined that "it was the Russian Marxists, and not Marx and Engels whom [the events in Russia] proved to be right" (1960: 184). Recently, P. Sweezy expressed the same idea: "The revolutions that put socialism on history's agenda took place not in economically developed countries, as Marx and Engels thought they would, but in countries where capitalism was still in early stages" (1993: 6). Thus these scholars seem to accept the Leninist argument axiomatically.

As a thoroughgoing materialist, Marx, it is well-known, did not leave any blueprint for the future society. In the same way, it goes without saying, there is no unique model of socialist revolution in Marx's writings -- the "German model" as Lenin would say in his polemic with the Mensheviks. There could, indeed, be innumerable kinds of situations with corresponding correlations of social forces in which a socialist revolution would break out and proceed. However, even allowing for the very specific situation of Russia in October, 1917, the statements cited above could be taken to be true only if it could be shown that the October events really amounted to the inauguration of a proletarian or socialist revolution, *content-wise*, in the sense of Marx. Only such a demonstration could invalidate the original Marxian "prognostication." Now, by a social revolution (in general) Marx means, as he emphasizes in one of his early polemics, the "dissolution of [society's] old relations." (1976b; 418), or equivalently, as he says fifteen years later, a change in society's "economic basis" constituted by the "relations of production" (1958: 13). An immediate consequence of this conception is that a social revolution is not a momentary event coinciding with the seizure of power. It is *epochal*. Particularly for the proletariat, the "epoch of social revolution begins" -- in the famous phrase of Marx's 1859 "Preface" -- with the installation of the proletariat as the ruling class on the ruins of the old state machinery, it being only the "first step in the workers' revolution," as the *Communist Manifesto* declares. This proletarian rule, whose necessary point of departure is workers' self-emancipation as a postulate, continues to exist throughout the "revolutionary transformation period," preparing the proletariat for its self-elimination, until the inauguration of the first phase of the Association.

We saw above that Lenin justified his call for a socialist revolution in 1917 mainly on the basis of the assumption of state power by the Russian bourgeoisie, signifying, according to him, the completion of the bourgeois democratic revolution -- at least to the extent sufficient for a socialist revolution to occur. We would, on the other hand, suggest that, to the extent that Lenin predicated the *completion* of the bourgeois democratic revolution (sufficient for a socialist revolution to take place) simply on the passage to political power of the bourgeoisie, Lenin was *revising* the concept of social revolution in Marx inasmuch as a social revolution in Marx means nothing less than a transformation of the social relations of production, and not simply a change in the political "edifice," to use Marx's term of 1859. If the "bourgeois democratic content of the revolution signifies purifying the country's social relations from medievalism, serfdom, feudalism," as Lenin said correctly in a later pronouncement (1982c: 589), then the passing of political power into bourgeois hands in February (1917) did certainly not "complete the bourgeois democratic revolution" -- at least to the extent sufficient for a socialist revolution to break out -- inasmuch as "the landlord-tenure system was *not* destroyed before October" (Lenin 1982c: 62; italics in original). In this sense the material premise of a socialist revolution, in the sense of Marx, was lacking in its Leninist configuration.

On the other hand, the seizure of political power in October (1917) could not be strictly called a proletarian conquest of power even when we ignore the historians' debate on the extent of the eventual proletarian participation in this seizure. As is well known, it was not the proletariat or their authentic representatives in the soviets and the factory committees that democratically took the decision and the initiative of seizing power. It was the Bolshevik central committee which had taken the vital decision to seize power (Carr 1964: 193).[4]

Seizing the power independently of the soviets, the Bolshevik leadership placed the second Congress of the Soviets before *a fait accompli*. Similarly, the existing Provisional Government was dismissed not by the Congress of Soviets, not even by the Petrograd Soviets, but by the latter's so-called Military Revolutionary Committee which was "exclusively under the Bolsheviks excepting for a single Socialist Revolutionary" (Carr 1964: 95). This singular operation "deprived simultaneously the Congress of Soviets and the Petrograd Soviet of all right to paternity regarding the founding act of the new order, and in fact deprived them of any claim to legitimacy" (Ferro 1980: 182). An undisputed authority on the history of the soviets has observed:

The October revolution was prepared and accomplished by the Bolsheviks under the slogan of "all power to the soviets." However, an examination of the historical reality shows that only a fraction of the workers', soldiers' and peasants' deputies themselves wanted the seizure of power. The majority of the soviets and the masses represented by them of course greeted the fall of the Provisional Government, but refused to have a Bolshevik hegemony (Anweiler 1958: 258-59).

Thus the Bolshevik practice of seizure of power had little to do with the Marxian principle of the "conquest of political power [as] the great duty of the *proletariat*" (*General Council* 1964b: 445; italics added). As Marx emphasized, "the working class is revolutionary or it is nothing" (1973e: 446).[5]

Sweezy has stressed that the Russian Revolution was a "genuine socialist revolution" because of the "well-established fact" that the regime that came to power was "clearly socialist in character." In support of his contention, he has argued that "the mission of life" of the "parties and their leaders . . . the seasoned Marxists, was to overthrow an unjust and exploitative system and replace it with one based on the principles of socialism as expounded by Marx and Engels" (1990: 6). What Sweezy says about the conviction and other subjective aspects of the revolutionary leaders is undoubtedly true. We submit, however, that this cannot be the materialist way of judging a regime. There is no a priori reason to accept what Lenin and his companions were claiming the October seizure of power to be and the regime that emerged from it. Judgment has to be based, following Marx's well-known text of 1859, on the objective, material conditions of life under the regime. Could we say that the regime in question was, indeed, a proletarian regime in the sense of Marx, as its rulers claimed it to be, on the basis of objective criteria?[6]

Having already identified the proletarian power with the Bolshevik power Lenin asserted six months after the seizure of power: "We, the party of the Bolsheviks conquered [*otvoevali*] Russia from the rich for the poor . . . . We must now govern Russia . . . . We must now consolidate what we ourselves have decreed, legislated, charted" (1982b: 596, 620). This was natural because "till now we have not reached the stage where the laboring masses could participate in government"

(Lenin 1982c: 115).[7] Thus, as E.H. Carr notes, well before Lenin's death "central Soviet organs and local executive committees both ultimately recognized an authority *outside the soviet system*" (1964: 219; italics added). Similarly, the authority of the party over "every aspect of policy and every branch of administration" was "openly recognized and proclaimed," and it was the Bolshevik party which "gave life and direction and motive power to every form of public activity in the USSR, and whose decision was binding on every organization of a public or semi-public character" (Carr 1964: 229,230,232).[8] Needless to add, the ruling party, far from being "the working class constituting itself into a party" -- as Marx would have it -- was a self-recruiting, self-proclaimed vanguard, whose capacity to immunize itself from the working masses would be -- to offer an analogy from mathematics -- the envy of an Eratosthenes devising his famous sieve for eliminating the composite numbers. This was indeed a dictatorship over the proletariat.[9]

Before the seizure of power, Lenin, consistently with Marx's thought on the proletarian regime, had stressed the need to destroy the old state apparatus with its bureaucracy, police and the standing army and its replacement by a new type of state (itself transitory) with freely elected and revocable officials at all levels, the police and the standing army being replaced by the armed working masses à la Commune of 1871. In his different polemical writings, Lenin had, in fact, accused the "Plekhanovs and the Kautskys," as well as the "Socialist Revolutionaries and the Mensheviks," of having "forgotten and perverted" this "essence of the Paris Commune." However, the reality of the regime completely contradicted Lenin's words. Indeed, he had to admit later that the Bolsheviks "effectively took over the old state apparatus from the tsar and the bourgeoisie" (1982c: 695). Thus instead of all officers being elected and subject to recall à la Commune, the body of appointed officials, organically linked with the new central establishments and hierarchically organized from top downward -- responsible only to their superiors -- increased in gigantic strides. Similarly, there arose a special police apparatus of which the core -- the security police -- installed five weeks after the seizure of power, grew to over a quarter million by 1921 (Schapiro 1984: 186). As regards the army, with the creation of the Red Army, a first breach in the Soviet system already occurred during the first half of 1918, as Anweiler emphasizes. The principle of election of officers -- this "specific mark of one of the consequent Soviet principles" -- was abolished, the rights of soldiers' committees were clipped, and the erstwhile tsarist officers were placed in responsible positions in increasing numbers (Anweiler 1958: 287).

In its turn, industry was organized on the principle of direction from above as opposed to the principle of direct administration in the factories exercised by the elected factory committees. Lenin now discovered that "the Russian is a bad worker in comparison with the [workers of the] advanced nations" (1982b: 610). Therefore, instead of collectively administering the affairs of the work places, through their own elected organs -- a practice earlier championed by the Bolsheviks, but now denounced as "petty bourgeois spontaneity" -- the masses must show "*unquestioning obedience* to the *single will* of the leaders of the labor process," and must accept "unquestioning subordination during working time to the one-person decisions of the Soviet directors, of the Soviet dictators [*diktatorov*], elected or nominated by the Soviet institutions [and] provided with dictatorial powers [*diktatorskimi polnomochiyami*]" (Lenin 1982b: 618, 630; italics in original). Thus we find little in the state or in the economy to justify the rulers' claim that the regime in question was indeed a proletarian regime. As a distinguished American historian has remarked:

"All power to the soviets" appeared to be a reality on the 26th of October, 1917, but it was mostly power to the Bolsheviks in those soviets . . . . By July, 1918 . . . the locus of decision making . . . shifted from the soviets . . . to the communist party . . . . The whole system of soviets and executive committees was reduced to an administrative and propaganda auxiliary of the party . . . . Deprived of power in the soviets and in the factories, the Russian proletariat . . . found that the triumph of the dictatorship in its name was a very hollow victory (Daniels 1967: 223-24).

Many Marxists, while accepting the Soviet regime of the early years as proletarian, have justified the regime's extraordinary measures on the score of Russia's backwardness and the absence or failure of the anticipated revolutions in Europe. The latter two factors are of course true, and they, in conjunction with a hostile international environment, undoubtedly contributed to the adoption of the exceptional measures. However, the basic question is, who made the decisions on those measures and who enforced them. If the makers and enforcers of decisions were not the immediate producers themselves but, in their name, an autonomized and self-designated vanguard outside the latter's control, then one would be hard put to claim that those measures were undertaken by the "proletariat organized as the ruling class" to defend the "socialist revolution." Under a proletarian rule, whatever constraint and coercion remained for the proletariat would be selfinflicted, would be the work of the coerced themselves.[10] Following Lenin's assertion, if Russia's laboring masses were not yet capable of administering the state and their work places (requiring guidance from above), and if, one month after the seizure of power, "the overwhelming majority of the Russian people were yet unable to know the full extent and significance of . . . the socialist revolution starting on October 25" (1982b: 456, 458), then one has to admit that Russia's immediate producers were not yet ready for a social revolution which would usher in a society of free and associated labor,[11] and, consequently, the October seizure of power could not have inaugurated a socialist revolution in the sense of Marx.[12]

Thus, given Russia's material backwardness and the (subjective) unpreparedness of its laboring masses to emancipate themselves -- as seen in Lenin's own declarations, as well as the regime's practical measures -- we are back to Marx's profound materialist proposition: "Humanity always sets itself only those tasks which it can solve, . . . [and] the task itself arises only where the material conditions of their solution already exist or are at least in the process of coming into existence" (1958: 14).[13] If such conditions were not present then "all attempts at making the present society explode would be Quixotism" (Marx 1953: 77). What Marx said, referring to the period of the utopian socialists -- while trying to explain their failure in that context -- seems not only to sum up the general conditions of a socialist revolution but also to have considerable relevance for the Russian situation of 1917: "Neither the working classes themselves were sufficiently trained and organized by the march of capitalist society itself to enter as historical agents upon the world's stage, nor were the material conditions of their emancipation sufficiently matured in the old world itself" (1971: 165-66).[14] It seems one could invert Deutscher's statement, cited earlier, and say that it was Marx, and not the Russian Marxists, whom the Russian events ultimately proved right. It should be stressed that our refusal to accept, in retrospect, the Bolshevik seizure of power as the start of a socialist revolution in Russia is not due to the absence of a socialist society in post-October Russia. It is because, first, the seizure of power was not a self-emancipating act of the laboring masses (themselves), not their own "self-activity" [*Selbsttätigkeit*] as Marx would say, and secondly -- as a natural consequence -- the regime issued in October was not the proletariat organized as the ruling class, the very first step in a socialist revolution.

NON-RESTORATION OF CAPITALISM

There seems to be a general consensus that at present we are witnessing a return of capitalism in the ex-USSR. This of course would be the logical conclusion also for the partisans of the non-capitalist (including socialist) tendency. Just as they affirm the non-capitalist character of the Soviet economy on the basis of the non-existence of juridical private property in the means of production and the absence of the *forms* of exchange (and distribution) similar to those under contemporary Western capitalism, in the same way the so-called privatization and marketization would signify, for them, the restoration of capitalism in the ex-USSR. In both cases the great absentee from their analysis is the (social) relations of production which, moreover, most of the partisans of the noncapitalist thesis equate, if not identify, with the forms of property, thus confusing property *forms* with property *relations*.

From the standpoint of our analysis of the Soviet economy, detailed in the earlier chapters, there could be no restoration of capitalism. This would be the logical position of those who have characterized the erstwhile Soviet economy as capitalist. Now, throughout the book, the analysis has centered on the Soviet economy of the planning period, inasmuch as this was the economy, starting after the so-called reconstruction period of the 1920s, and continuing to function for most of the period without major changes, that came to be characterized as the Soviet model. Even the early Soviet regime, preceding Stalin's consolidation of power in the late 1920s, could in no way be called a proletarian regime (in the sense of Marx). The overwhelming majority on the left, representing different tendencies -- non-capitalist and capitalist -- holds that the Soviet regime of the early period was a proletarian regime and that, as such, its relations of production were basically non-capitalist. The Soviet economy remained non-capitalist for the rest of its history for all excepting those who have subscribed to the capitalist tendency. As regards the partisans of the latter tendency, there has been no consensus. For some -- like T. Cliff and R. Dunayevskaya, -- capitalism was restored under Stalin and continued to prevail for the rest of the period while for others -- mainly the Chinese communists under Mao and their international sympathizers -- capitalism returned to the USSR after Stalin. For two eminent partisans of the capitalist tendency -- A. Bordiga and C. Bettelheim -- there could be no restoration of capitalism in the Soviet economy. For Bordiga, given the dominance of pre-capitalism in Russia in the 1917, the "October revolution" was socialist only politically, it was capitalist economically. Once the pre-bourgeois property relations were destroyed, the state industry was based on wage labor and commodity production (and exchange). For Bordiga, the Stalinist counter-revolution was a political counterrevolution and only indicated the decisive victory of the capitalist base over the socialist superstructure (Bordiga 1975; Tacchinardi and Peregalli 1990). As to Bettelheim, earlier a fervent Leninist and an upholder of the thesis of state capitalism in Russia in the post-Lenin period, he has ultimately situated the beginning of Soviet capitalism right at the start of the Bolshevik rule, which, according to him, initiated a capitalist revolution by generalizing wage labor (Bettelheim 1974, 1977, 1982, 1983, 1985a).[15]

To what extent could we say that the Soviet regime, preceding the Stalinist consolidation of power, was non-capitalist and that capitalism was restored in the USSR only later? The question can be settled correctly, following Marx's method, only on the basis of a study of the relations between the immediate producers and their conditions of production, in other words, the social relations of production. What, then, was the nature of these relations in the immediate post-October period?

If the official (ideological) discourses of the period are ignored, and one observes, following Marx's method, the contradictions of material life, we have to take into consideration, on the one hand, the liquidation of the factory committees as centers of the workers' collective self-administration and, on the other, the "transformation of the soviets from organs of the proletarian self-rule and vehicles of radical democracy into organs allowing the party elite to lead the masses" (Anweiler 1958: 303). This meant, for the workers in the factories, mines, construction, and transport, separation from and subordination to the conditions of production, and, naturally, they remained wage laborers.[16] The rest of the urban immediate producers were, on the whole, self-employed simple commodity producers. On the other hand, commodity production in the countryside was greatly stimulated in the wake of the destruction of the largely pre-capitalist agrarian relations after the seizure of power. Under the so-called war communism (1918-1920/21), workers' wage labor position was coupled with the severest measures of labor discipline imposed on them by the new rulers. Compulsory labor service, labor books, forced labor camps, one-person management, Taylor system, piece wage, were all imposed on the proletariat by the Party-State in the name of the proletarian rule (Carr 1963: 198-216).[17]

On the other hand, in spite of all official attempts to suppress commodity relations, the latter continued to prevail. Nove writes about the "sleepless, leather jacketed commissars working round the clock in a vain attempt to replace the free market" (1982:74).[18] Under the New Economic Policy (NEP) (1921-1927/28), there was no basic change in the production relations. Rather, commodity production -- simple and capitalist -- now freed from many of the earlier restrictions, developed faster. "In less than a year NEP had reproduced the characteristic essentials of a capitalist economy" (Carr 1963: 323). According to the official data on class composition of Russia's total population (including nonworking dependents), workers and employees constituted about 15 percent in 1924 rising to around 18 percent in 1928, while independent commodity producers "individual farmers and non-cooperated handicrafts persons" -- constituted almost 75 per cent in 1924 and remained at about the same level in 1928 (*Narkhoz* 1987: 11). The Soviet economy under NEP was conceived as a market economy with "commanding heights" -- banking, foreign trade, large scale industry -- in the hands of the state. "The heights were governed, in their relations with the rest of the economy, by the laws of market" (Carr and Davies 1974: 665). In fact, "in the 1920s commodity money relations . . . penetrated all the pores of the economic organism and became the main link connecting its various parts" (Shmelev and Popov 1989: 13). At the same time, the industrial "trusts" -- associations of state owned enterprises -- had the legal position of juridical persons "to whom the state has accorded," by a decree of 1923, "independence in the carrying out of their operations . . . acting on the principle of commercial calculation with the aim of deriving profits," including the right to issue long-term bonds (Baykov 1970: 108,110; Shmelev and Popov 1989: 9). Beginning with 1925, the industrial managers had the "unrestricted legal right to hire and fire [workers]" (Carr and Davies 1974: 491). Thus, in the period preceding Stalin's consolidation of power, the Soviet economy was characterized by "an overwhelmingly private agriculture, legalized private trade and small-scale private manufacturing," with the "vast majority of those engaged in manufacturing and mining working for the state" (Nove 1982: 86). At the same time, unemployment continued at a high level. The percentage of the unemployed to the employed labor was 14.6 in 1924 and 13.2 in 1929,[19] and this, in spite of the right to work guarantees by the RSFSR labor codex (1918).

The development of the capitalist production relations in the USSR in the pre-Stalin period should come as no surprise to anyone reading Lenin's own discourses during the period in question.[20] In contrast to most of his associates, Lenin was more candid in his assessment of the Soviet reality. Just as he clearly referred to the effective non-participation of the Soviet laboring masses in the affairs of the state, as seen above, in the same way he unambiguously pointed out the development of *capitalism* in Russia in actual reality. Thus, right in the midst of war communism, speaking against the illusions of some of his associates, Lenin told the 1919 party congress that "even in Russia capitalist commodity economy is alive, operates, develops [and] generates the bourgeoisie as *in every capitalist society [kak i vo vsyakom kapitalisticheskom obshchestve]*" (1982c: 120; italics added). With the start of NEP, Lenin, in fact, insisted on the need to develop capitalist production relations in his country because of his conviction that there could be no direct "transition from *pre-capitalist* relations to socialism" (1982c: 548; italics in original). It should be stressed that Lenin's concept of state capitalism, to which he wanted to channel the Soviet economy, is based on capitalist production relations, with only the control on juridical ownership of the means of production by the (proletarian) state. It is the *"development of capitalism under the control and regulation of the proletarian state"* (Lenin 1982c: 571; italics added). Speaking particularly of concessions as a specific "form of state capitalism," Lenin underlined that "the concessionaire is a capitalist" (and that) "he conducts his business in a capitalist way for the sake of profit" (1982c: 545).[21] The regime's efforts to develop capitalism, in fact, bore fruit as is seen in the increase in the share of workers and employees in the Soviet population from 15 percent in 1924 to 18 per cent in 1928 -- which we mentioned earlier, citing official data -- though this rate of growth of wage labor in the Soviet economy would be dwarfed soon under Stalin's "revolution." In view of this reality of capitalist development in the pre-Stalin USSR, it is difficult to accept Cliff's assertion -- with reference to the genesis of state capitalism under Stalin -- that "changes in the relations of production" occurred under bureaucracy (1964: 174), or Dunayevskaya's contention -- in the context of Stalin's counter-revolution -- that "along with the bureaucratization of the apparatus . . . the relations of production were undergoing a transformation" (1992: 74).[22] Clearly, the position of both these Marxists is much closer to Trotsky's than to Lenin's in this respect. Bordiga, whom we cited earlier, was one of the few Leninists who had no inhibition to inquire into Russia's social relations of production in the pre-Stalin period of the Soviet regime. (His characterization of the Bolshevik seizure of power as a revolution, which was socialist politically and capitalist economically, would, however, be hard to defend).

Thus it is far from clear in what sense one could speak of restoration of capitalism or the establishment of state capitalism in the USSR under Stalin. Under Stalin's "revolution from above" capitalism was not reborn. What basically happened was that wage labor was generalized extremely rapidly and on a vast scale, combined with constraints and special operational forms of the economy not inconsistent with a capitalist "war economy in peacetime," particularly given the "catching up with-and-surpassing" exigency of capital accumulation in a situation of economic-technological backwardness. Thus in less than a decade -- between 1928 and 1937 -- the proportion of "workers and employees" in the total Soviet population (including non-working dependents) rose dramatically from 18 per cent to 46 per cent (Vinogradov et al. 1978: 467; *Narkhoz* 1987: 11) within a context of original expropriation of the peasant masses at an unprecedented speed and scale. The Soviet proletariat's double freedom was of course greatly limited starting with the end of the 1930s (and continuing until Stalin's death) when most of the repressive measures of war communism were reintroduced, undoubtedly on a vaster scale, given the extent of proletarianization (for millions of peasants there was a reversal to semi-feudal conditions).[23] However, such constraints on laborer's freedom over a limited period of time do not contradict, as we have argued earlier in the book, the existence of capital at certain historical situations.[24] As already mentioned, the Stalinist mode of accumulation of *capital* (entirely within Marx's theoretical framework) achieved, for the first time in Russian and Soviet history, peacetime full employment and job security which, though considered by many Marxists as a gain of the October revolution, was beyond Stalin's predecessors. This only confirms the validity of the Marxian proposition that it is the accumulation of capital which is the "independent variable," laborer's employment and wages the "dependent variable."

Once again, given this reality of capitalist relations of production and the specific way they were being reproduced at an expanded scale -- it is absurd to claim, as the Chinese communists and their international partisans started to do after the Krushchev leadership assumed power, that capitalism was restored in the USSR in the post-Stalin period. If anything, many of the draconian measures applied earlier against the Soviet immediate producers (including the peasants) were removed along with a relative improvement in their living conditions in the post-Stalin period, of course, mainly because the earlier measures no longer corresponded to the needs of capital in the new situation. As all know, until the end of the regime, there was no basic change in the mode of functioning of the Soviet economy, least of all in *wage labor* relations on which the entire economy, on the whole, was based. Hence, given the continuation of the capitalist production relations, there could be no restoration of capitalism in the ex-USSR. On the other hand, if by restoration of capitalism is meant the restoration of the type of economy (and society) that prevailed in pre-October (1917) Russia, then it cannot be *capitalism* that would be restored, since the then Russian economy was very partially capitalist in which, again, formal subsumption of labor (under capital) played a significant role. On Lenin's own assessment, the "chief manifestations" of pre-capitalist relations until 1917 were "monarchy, estates system, land tenure and use, the [inferior] status of women . . . ." (1982c: 589) in a situation where "the most developed forms of capitalism embraced effectively a small top crest of industry and very little touched agriculture" (1982b: 532). In fact, as we saw above, Lenin was speaking precisely in terms of transition to socialism (in Russia) from *pre-capitalism*, and not capitalism.[25]

A final word. The partisans of the socialist, as well as of the NSNC thesis, -- particularly the Trotskyists like E. Mandel subscribing to the latter -- have yet to explain how this transition to capitalism could be effected from a regime, considered to have been superior to capitalism, without any massive resistance of the immediate producers. Mandel, in particular, outdoing, in some respects, the Soviet spokespersons themselves in the appraisal of the regime's achievements, has stressed that, in view of the "gains from the October revolution" such as full employment and state ownership of the means of production, restoration of capitalism in the USSR could "result only after breaking the resistance of the Soviet working class" following "violent social and political confrontations" (1981: 38; 1990: 58). There is nothing yet to validate this sweeping assertion. On the other hand, if one holds that the social formation in Russia has continued to be based on capitalist relations of production, whatever be the changes in the property forms or forms of exchange and distribution, the reaction of the workers of the ex-USSR to the new situation is not very difficult to explain. Apparently these workers do not find the so-called gains from the October revolution worth fighting and dying for. Of course, they had job security. But they know that it was full employment under *wage labor* in conditions which, in many respects -- including the real wage level -- were inferior to the conditions of employed wage laborers in advanced capitalist countries. However, the most important point to stress about these workers' massive *indifference* to the changes, initiated -- as usual -- from "above," is that they have never considered as their own the famous state owned means of production -- the second and perhaps a more important "gain from October". "Removed from direct administration and disposal of social ownership, having no influence on the system of remuneration, and participating in no way in the distribution of national income and produced product," the Soviet workers naturally "perceived" such "state ownership" as "alien" and "not their own" (Butenko 1988: 16, 18). It is in this situation of "apathy enveloping millions" and "gradually exhausting all motivational basis," that the "standard 'socialist toiler' [*sotsialisticheskoi truzhenik*], a product of 70 years of Soviet rule" (Loginov 1992: 12), has worked, "alienated from ownership, from power, from results of labor," as the Soviet Academy of Sciences recognized two years before the end of the regime (Voprosy teorii 1989: 2).[26]

NOTES

1. Incidently, Carr is wrong in stating that the International was "sponsored" by Marx (and Engels) (1964: 19). It was basically the English and the French workers who, on their own initiative, founded the International. Marx was simply a member of the audience at the first international workers' meeting in London (1864, September), as "a mute figure on the platform" [*als stumme Figur auf der Platform*], in Marx's own words. Later he was accepted as a representative of the German workers and designated as a member of the sub-committee in charge of drafting the International's rules. He was eventually asked to draft the provisional rules of the International. A firm believer in workers' self-emancipation, Marx would never claim to guide the workers. See C. Abramsky (1964: 73,74,76).

2. Significantly, Marx's Inaugural Address to the International ends with the well-known last lines of the *Communist Manifesto*.

3. It is not without reason that in the *locus classicus* on the vanguard party, *What is to be done*? (1902), Lenin, contrary to his usual polemical practice, does not try to justify his stand on the select band of "professional revolutionaries," and the workers' guided liberation, by any quotation from Marx's texts. Here Kautsky replaces Marx to provide the necessary rationale.

4. This was quite consistent with Lenin's conviction (contrary to Marx's) that the workers on their own -- unguided by an organized group of "professional revolutionaries" -- are incapable of liberating themselves.

5. Even before the seizure of power Lenin had already treated the Bolshevik power and the proletarian power as equivalent, and, in justification of the Bolshevik rule, pointed out that if Russia since 1905 could be ruled by 130,000 landowners it was wrong to hold that "240,000 members of the Bolshevik party will not be able to rule Russia in the interest of the poor and against the rich" (1982b: 381,367-68).

6. We assume that by socialist regime Sweezy means proletarian regime inaugurating the transition to socialism, inasmuch as, under socialism, in the sense of Marx, political power ceases to exist along with the proletariat holding it.

7. Carr cites Lenin's 1921 statement, "Can every worker know how to administer the state? Practical people know this is a fairy tale," and then comments: "this reads like an explicit repudiation of his own earlier position" (1964: 247). Indeed, as a distinguished Marxist historian has stressed, everything that the Bolsheviks had promised to the people before, and on the occasion of the seizure of power, was later repudiated (Reiman 1987: 17-19).

8. Osinsky complained at the 1919 party congress that "even the central committee as a collegiate organ does not properly speaking exist," since "comrades Lenin and Sverdlov decide current questions by way of conversation with each other or with individual comrades" (Carr 1964: 193).

9. Carr notes: "Lenin described the attempt to distinguish between the dictatorship of the class and the dictatorship of the party as proof of 'an unbelievable and inextricable confusion of thought'" (1964: 230-31).

10. For an insightful discussion on this implication of the proletarian rule, see H. Marcuse (1958: 21-23) who, however makes the common mistake of confusing the "revolutionary dictatorship of the proletariat" with the "first phase of communism."

11. We leave aside the question as to what extent the Bolsheviks themselves thwarted and destroyed the creative initiative of the laboring masses. As Anweiler notes, "while the Bolsheviks set about disciplining the spontaneous sovereignty of the soviets, they simultaneously removed the premises of soviet democracy" (1958: 286). As regards the emasculation of the factory committees by the new regime, leading to "the control of the workers by the state -- the so-called workers' state -- and not the control of the state by the workers," see Ferro (1980: 192-97).

12. A striking example of uncritically accepting the Leninist, nay, the post-Lenin, official Soviet position on the character of the regime, going so far as to qualifying the latter as the "first socialist state...about to resolve the problem" [*questa soluzione tanto vicina*] of creating a "society of free and equal individuals," we see in the well-known Italian philosopher G. della Volpe (1962: 43-48,82-83). We should emphasize that the subjective and objective unpreparedness of Russia for a *socialist* revolution does not at all imply that there could have been no revolution in Russia in 1917, with its working class playing a major if not a leading role. In the middle of the last century, when "the communists turned their main attention to Germany," as the *Communist Manifesto* says in its last section, Germany was a semi-feudal land, and was "on the eve of a bourgeois revolution" (and not a socialist revolution). It is possible that the immense majority of the laboring masses -- including the peasant masses -- of the semifeudal Russia were immediately ready for a thoroughgoing bourgeois democratic revolution, and, if allowed unfettered initiative, would themselves have then decided -- in course of the "revolution in permanence" (Marx 1966b: 99) -- on the best way to advance toward a society of free and associated labor.

13. In his critique of Bakunin, Marx observed that a radical social revolution is "tied with certain historical conditions of economic development; the latter are its premises. It is therefore only possible where with the capitalist production, the industrial proletariat occupies at least a significant position in the mass of population," and then added that "Bakunin understands nothing of social revolution . . . . Its economic conditions do not exist for him" (1973c: 633).

14. Lenin seemed to have a precise idea of when Russia would enter the first phase of communism. Carr writes: "In 1918 Lenin put the 'transition period' at 'ten years or perhaps more,'. . . and on May 1, 1919, he predicted that 'a majority of those present who have not passed the age of 30 or 35 will see the dawn of communism'." (1964: 241). Could anyone be more utopian (in the precise Marxian sense of the term)?

15. The thesis characterizing the Soviet economy as capitalist has a long ancestry, starting almost immediately after the Bolshevik seizure of power. This was the work of the anarchists and the so-called council communists. This is not the occasion to go into this history. For a good account, including a representative choice of texts, see Bongiovanni (1975: 35-172).

16. Concerning the period under consideration, two contemporary historians note that the political strength of the Soviet industrial workers, the "heroes of the October revolution, . . . greatly diminished," that "the workers had effectively lost their hard won right to strike; the penalties against strikes were more severe than before the revolution" (Perrie and Davies 1991: 41).

17. On the eve of the seizure of power, Lenin already noted that "new means of control" such as "grain monopoly, bread rationing, general labor conscription, labor book, . . . were created *not* by us but by capitalism . . . . The organizational forms of labor we shall not

invent but take ready-made from capitalism . . . ." (1982b: 365, 366, 367; italics in original). In his turn, L. Trotsky told the Soviet trade unionists in 1920 that "the human being is a fairly lazy animal," that the "replacement of capitalism by socialism" is not possible without "governmental coercion and militarization of labor," and that "the worker is subjected to the state in all the relations." He of course rationalized this governmental coercion by qualifying it as "militarization of labor by the will of the laborers themselves" (1963: 202,213,252).

18. This clearly shows that, independently of the will of individuals, it is the *economy* -- in the sense of Marx (1962a: 96) -- that prevailed over politics. Generalizing for the whole Soviet period, a distinguished Hungarian scholar has noted: "Since the period of war communism not even the most rigidly centralized mechanisms have abolished monetary economy or -- apart from war and other extraordinary circumstances -- the free movement of labor" (Szamuely 1974: 22). See also S. Malle (1985: 167, 193).

19. Calculated from data in Schwarz (1956: 51), Carr (1963: 323), Carr and Davies (1974: 503). Carr notes that "a decree of September 10, 1921, . . . described the wages system a fundamental factor in the development of industry," and that "wages were now primarily a matter of the relation between the worker and the undertaking in which he[she] worked." Carr also refers to "the drastic dismissals of workers . . . in response to the dictates of *khozraschët*" (1963: 320,321-22).

20. The historian M. Reiman points out that "the Leninist period did not immediately lead to Stalinism. . . . The radical change leading to the true period of Stalinism started in 1928/29" (1987: 34-40).

21. Trotsky wished away the reality of capitalist relations under NEP by his strange assertion that "capitalism does not exist although its *forms* persist" in the "industries" which are "in the hands of the workers' state" (1972: 245; italics added). This is clearly a step backward compared to Lenin. An Italian scholar has neatly summed up Trotsky's position: "If the power is in the hands of the workers and their party, then, in spite of the presence of all the commodity categories, wage, surplus value, . . . there is no class exploitation, no capitalism, although its forms are there" (Bongiovanni 1975: 180). Later, almost throughout the Soviet period, the regime would justify its socialism by a similar distinction between the existing "forms" of capitalism -- like commodity relations, money, wage labor -- and their opposite, "socialist content."

22. When it came to concretely analyzing the economy under Stalin, Dunayevskaya was definitely on more solid grounds. In fact, her analysis of the USSR's first three Five Year Plans remains one of the best in the literature on the Soviet economy (1992: 35-70).

23. It seems that during most of this classical period of Soviet "socialism," there were three forms of labor in the process of material production: (capitalist) wage labor in the state enterprises and institutions with wage at a lower-than-living wage level, pre-capitalist form of labor in the collective farms with different kinds of obligations and "without almost any pay," and forced labor in the camps where "at any one time there were between 11 and 13 million individuals" (Manevich 1991: 136). Regular, open use of state violence to proletarianize the immediate producers well corresponds to the original accumulation of capital as we know from Marx.

24. Citing Stalin's pronouncement -- made against the theory of equilibrium in justification of collectivization of agriculture -- that "it is sufficient to take the theory of reproduction from the treasury of Marxism," M. Rubel observes: "To plan [under Stalin]

meant to organize at the national level the methods described by Marx concerning the 'original accumulation of capital,' machinery and big industry as the sources of surplus value" (1974: 79,95).

25. When Lenin asserted the impossibility of pre-capitalist Russia to make the transition to socialism without traversing the *capitalist* road -- albeit under a workers' state -- what else was he doing but admitting that the material premises for a *socialist revolution* did not yet exist in Russia? Within its Marxian meaning socialist revolution always signifies inaugurating the period of transition *from capitalism to socialism*. By a socialist revolution the proletariat does not first inaugurate or develop capitalism in order to go over to socialism subsequently. During what Marx calls the "revolutionary transformation period," capitalist relations, while still continuing, would not develop further but would be gradually declining, undergoing increasing revolutionization until they cease to exist giving place to emancipatory social relations. In the opposite case, if there could be no direct transition to socialism because of the existence of pre-capitalist relations before the latter would yield place to capitalist relations -- albeit under "state capitalism," as Lenin held -- then the revolution in question would be a bourgeois revolution, content-wise, even when it is led by the proletariat -- revolution being understood in the sense of Marx.

26. The alienation and apathy of the Soviet workers in regard to the regime did not, however, mean their simple passivity in the face of the regime. Workers' opposition to the regime manifested itself to a non-negligible extent throughout the Soviet rule in different forms. Thus only seven months after the much-proclaimed "victory of the socialist revolution" the worker-poet Alexis Gastev told the congress of the National Economic Council: "We are up against an immense sabotage by millions of individuals. I laugh when I am told that this is bourgeois sabotage . . . . We are [in fact] dealing with a national, popular, proletarian sabotage" (Heller and Nekrich 1982: 47). Workers' continuing opposition to the regime is seen again -- even before Stalin's "second revolution" had started -- in the exceptionally large number of individuals detained in Soviet prisons, a number that was higher than the highest number ever attained in Tsarist prisons -- the two numbers being, respectively, 185000 (1927) and 183864 (1912) (Heller and Nekrich 1982: 179). Millions thrown in prisons and forced labor camps, subsequently, in the Stalin period were, of course, the most eloquent testimony to the massive opposition to the regime by the Soviet workers (and peasants). In the post-Stalin period the most dramatic instance of the workers' opposition to the regime was seen in the open rebellion of the whole body of workers of the town of Novocherkassk in 1962 (Haynes and Semyonova 1979: 76-81). For a good, synthetic account of the Soviet workers' many-sided opposition to the regime during the last days of Stalin and in the post-Stalin era, see Schlögel (1984:47-131).

BIBLIOGRAPHY

Abramovitz, Moses. "Catching Up, Forging Ahead and Falling Behind." *Journal of Economic History* 46, no. 2 (June 1986).

Abramsky, C. "Marx and the General Council of the International Workingmen's Association." In *La Première Internationale: Colloques internationaux du CNRS*. Paris: CNRS, 1964.

Aganbegyan, A. "Generalnyi kurs ekonomicheskoi politiki." *Ekonomika i organizatsiia promyshlennogo proizvodstva* (hereinafter *EKO*) no. 11 (1985).

————. *Sovetskaya ekonomika - vzglyad na budushchee.* Moscow: Ekonomika, 1988.

————. *Inside Perestroika: The Future of the Soviet Economy.* N.Y.: Harper and Row, 1989.

Althusser, L. *Lire le Capital.* Paris: Maspero, 1965.

————. "Avertissement." In Karl Marx. *Le Capital.* Edited by L. Althusser. Vol. 1. Paris: Garnier Flammarion, 1969.

————. "Enfin la crise du Marxisme!" In Il Manifesto. *Pouvoir et opposition dans les sociétés post révolutionnaires.* Paris: Edition du Seuil, 1978.

Amann, R. "Technical Progress and Soviet Economic Development: Setting the Scene." In *Technical Progress and Soviet Economic Development,* edited by R. Amann and J. Cooper, Oxford: Basil Blackwell, 1986.

Anchishkin, A. *Prognozirovanie rosta sotsialisticheskoi ekonomiki.* Moscow: Ekonomika, 1973.

Anweiler, Oskar. *Die Rätebewegung in Russland 1905-1921.* Leiden: E.J. Brill, 1958.

Bahro, R. *The Alternative in Eastern Europe.* London: NLB, 1978.

Bajt, A. "Investment Cycles in European Socialist Economies," *Journal of Economic Literature* December 1971.

Basin, Yu G. "Khoziaistvennyi raschët i ego pravovnie formi." *Sovetskoe gosudarstvo i pravo* no. 7 (1968).

Baumol, William J. *Business Behavior, Value and Growth*. N.Y.: Harcourt Brace and World, 1967.

Baykov, A. *The Development of the Soviet Economic System*. London: Cambridge University Press, 1970.

Becker, A. "National Income Accounting in the U.S.S.R." In *Soviet Economic Statistics*, edited by V.G. Treml, and J.P. Hardt, Durham, N.C.: Duke University Press, 1972.

—————. *Sitting on Bayonets: The Soviet Defense Burden and the Slowdown of Soviet Defense Spending*. Santa Monica: Rand Corporation, 1985.

Becker, A; R. Moorsteen, and R. Powell, *The Soviet Capital Stock: Revisions and Extension 1961-1967*. New Haven, Conn.: The Economic Growth Center, 1968.

Bergson, Abram. *The Structure of Soviet Wages*. Cambridge, Mass.: Harvard University Press, 1944.

—————. "National Income." In *Economic Trends in the Soviet Union*, edited by Abram Bergson and Simon Kuznets, Cambridge, Mass.: Harvard University Press, 1963.

—————. *The Economics of Soviet Planning*. New Haven, Conn.: Yale University Press, 1964.

—————. "Income Inequality Under Soviet Socialism." *Journal of Economic Literature* 22, no. 3 (September 1984).

Berle, A.A., and G.C. Means. *The Modern Corporation and Private Property*. Revised Edition. N.Y.: Harcourt Brace, 1968.

Berliner, J.S. *Factory and Manager in the USSR*. Cambridge, Mass.: Harvard University Press, 1957.

—————. "Managerial Incentives and Decision-making: A Comparison of the United States and the Soviet Union." In *Readings on the Soviet Economy*, edited by F. Holzman, Chicago: Rand McNally, 1962.

—————. "Marxism and the Soviet Economy." In *The Soviet Economy: A Book of Readings*, edited by M. Bornstein, and D. Fusfeld, Homewood, Ill.: Richard Irwin, 1966.

—————. "Real Income and Consumption Statistics: Summary and Assessment." In *Soviet Economic Statistics*, edited by V.G. Treml and J.P. Hardt, Durham, N.C.: Duke University Press, 1972.

—————. *Soviet Industry from Stalin to Gorbachev: Essays on Management and Innovation*. Ithaca, N.Y.: Cornell University Press, 1988.

—————. "Restructuring the Soviet Planned Economy." In *From Socialism to Market Economy: The Transition Problem*, edited by W.S. Kern, Kalamazoo, Mich.: W.E. Upjohn Institute, 1992.

Bettelheim C. *Calcul économique et formes de propriété*. Paris: Maspéro, 1970.

—————. *Les luttes de classes en URSS: première période 1917-1923*, Paris: Maspero/Seuil, 1974.

————. *Les luttes de classes en URSS: deuxième période 1923-1930* Paris: Maspero/Seuil, 1977.

————. *Les luttes de classes en URSS: troisième période 1930-1941*. Vol. 1, 2. Paris: Maspero/Seuil, 1982, 1983.

————. "La pertinence des concepts marxiens de classe et de lutte de classes pour l'analyse de la société soviétique." Mimeographed. Paris, 1985a.

————. "The Specificity of Soviet Capitalism." *Monthly Review* September 1985b.

Bobrowski, C. *Formation du système soviétique de planification*. Paris: Mouton, 1956.

Bongiovanni, Bruno, *L'antistalinismo di sinistra e la natura sociale dell' URSS*. Milan: Feltrinelli, 1975.

Bordiga, Amadeo. "La Russia sovetica dalla revoluzione ad oggi" (1946) and "Quarant'anni di una organica valutazione degli eventi di Russia" (1957). In *L'antistalinismo di sinistra e la natura sociale dell'URSS*, edited by Bruno Bongiovanni, Milan: Feltrinelli, 1975.

Bornstein, Morris. "Soviet Price Theory and Policy." In *The Soviet Economy: A Book of Readings*, edited by Morris Bornstein and Daniel Fusfeld, Homewood, Ill.: Richard Irwin, 1970.

————. "Unemployment in Capitalist Regulated Market Economies and Socialist Centrally Planned Economies." *American Economic Review* (May 1978).

————. "Soviet Price Policies." *Soviet Economy* 3, no. 2 (1987).

Brody, Andras. "About Investment Cycles and Their Attenuation." *Acta Oeconomica* 31 nos. 1-2 (1983).

Brown, E.C. *Soviet Trade Unions and Labor Relations*. Cambridge, Mass.: Harvard University Press, 1966.

Budarin, V.A. "Konkurentsiya." *Bol'shaya Sovetskaya Entsiklopedia*. Vol. 13. Moscow: Sovetskaya Entsiklopedia, 1978.

Buick, Adam, and Crump, John. *State Capitalism: The Wages System under New Management*. London: Macmillan, 1986.

Butenko, A.P. "O Kharaktere sobstvennosti v usloviyakh real'nogo sotsializma." *EKO* 2 (1988).

Carr, E.H. *Socialism in One Country*, Vol. 1. London: Macmillan, 1958.

————. *The Bolshevik Revolution*. Vol. 2. London: Macmillan, 1963.

————. *The Bolshevik Revolution*. Vol. 1. London: Macmillan, 1964.

————. *The October Revolution Before and After*. N.Y.: Alfred Knopf, 1969.

Carr, E.H. and R.W. Davies. *Foundation of a Planned Economy 1926-1929*, vol 1. Harmondsworth, Middlesex, England: Penguin Books, 1974.

Chapman, Janet. *Real Wages in Soviet Russia since 1928*. Cambridge, Mass.: Harvard University Press, 1963.

————. "Soviet Wages Under Socialism." In *the Socialist Price Mechanism*, edited by Alan Aboucher, Durham, N.C.: Duke University Press, 1977.

Chavance, B. *Le capital socialiste*. Paris: Sycomore, 1980.

Cliff, T. *State Capitalism in Russia*. London: Pluto Press, 1964.

Cohn, Stanley H. *Economic Development of the Soviet Union*. Lexington, Mass.: Heath, 1969.

————. "National Income Growth Statistics." In *Soviet Economic Statistics*, edited by V.G. Treml and J.P. Hardt, Durham, N.C.: Duke University Press, 1972.

————. "Analysis of the Soviet Growth Model." In *The Soviet Economy: A Book of Readings*, edited by M. Bornstein, and D. Fusfeld, Homewood, Ill.: Richard Irwin, 1974.

————. "Sources of Low Productivity in Soviet Capital Investment." In U.S. Congress Joint Economic Committee. *Soviet Economy in the 1980s: Problems and Prospects*, Part I. Washington, D.C.: Government Printing Office, 1982.

————. "Soviet Intensive Economic Development Strategy in Perspective." In U.S. Congress Joint Economic Committee. *Gorbachev's Economic Plans*, Part 1. Washington, D.C.: Government Printing Office, 1987.

Constitution of the Union of Soviet Socialist Republics (1977). Moscow: Novosti, 1984.

Cooper, Julian. "Technology in the Soviet Union." *Current History* (October 1986).

Culbertson, W.P, Jr., and R.C. Amachar. "Inflation in the Planned Economies." *The Southern Economic Journal* 45, no. 2 (October 1978).

Dallago, Bruno. *Suiluppo e cicli nelle economie est Europee*. Milan: Franco Angeli, 1982.

Daniels, Robert V. *The Red October*. N.Y.: Charles Scribner, 1967.

Danilov, V.P. *Rural Russia Under the New Regime*. Bloomington: Indiana University Press, 1988.

Davies, R.W. "The Soviet Planning Process for Rapid Industrialization." *Economics of Planning* 6, no. 1 (1966).

————. "The Soviet Rural Economy in 1929-1930." In *Essays in Honour of E.H. Carr*, edited by C. Abramsky, London: Macmillan, 1974.

————. *The Industrialization of Soviet Russia*. Vol. 1. *The Socialist Offensive: The Collectivization of Soviet Agriculture 1929-1930*. London: Macmillan, 1980a.

————. *The Industrialization of Soviet Russia*. Vol. 2. *The Soviet Collective Farm 1929-1930*. London: Macmillan, 1980b.

————. *The Industrialization of Soviet Russia*. Vol. 3. *The Soviet Economy in Turmoil*. Cambridge, Mass.: Harvard University Press, 1989.

————. "Introduction." In *From Tsarism to the New Economic Policy: Continuity and Change in the Economy of the USSR*, edited by R.W. Davies, Ithaca, N.Y.: Cornell University Press, 1991.

della Volpe, G. *Rousseau e Marx*. Rome: Editori Riuniti, 1962.

Deutscher, Isaac. *Russia in Transition*. N.Y.: Grove Press, 1960.

Diamond, D.B., L.W. Bettis, and R.E. Ramsson, "Agricultural Production." In *The Soviet Economy: Toward the Year 2000*. edited by Abram Bergson and Herbert Levine, London: Allen and Unwin, 1983.

Dobb, Maurice. *Soviet Economic Development Since 1917*. N.Y.: International Publishers, 1966.

Dunayevskaya, Raya. *The Marxist-Humanist Theory of State Capitalism*. Chicago: News and Letters, 1992.

Eason, W.W. "Labor Force." In *Economic Trends in the Soviet Union*. edited by A. Bergson, and S. Kuznets, Cambridge: Harvard University Press, 1963.

Eatwell, J. "Competition." In *Classical and Marxian Political Economy*, edited by J. Bradley, and M. Howard, N.Y.: St. Martins Press, 1982.

"Ekonomika SSSR v 1990 godu." *Ekonomika i Zhizn* no. 5 (January 1991).

Ellman, M. "Money in the 1980's: From Disequilibrium to Collapse." In *The Disintegration of the Soviet Economic System*, edited by M. Ellman and V. Kontorovich, London: Routledge, 1992.

————. "General Aspects of Transition." In *Economic Transition in Eastern Europe*, edited by M. Ellman, E. Gaider, and G.W. Kolodko. Oxford: Basil Blackwell, 1993.

Eucken, W. "On the Theory of Centrally administered Economy." In *Comparative Economic Systems*, edited by M. Bornstein, Homewood, Ill.: Richard Irwin, 1969.

Ezhov, A. "Sovershenstvovanie mekhanizma planovogo upravleniia tsenami." *Voprosy ekonomiki* no. 1 (1982).

Fainsod, Merle. *Smolensk Under Soviet Rule*. Cambridge, Mass.: Harvard University Press, 1958.

Fal'tsman, V. "Povyshenie otdachi osnovnykh fondov promyshlennosti." *Voprosy ekonomiki* no. 3 (1985).

————. "Dinamika natsional'nogo bogatstva SSSR." *Ekonomika i matemeticheskie metody* 27, no. 2 (1991).

————. "Krizis soiuza i budushchee ekonomiki Rossii." *Voprosy ekonomiki* no. 4-6 (1992).

Feher, F., A. Heller, and G. Markus. *Dictatorship over Needs*. Oxford: Basil Blackwell, 1983.

Ferro, Marc. *Des soviets au communisme bureaucratique*. Paris: Gallimard, 1980.

Fine, B. "Competition". In *A Dictionary of Marxist Thought*, edited by T. Bottomore, Oxford: Basil Blackwell, 1983.

Galasi, P., and E. Sik. "Allocation du travail dans l'économie socialiste." *Économies et Sociétés* (October 1982).

Galbraith, J.K. *The New Industrial State.* N.Y.: The New American Library, 1978.

Garvy, G. *Money, Banking and Credit in Eastern Europe.* N.Y.: Federal Reserve Bank of N.Y., 1966.

General Council of the First International 1864-1866: Minutes. Moscow: Foreign Languages Publishing House, 1964a.

General Council of the First International 1870-1871: Minutes. Moscow: Foreign Languages Publishing House, 1964b.

Georgescu-Roegen, N. "Dynamic Equilibrium and Economic Growth". *Économie Appliquée* 27, no. 4 (1974).

Gerschenkron, Alexander. *Economic Backwardness in Historical Perspective.* Cambridge, Mass.: Harvard University Press, 1966a.

—————. "Industrial Enterprise in Soviet Russia." In *The Corporation in Modern Society*, edited by E. Mason, N.Y.: Atheneum, 1966b.

Glushkov, N. "Tsenoobrazovanie i khoziaistvennyi mekhanizm." *EKO* no. 9 (1982).

Goldman, M. "Economic Growth and Institutional Change in the Soviet Union." In *The Soviet Economy: A Book of Readings*, edited by M. Bornstein, and D. Fusfeld, Homewood, Ill.: Richard D. Irwin 1970.

—————. *Gorbachev's Challenge: Economic Reform in the Age of High Technology.* N.Y.: W.W. Norton, 1987.

Gomulka, S. "Soviet Growth Slowdown: Duality, Maturity and Innovation." *America Economic Review* (May 1986).

Gorbachev, M.S. Politicheski doklad tsentral'nogo komiteta KPSS XXVII s'ezdu kommunisticheskoi partii sovetskogo soiuza." *Pravda*, 26 February 1986a.

—————. "O pyatletnem plane ekonomicheskogo i sotsial'nogo razvitiya SSSR na 1986-1990 gody i zadachakh partiinykh organizatsii po ego realizatsii." *Pravda*, 17 June 1986b.

—————. "O zadachakh partii po korennoi perestroike upravleniya ekonomikoi" *Pravda*, 26 June 1987.

—————. "Na putyakh k rynochnoi ekonomike." *Pravda*, 18 September 1990.

Granick, David. *Job Rights in the Soviet Union: Their Consequences.* Cambridge: Cambridge University Press, 1987.

Gregory, Paul R., and Robert, C. Stuart. *Soviet Economic Structure and Performance.* N.Y.: Harper and Row, 1990.

Grossman, G. "Gold and Sword: Money in the Soviet Command Economy." In *Industrialization in Two systems: Essays in Honor of Alexander Gerschenkron*, edited by M. Rosovsky, N.Y.: Wiley, 1966.

—————. "Price Control, Incentives and Innovation in the Soviet Economy." In *The Socialist Price Mechanism*, edited by A. Aboucher, Durham, N.C.: Duke University Press, 1977.

Grunberger, Richard. *A Social History of the Third Reich.* N.Y.: Penguin Books, 1983.

Hanson, Philip. "East-West Comparisons and Comparative Economic Systems." *Soviet Studies* no. 3 (January 1971).

—————. *From Stagnation to Catastroika: Commentaries on the Soviet Economy 1983-1991.* N.Y.: Praeger, 1992.

Haynes, V. and O. Semyonova, eds. *Workers Against the Gulag.* London: Pluto Press, 1979.

Hegel, G.W.F. *Wissenschaft der Logik.* Edited by G. Lasson. Vol. 1. Hamburg: Felix Meiner, 1963a.

—————. *Wissenschaft der Logik.* Edited by G. Lasson. Vol. 2. Hamburg: Felix Meiner, 1963b.

Heller, M. and A. Nekrich. *L'Utopie au pouvoir.* Paris: Calmann-Lévy. 1982.

Hicks, J.R. *The Social Framework.* Oxford: Clarendon Press, 1971.

Hilferding, R. "State Capitalism or Totalitarian State Economy" (1940). In *A Handbook of Socialist Thought,* edited by J. Howe, London: Victor Gollancz, 1972.

—————. *Das Finanzkapital.* Frankfurt am Main: Eurpäische Verlagsantalt, 1973.

Hofmann, Werner. *Die Arbeitsverfassung der Sowjetunion.* Berlin: Duncker und Humblot, 1956.

—————. "Das'Wertgesetz' in der Erwerbsgesellschaft unserer Tage und in der sozialistischen Planwirtschaft." In *Kritik der politischen Ökonomie heute: 100 Jahre "Kapital",* edited by Walter Euchner and Alfred Schmidt, Frankfurt am Main: Europäische Verlagsanstalt, 1968.

Holzman, Franklyn D. "Soviet Inflationary Pressures, 1928-1957: Causes and Cures." In *Readings on the Soviet Economy,* edited by F.D. Holzman, Chicago: Rand McNally, 1962.

Hunter, Holland. "Foreward." In *Soviet Industry from Stalin to Gorbachev: Essays on Management and Innovation,* edited by J. S. Berliner, Ithaca, N.Y.: Cornell University Press, 1988.

Jasny, N. *Soviet Industrialization 1928-1952.* Chicago: University of Chicago Press, 1961.

"K gumannomu demokraticheskomu sotsializmu" *Pravda,* 27 June 1990.

Karagedov, R.S. "Ob organizatsionnoi strukture upravleniia promyshlennost'iu." *EKO* no. 8 (1983).

—————. "Ekonomnika defitsita: po stranitsam knigi Ya. Kornai." *EKO,* no. 12 (1987).

Katsenelinboigen, A.J. *The Soviet Union: Empire, Nation, System.* New Brunswick: Transaction Publishers, 1990.

Kautsky, K. *Das Erfurter Program.* Berlin: Dietz Verlag. 1965.

Khachaturov, T. "Ekonomicheskaya reforma i voprosy effectivnosti kapital'nykh vlozhenii." *Voprosy ekonomiki* no. 7 (1967).

————. "Ekonomicheskie metody upravleniia sotsialisticheskim obshchest-vennym proizvodstvom." *Voprosy ekonomiki* no. 6 (1984).

Khandruev, A. "In Search of Reasonable Compromise: Inflation and Problems of Soviet Economic Stabilization." In *St. Petersburg-Leningrad Papers: How to Save the Soviet Economy*? London: Center for Research into Communist Economies, 1991.

Khanin, G. "Ekonomischeskii rost al'ternativnaya otsenka." *Kommunist* no. 17 (1988).

————. "Ekonomicheskii rost v SSSR v 80-e gody." *EKO* no. 5 (1991).

Khudokormov, G., ed. *Political Economy of Socialism*. Moscow: Progress Publishers, 1985.

Kirichenko, V., and I. Pogosov, "Novye printsipy statistiki: pervye rezul'taty." *EKO*, no. 10 (1991).

Kodet, Z. "Monopoly and Competition in a Socialist Economy." *Czechoslovak Economic Papers* no. 5 (1966).

Kornai, J. *Economics of Shortage*. Amsterdam: North Holland, 1980.

————. "Some Properties of the East European Growth Pattern." *World Development*. Vol. 9, no. 9/10 (1981).

————. *Growth, Shortage and Efficiency: A Macrodynamic Model of the Socialist Economy*, Berkeley: University of California Press, 1982.

————. "Equilibrium as a Category in Economics," *Acta Oeconomica* 30 no. 2 (1983).

————. *The Socialist System: The Political Economy of Communism*. Oxford: Clarendon Press, 1992.

Kossov, V. "Zakonomernosti razvitiya tyazheloi promyshlennosti." *Voprosy ekonomiki* no. 11 (1984).

Kotliar, A. "Polnaia zaniatost' i sbalansirovannost' faktorov sotsialisticheskogo proizvodstva." *Voprosy ekonomiki* no. 7 (1983).

————. "Sistema trudoustroistva v SSR." *Ekonomicheskie nauki* no. 3 (1984).

Kozlov, G., ed. *Political Economy: Socialism*. Moscow: Progress Publishers, 1977.

KPSS (Kommunisticheskaya Partiya Sovetskogo Soiuza) *v Rezoliutsiyakh i Resheniyakh S'ezdov, Konferentsii i Plenumov* Tsk. Vol. 3. Moscow: Izdatel'stvo politicheskoi literaturi, 1970.

KPSS v Rezoliutsiyakh i Resheniyakh S'ezdov, Konferentsii i Plenumov Tsk. Vol. 5. Moscow: Izdatel'stvo politicheskoi literaturi, 1971.

Kronrod, Ya. A. ed. *Zakon stoimosti i ego ispol'zovanie v narodnom khoziaistve*. Moscow: Gospolitizdat, 1959.

Kuczynski, W. "The State Enterprise under Socialism." *Soviet Studies* (July 1978).

Kurman, A. *Dvizhenie rabochikh kadrov promyshlennogo predpriyatia*. Moscow: Statistika, 1971.

Kuromiya, H. *Stalin's Industrial Revolution: Politics and Workers, 1928-1932*. Cambridge: Cambridge University Press, 1988.

Kurowski, L. *Les finances dans les états socialistes*. Paris: Librairie Générale du Droit et de Jurisprudence, 1962.

Kushnirsky, F.I. *Soviet Economic Planning 1965-1980*. Boulder: Westview Press, 1982.

Kuznets, Simon. "A Comparative Appraisal." In *Economic Trends in the Soviet Union*, edited by Abram Bergson and Simon Kuznets, Cambridge, Mass.: Harvard University Press, 1963.

Kvasha, Ya. "Kontsentratsiya proizvodstva i melkaya promyshlennost'." *Voprosy ekonomiki* no. 5 (1967).

Laibman, David. *Value, Technical Change and Crisis*. Armonk, NY: M.E. Sharpe, 1992.

Lange, Oskar. "The Role of Planning in Socialist Economy." In *Comparative Economic Systems*, edited by M. Bornstein, Homewood Ill.: Richard Irwin, 1969.

—————. *Papers in Economics and Sociology* Oxford: Pergamon, 1970.

Lanyi, K. "Enterprises, Markets, Competitive Situation." *Acta Oeconomica* 24, no. 1-2 (1980).

Lavigne, Marie. *Le capital dans l'économie soviétique*. Paris: SEDES, 1960.

—————. *Les économie socialistes soviétique et européennes*. Paris: A. Colin, 1979.

Legislative Acts of the USSR. Book 2. Moscow: Progress Publishers, 1982.

Legislative Acts of the USSR. Book 3. Moscow: Progress Publishers, 1983.

Lenin, V.I. *Razvitie kapitalizma v Rossii*. (1899, 1908). Moscow: Politizdat, 1958.

—————. "O lozunge soedinennykh shtatov Evropy" (1915). *Izbrannye Proizvedeniya* (hereafter *IP*). Vol. 1. Moscow: Politizdat, 1982a.

—————. *Gosudarstvo i revoliutsia* (1917). *IP*. Vol. 2. Moscow: Politizdat, 1982b.

—————. "Zadachi proletariata v nashei revoliutsi" (1917). *IP*. Vol. 2. Moscow: Politizdat, 1982b.

—————. "Grozyashchaya katastrofa i kak s nei borot'sya (1917)." *IP*. Vol. 2. Moscow: Politizdat, 1982b.

—————. "Uderzhat li bol'sheviki gosudarstvennuiu vlast'" (1917). *IP*. Vol. 2. Moscow: Politizdat, 1982b.

—————. "Tezisy ob uchreditel'nom sobranii" (1917). *IP*. Vol. 2. Moscow: Politizdat, 1982b.

—————. "Tretii vserossiiskii s'ezd sovetov rabochykh, soldatskikh i krest'yanskikh deputatov" (1918). *IP*. Vol. 2. Moscow: Politizdat, 1982b.

————. Sed'moi extrennyi s'ezd RKP(b)(1918). *IP*. Vol. 2. Moscow: Politizdat, 1982b.

————. "Rech'na I vserossiiskom s'ezde sovetov narodnogo khoziaistva" (1918). *IP*. Vol. 2. Moscow: Politizdat, 1982b.

————. "Ocherednye zadachi sovetskoi vlasti" (1918). *IP*. Vol. 2. Moscow: Politizdat, 1982b.

————. "Proletarskaya revoliutsiya i renegat' Kautskii" (1918). *IP*. Vol. 3. Moscow: Politizdat, 1982c.

————. "VIII s'ezd RKP(b)" (1919). *IP*. Vol. 3. Moscow: Politizdat, 1982c.

————. "O prodovol'stvennom naloge" (1921). *IP*. Vol. 3. Moscow: Politizdat, 1982c.

————. "Kongress kommunisticheskogo internatsionala" (1921), *IP*. Vol. 3. Moscow: Politizdat, 1982c.

————. "K chetyrekhletnei godovshchine oktyabr'skoi revoliutsii" (1921). *IP*. Vol. 3. Moscow: Politizdat, 1982c.

————. "O znachenii zolota teper' i posle polnoi pobedy sotsializma" (1921). *IP*. Vol. 3. Moscow: Politizdat, 1982c.

————. "Pismo k s'ezdu" (26.12.1922). *IP*. Vol. 3. Moscow: Politizdat, 1982c.

————. "O kooperatsii" (1923). *IP*. Vol. 3. Moscow: Politizdat, 1982c.

Levine, David P. *Economic Studies: Contributions to the Critique of Economic Theory*. London: Routledge and Kegan Paul, 1977.

Levine, Herbert. "Pressure and Planning in the Soviet Economy." In *The Soviet Economy: A Book of Readings*, edited by M. Bornstein and D. Fusfeld, Homewood, Ill.: Richard Irwin, 1974.

Levitski, B. "Die Nomenklaturein wichtiges Instrument sowjetischer Kaderpolitik." *Osteuropa* (June 1961).

Lewin, Moshe. *Political Undercurrents in Soviet Economic Debates*. Princeton, NJ: Princeton University Press, 1974.

————. *The Making of the Soviet System: Essays in the Social History of Interwar Russia*, N.Y.: Pantheon, 1985.

Loginov, V. "Prichiny krizisa sovetskoi ekonomiki: vosproizvodstvennyi aspekt." *Voprosy ekonomiki* no. 4-6 (1992).

Lorenz, R. *Sozialgeschichte der Sowjetunion*. Vol. 1 (1917-1945). Frankfurt am Main: Suhrkamp Verlag, 1976.

Lukács, G. *Geschichte und Klassenbewusstsein*. Neuwied and Berlin: Hermann Luchterhand Verlag, 1970.

Luxemburg, Rosa, *Die Akkumulation des Kapitals* (1912). Frankfurt:, Verlag Neue Kritik, 1966.

Malle, Silvana. *The Economic Organization of War Communism 1918-1921*. Cambridge: Cambridge University Press, 1985.

————. *Employment Planning in the Soviet Union.* N.Y.: St. Martin's Press, 1991.

Mandel, Ernest. "Ten Theses." *Critique* no. 3 (Autumn 1974).

————. "On the Nature of the Soviet State." *New Left Review* (March-April 1978.

————. "The Laws of Motion of the Soviet Economy." *Review of Radical Political Economics* (Spring 1981).

————. *Traité d'Économie Marxiste.* Paris: Ch. Bourgeois , 1986a.

————. "In Defense of Socialist Planning." *New Left Review* (September October 1986b).

————. "A Theory Which Has not Withstood the Test of Facts." *International Socialism,* no. 49, December 1990.

Manevich, E. *Labor in the USSR.* Moscow: Progress Publishers, 1985a.

————. "Khoziaistvennyi mekanizm i ispol'zovanie trudovykh resursov." *EKO* no. 12 (1985b).

————. "Zarabotnaya plata v uslovyakh rynochnoi ekonomiki." *Voprosy ekonomiki* no. 7 (1991).

Manuel d'Economie Politique. Academie des Sciences de l'URSS. Paris: Editions Sociales, 1956.

Marcuse, Herbert. *Soviet Marxism: A Critical Analysis.* N.Y.: Columbia University Press, 1958.

————. "Industrialisierung and Kapitalismus in Werk Max Webers." *Kultur und Gesellschaft.* Frankfurt: Suhrkamp Verlag, 1965.

Markina, N.G., and A.V. Orlov. "Tovarooborot." *Bol'shaya Sovetskaya Entsiklopedia.* Moscow, Vol. 26, *Sovetskaya Entsiklopedia,* 1977.

Marris, Robin. *The Economic Theory of Managerial Capitalism.* N.Y.: The Free Press, 1964.

Marx, K. *Grundrisse der Kritik der politischen Ökonomie,* (1857-58). Berlin: Dietz Verlag, 1953.

————. *Theorien über den Mehrwert.* Vol. 1. Berlin: Dietz Verlag, 1956.

————. *Zur Kritik der politischen Ökonomie* (1859). Berlin: Dietz Verlag, 1958.

————. *Theorien über den Mehrwert.* Vol. 2. Berlin: Dietz Verlag, 1959.

————. *Das Kapital.* Vol. 1 (1867, 1873). Berlin: Dietz Verlag, 1962a.

————. *Theorien über den Mehrwert.* Vol. 3. Berlin: Dietz Verlag, 1962b.

————. "Randglossen zu Adolph Wagners 'Lehrbuch'." In K. Marx and F. Engels. *Werke* (hereafter *MEW*), Vol. 19. Berlin: Dietz Verlag, 1962c.

————. *Das Kapital.* Vol. 3. Berlin: Dietz, Verlag, 1964.

————. "Le Capital." Vol. 1 (1875), and "Misère de la Philosophie" (1847). In K. Marx *Oeuvres: Economie.* Vol. 1 Edited by M. Rubel. Paris: Gallimard, 1965.

—————. "Ökonomisch-philosophische Manuskripte" (1844), and "Aus den Exzerptheften" (1844). In K. Marx and F. Engels. *Studienausgabe* (hereafter *MESA*). Vol. 2. Frankfurt am Main: Fischer Taschenbuch Verlag, 1966a.

—————. "Manifest der kommunistischen Partei" (1848) and "Randglossen zum Programm der deutschen Arbeiterpartei" (1875). In *MESA*. Vol. 3. Frankfurt am Main: Fischer Taschenbuch, 1966b.

—————. *Resultate des unmittelbaren Produktionsprozesses* (1863-65). Frankfurt: Verlag Neue Kritik, 1969.

—————. "Wages, Price and Profit" (1865). In K. Marx, and F. Engels *Selected Works.* Moscow: Progress Publishers, 1970.

—————. "The Civil War in France", and "Outlines of the 'Civil War in France' (1871)." In K. Marx, and F. Engels. *On the Paris Commune,* Moscow: Progress Publishers, 1971.

—————. "Die heilige Familie" (1845). In *MEW*. Vol. 2. Berlin: Dietz Verlag, 1972a.

—————. *Briefe über "Das Kapital".* Erlangen: Politladen, 1972b.

—————. *Das Kapital.* Vol. 2. Berlin: Dietz Verlag, 1973a.

—————. *Die deutsche Ideologie* (1845-46). In *MEW*. Vol. 3. Berlin: Dietz Verlag, 1973b.

—————. "Konspekt von Bakunins Buch 'Staatlichkeit und Anarchie'" (1874-75). In *MEW*. Vol. 18. Berlin: Dietz Verlag, 1973c.

—————. "Lohnarbeit und Kapital" (1849). In *MEW*. Vol. 6. Berlin: Dietz Verlag, 1973d.

—————. "Brief an J.B.V. Schweitzer" (1865). In *MEW*. Vol. 16. Berlin: Dietz Verlag, 1973e.

—————. "Zur Kritik der politischen Ökonomie Manuskript (1861-1863)." In K. Marx, and F. Engels. *Gesamtausgabe* (hereafter MEGA), Section 2, Vol. 3, Part 1, Berlin: Dietz Verlag, 1976a.

—————. "Kritische Randglossen . . ." In *MEW.* vol 1, Berlin: Dietz Verlag, 1976b.

—————. "Zur Kritik der politischen Ökonomie (Manuskript 1861-1863)." In *MEGA,* Section 2 Vol. 3, Part 6. Berlin: Dietz Verlag, 1982.

Mathews, M. "Top Incomes in the USSR: Toward a Definition of the Soviet Elite." *Survey* (Summer 1975).

McAuley, A. *Economic Welfare in the Soviet Union.* Madison: University of Wisconson Press, 1979.

McNulty, P. "A Note on the History of Perfect Competition." *Journal of Political Economy* 75, no. 6 (1967).

—————. "Economic Theory and the Meaning of Competition." *Quarterly Journal of Economics* (November 1968).

Medikov, V. Ya. "Privychnoe i neochevidnoe v ispol'zovanii moshchnostei." *EKO* no. 3 (1985).

Merl, Stephan. *Der Agrarmarkt und die Neue Ökonomische Politik: die Anfänge staatlicher Lenkung der Landwirtschaft in der Sowjetunion 1925-1928.* Munich: Oldenbourg Verlag, 1981.

Meszaros, I. "La question du pouvoir politique." In Il Manifesto. *Pouvoir et opposition dans les sociétés post révolutionnaires.* Paris: Seuil, 1978.

Mikul'skii, K. "Vysvobozhdenie rabotnikov i pravo na trud: upravlenie protsessom pereraspredeleniya." *Voprosy ekonomiki* no. 2 (1989).

Moorsteen, R., and R.P. Powell. *The Soviet Capital Stock 1928-1962,* Homewood, Ill.: Richard Irwin, 1966.

Narkhoz 1967. Narodnoe khoziaistvo SSSR: statisticheskii ezhegodnik v 1967g. Moscow, 1968.

Narkhoz 1970. Narodnoe khoziaistvo SSSR: statisticheskii ezhegodnik v 1970g. Moscow, 1971.

Narkhoz 1922-1972. Narodnoe khoziaistvo SSSR 1922-1972: Iubileinyi statisticheskii ezhegodnik. Moscow, 1972.

Narkhoz 1975. Narodnoe khoziaistvo SSSR: statisticheskii ezhegodnik v 1975g. Moscow, 1976.

Narkhoz 1980. Narodnoe khoziaistvo SSSR: statisticheskii ezhegodnik v 1980g. Moscow, 1981,

Narkhoz 1922-1982. Narodnoe khoziaistvo SSSR 1922-1982: Iubileinyi statisticheskii ezhegodnik, Moscow, 1982.

Narkhoz 1984. Narodnoe khoziaistvo SSSR: statisticheskii ezhegodnik v 1984g. Moscow, 1985.

Narkhoz 1985. Narodnoe khoziaistvo SSSR: statisticheskii ezhegodnik v 1985g. Moscow, 1986.

Narkhoz 1987. Narodnoe khoziaistvo SSSR za 70 let. Moscow, 1987.

Narkhoz 1989. Narodnoe khoziaistvo SSSR: statisticheskii ezhegodnik v 1989g. Moscow, 1990.

Narkhoz 1990. Narodnoe khoziaistvo SSSR: statisticheskii ezhegodnik v 1990g. Moscow, 1991.

Norman, E.H. *Origins of the Modern Japanese State: Selected Writings of E.H. Norman.* New York: Pantheon Books, 1975.

Notkin, A.I. "Rates of Development of Socialist Production and the Rise in Public Consumption." In *Production, Accumulation and Consumption.* S. Pervushin, A. Notkin, I.A. Kvasha, S. Kheinman, V. Venzher. White Plains, N.Y.: IASP, 1967.

Nove, A. *An Economic History of the U.S.S.R.* Harmondsworth, Middlesex, England: Penguin, 1982.

Nove, A., and D. Morrison. "The Contribution of Agriculture to Accumulation in the 1930s." In *L'industrialisation de l'URSS dans les années trente,* edited by Charles Bettelheim, Paris: Editions de l'École des Hautes Études en Sciences Sociales, 1982.

Nove, A., and D.M. Nuti, eds. *Socialist Economics*. Harmondsworth, Middlesex, England: Penguin, 1972.

Nuti, D.M. "Socialism on Earth." *Cambridge Journal of Economics* no. 5 (1981).

Ofer, Gur. "Soviet Economic Growth: 1928-1985." *Journal of Economic Literature* 25 (December 1987).

Ollman, B. *Dialectical Investigations*. N.Y.: Routledge, 1993.

"Osnovnye napravleniya po stabilizatsii narodnogo khoziaistva i perekhodu k rynochnoi ekonomike." *Pravda*, 18 October 1990.

Pavlevski, J. "Le niveau de vie en Union Soviétique. *Cahiers de l'ISEA* 3, no. 2 (1969).

Pavlov G. and L. Pchelkina "Balansy proizvodstvennykh moshchnostei -- osnova razrabotki plana proizvodstva." *Planovoe Khoziaistvo* no. 9 (1981)

Perrie, M., and R.W. Davies, "The Social Context." In *From Tsarism to the New Economic Policy*, edited by R.W. Davies, Ithaca, N.Y.: Cornell University Press, 1991.

Pervushin S. "Ob odnoi iz glubinnykh prichin krizisnogo sostoyaniya sovetskoi ekonomiki." *Voprosy ekonomiki* no. 8 (1991).

Petty W. *Treatise on Taxes and Contributions*. In *The Economic Writings of Sir William Petty*, edited by C.H. Hull, N.Y.: A. Kelley, 1963-66.

Pitzer, S., and A. Baukol. "Recent GNP and Productivity Trends." *Soviet Economy* 7, no. 1 (January-March 1991).

Plyshevsky, B. "Sotsialisticheskoe nakoplenie na sovremennom etape." *Planovoe Khoziaistvo* no. 3 (1986).

Polyakov, V., and V. Rakhmilovich. "Les entreprises d'État en URSS." *Revue Internationale du Travail* (May-June 1977).

Popov, G. "Pol'nyi khozraschët osnovnogo zvena ekonomiki." *EKO* no. 7 (1984).

Pouliquen, A. "L'organisation du travail agricole collectif et le contrôle social de l'activité économique en URSS." *Revue d'études comparatives est-ouest* (September 1982).

Prokopovitch, S.N. *Histoire économique de l'U.R.S.S.* Paris: Flammarion, 1952.

Pryor, F.L. "Growth and Fluctuations of Production in OECD and East European Countries." *World Politics* (January 1985).

Rapawy, S. "Labor Force and Employment in the USSR." U.S. Congress, Joint Economic Committee. *Gorbachev's Economic Plans*. Vol. 1. Washington, D.C.: Government Printing Office, 1987.

Reichelt, H. *Zur logischen Struktur des Kapitalbegriffs bei Karl Marx*. Frankfurt am Main: Europäische Verlagsanstalt, 1970.

Reiman, M. *Die Geburt des Stalinismus*. Frankfurt am Main: Europäische Verlagsanstalt, 1979.

————. *Lenin, Stalin, Gorbachev: Kontinuität und Brüche in der sowjetischen Geschichte*. Hamburg: Junius Verlag, 1987.

Resheniya partii i pravitel'stva po Khoziaistvennym Voprosam, vols 1 and 2. Moscow: Politizdat, 1967.

Ricardo, David. *Principles of Political Economy and Taxation*. In *Works and Correspondence of David Ricardo*, Vol. 1. edited by P. Sraffa, Cambridge: Cambridge University Press, 1951.

Rizzi, B. *La bureaucratisation du monde* (1939). Paris: Champ Libre, 1976.

──────. *Il colettivismo burocratico*. Milan: Sugarco, 1977.

Roemer, J. *Analytical Foundations of Marxian Economic Theory*. Cambridge: Cambridge University Press, 1981.

──────. "Can There be Socialism after Communism?" *Politics and Society* (September 1992).

Rosdolsky, Roman. *Zur Entstehungsgeschichte des Marxschen 'Kapital'*. 2 vols. Frankfurt am Main: Europäische Verlagsanstalt, 1968.

Rubel, M. "Notes et variantes." In Karl Marx. *Oeuvres*. Vol. 2. edited by M. Rubel Paris: Gallimard, 1968.

Rumyantsev, A., and P. Bunich. "Tsentral'noe planirovanie i samostoyatel'nost' predpryatny." *Kommunist* no. 5 (1968).

Rusanov, E. *Raspredelenie ispol'zovania trudovykh resursov*. Moscow: Ekonomika 1971.

Ryzhkov, N. "Ob ekonomicheskom polozhenii strany i kontseptsii perekhoda na reguliruemoi rynochnoi ekonomike." *Pravda*, 25 May 1990.

Sakharov, A. "A Letter from Exile." In *On Sakhrov*, edited by A. Babyonshev, N.Y.: Vintage Books, 1982.

Sapir, J. *Les fluctuations économiques en URSS (1941-1985)*. Paris: Editions de l'École des Hautes Études en Sciences Sociales, 1989.

Schapiro, L. *The Russian Revolutions of 1917: the Origins of Modern Communism*. N.Y.: Basic Books, 1984.

Schlögel, K. *Der renitente Held: Arbeiterprotest in der Sowjetunion 1953-1983*. Hamburg: Junius, 1984.

Schroeder, Gertrude E. "Consumption." In *The Soviet Economy: Toward the Year 2000*, edited by A. Bergson and H. Levine, London: Allen and Unwin, 1983a.

──────. "Soviet Living Standards: Achievements and Prospects." U.S. Congress, Joint Economic Committee. *Soviet Economy in 1980s: Problems and Prospects*. Vol. 2. Washington, D.C.: Government Printing Office, 1983b.

──────. "Anatomy of Gorbachev's Economic Reforms." *Soviet Economy* (July-September 1987).

──────. "The Soviet Economy on a Treadmill of Perestroika." In *Gorbachev's First Five Years*, edited by H.D. Balzer, Boulder, Colo.: Westview Press, 1991.

Schumpeter, J. *Capitalism, Socialism and Democracy*. N.Y.: Harper and Row, 1950.

──────. *History of Economic Analysis*. N.Y.: Oxford University Press, 1954.

Schwarz, S. *Les ouvriers en union soviétique*, Paris: Marcel Rivière, 1956.

Seliunin, V. and G. Khanin, "Lukavaia tsifra." *Novyi mir* no. 2 (1987).

Seurot, F. *Le système économique de l'URSS*. Paris: Presses Universitaires de France, 1989.

Shatalin, S. "Sotsial'noe razvitie i ekonomicheskii rost." *Kommunist* no. 14 (1986).

Shkredov V.P. *Ekonomika i pravo*. Moscow: Ekonomika, 1967.

————. *Metod issledovaniya sobstvennosti v "Kapitale" K. Marksa*. Moscow: Izdatel'stvo Moskovskogo Universiteta, 1973.

Shmelev, N. "Avansy i dolgi." *Novyi mir* no. 6 (1987).

Shmelev, N., and V. Popov, *The Turning Point: Revitalizing the Soviet Economy*. N.Y.: Doubleday, 1989.

Skorov, G.E., and A.V. Danilov, "The USSR's Experience of Eliminating Unemployment." In *Tripartite World Conference on Employment, Income Distribution and Social Progress and the International Division of Labor*. Mimeographed. Geneva: Ill.O, 1976.

Smith, A. *An Inquiry into the Nature and Causes of the Wealth of Nations*. N.Y.: Modern Library 1937.

Sorokin, G. Tempi rosta sovetskoi ekonomiki." *Voprosy ekonomiki* no. 2 (1986). *Der Sprach-Brockhaus*. Wiesbaden, 1956.

Stalin, J. *Selected Writings*. Westport, Conn.: Greenwood, 1970.

————. *Oeuvres Choisies*. Tirana: 8 Nëntori, 1980.

Stigler, G. "Perfect Competition, Historically Contemplated." In *Essays in the History of Economics*, edited by G. Stigler, Chicago: University of Chicago Press, 1967.

Sukhov, A. "Podvizhnost' rabochei sily i eë prichiny." *Ekomicheskie nauki* no. 4 (1974).

Sutton, A.G. *Western Technology and Soviet Economic Development 1930 to 1945*, Stanford: Hoover Institution Press, 1971.

Sweezy P.M. *Post-Revolutionary Society*. N.Y.: Monthly Review Press, 1980.

————. "Competition and Monopoly." *Monthly Review* (May 1981).

————. "After Capitalism — What?" *Monthly Review* (July-August 1985).

————. "Preface for a New Edition of 'Post Revolutionary Society.'" *Monthly Review* (July-August, 1990).

————. "Class Societies: The Soviet Union and the United States. Two Interviews." *Monthly Review* (December 1991).

————. "Socialism: Legacy and Renewal." *Monthly Review* (January 1993).

Szamuely, L. *First Models of the Socialist Economic System*. Budapest: Akademiai Kiado, 1974.

Tacchinardi, R., and A. Peregalli. *L'URSS e i teorici del capitalismo di stato*. Rome: P. Lacaita, 1990.

"Teaching of Political Economy in the Soviet Union." *American Economic Review*, September, 1944.

Toms, Miroslav. "Toward a Marxian Model of Capital Accumulation, Unemployment and Distribution with One Technique of Production." *Czechoslovak Economic Papers* no. 16 (1976).

Treml,V.G. "Perestroyka and Soviet Statistics." *Soviet Economy* 14 (January-March 1988).

Trotsky, L. *Terrorisme et Communisme (1920)* Paris: Union Générale d'Éditions, 1963.

————. *The First Five Years of the Communist International.* Vol. 2. N.Y.: Monad Press, 1972.

United Nations, Economic Commission for Europe, *Economic Survey of Europe*, various issues.

Vacic, A. "Distribution according to Work and Commodity Production." *Acta Oeconomica* 18 no. 3-4 (1977).

Val'tukh, K.K., and B.L. Lavrovskii, "Proizvodstvennyi apparat strany: ispol'zovanie i rekonstruksiia." *EKO*, no. 2 (1986).

Varga, E. *Deux Systemes*. Paris: ESI, 1938.

Vinogradov, V.A. Iu.F. Vorob'ev, I.A. Gladkov, E.I. Kapustin, N.N. Nekrasov, A.I. Pashkov, N.P. Fedorenko, N.N. Chekrovets. *Istoriya sotsialisticheskoi ekonomiki SSSR v7 tomakh.* Vol. 4. Moscow: Nauka, 1978.

"Voprosy teorii: diskussionnaya tribuna -- k sovremennoi kontseptsii sotsializma." *Pravda*, 14 July 1989.

Voslensky, M. *La nomenklatura*. Paris: Belfond, 1980.

Wädekin, K.E. *Fürungskräfte im sowjetischen Dorf.* Berlin: Duncker und Humblot, 1969.

————. "Attempts and Problems of Reforming a Socialized Agriculture: The Case of the USSR." *Economic and Political Weekly*, October 21, 1989.

————. "Lebensmittelversorgung in der UdSSR: Krise der Produktion oder des Marktes?" *Osteuropa* no. 5 (May 1990).

Webbs, Sydney and Beatrice Webbs. *Soviet Communism: a New Civilization? London: Longmans,* 3d ed. 1944.

Weber, Max. *Wirtschaft und Gesellschaft.* Tübingen: Verlag von J.C.B. Mohr, 1925.

Wilczynski, J. *The Economics of Socialism.* Chicago: Aldine, 1970.

Winiecki, J. *The Distorted World of Soviet-Type Economies.* Pittsburgh, Pa.: University of Pittsburgh Press, 1988.

Wronski, H. *Rémunération et niveau de vie dans les kolkhoz - le troudoden'.* Paris: SEDES 1957.

Yanowitch, M. "The Soviet Income Revolution." In *The Soviet Economy: A Book of Readings*, edited by M. Bornstein, and D. Fusfeld, Homewood, Ill.: Richard Irwin, 1966.

Zakharov, V. "Kredit i banki v sisteme upravleniya ekonomikoi." *Voprosy ekonomiki* no. 3 (1982).

Zaleski, E. *Planning for Economic Growth in the Soviet Union 1918-1932.* Chapel Hill, N.C.: University of North Carolina Press, 1962.

————. *La planification stalinienne. Croissance et fluctuations économiques en URSS 1933-1952.* Paris: Économica, 1984.

Zaostrovtsev, P. "Sotsialisticheskaya sobstvennost' i tovarnoe proizvodstvo pri sotsializme." *Voprosy ekonomiki,* no. 3 (1959).

Zarembka, Paul. "Development of State Capitalism in the Soviet System." *Research in Political Economy* 13, (1992).

Zaslavskaya, Tatyana. "The Novosibirsk Report." *Survey* (Spring 1984).

————. "Chelovecheskii faktor razvitiya ekonomiki i sotsial'aya spravedlivost'" *Kommunist* no. 13 (1986).

Zwass, A. "Money, Banking, and Credit." *Eastern European Economics* no. 17 (1978-79).

NAME INDEX

Abramovitz, 96-99
Abramsky, 160
Aganbegyan, 68, 72, 74, 89, 93,
    94, 103, 127, 135, 140, 141,
    145
Althusser, 1, 2, 9
Amachar, 141
Amann, 73
Anchishkin, 68, 69, 71, 72
Anweiler, 151, 152, 161

Bahro, 53, 54
Basin, 58, 60
Baukol, 97, 100
Baumol, 144
Baykov, 65, 87, 132, 156
Becker, 69, 71, 76
Bergson, 56, 57, 103
Berle, 31
Berliner, 81, 89, 93, 99, 107,
    126, 133, 141
Bernstein, 4
Bettelheim, xiv, 2, 3, 99, 144,
    155
Bettis, 100
Bobrowski, 87
Bongiovanni, 161, 162
Bordiga, 155, 157
Bornstein, 58, 136, 143

Brody, 139
Brown, 51
Budarin, 128
Buick, 119
Bunich, 103
Butenko, 159

Carr, 50, 86, 107, 148-152, 156,
    162
Chapman, 67, 81
Chavance, xiv, 118
Ciliga, 119
Cliff, 122, 128, 129, 155, 157
Cohn, 66, 67, 72, 86, 93, 133
Cooper, 73
Culbertson, 141

Dallago, 145
Daniels, 153
Davies, 49-51, 62, 80, 85, 86,
    88, 156, 157, 162
della Volpe, 161
Deutscher, 149, 154
Diamond, 100
Djilas, 108
Dobb, 57, 65
Dunayevskaya, 2, 122, 129, 155,
    162

SUBJECT INDEX

About the Author

PARESH CHATTOPADHYAY is Professor of Political Economy at the University of Quebec in Montreal. Dr. Chattopadhyay has been Professor of Economics at the Indian Institute of Management in Calcutta, and a Visiting Professor of Political Economy at the Universities of Paris and of Grenoble.

ISBN 0-275-94530-8

9 780275 945305

90000>

EAN

HARDCOVER BAR CODE